FUNERAL LITURGIES

Flor McCarthy is a Salesian priest who has worked as a catechist for many years in Dublin and has extensive parish experience in the U.S.A. as well as in Ireland. He is well known for his works on *Sunday and Holy Day Liturgies*.

FUNERAL LITURGIES

Flor McCarthy, S.D.B.

DOMINICAN PUBLICATIONS
FOWLER WRIGHT BOOKS LTD
COSTELLO PUBLISHING COMPANY INC.

First published (1987) by
Dominican Publications
St Saviour's, Dublin 1, Ireland

in association with

Fowler Wright Books Ltd
Burgess Street, Leominster, Herefordshire

and

Costello Publishing Company Inc.
P. O. Box 9, Northport, Long Island, NY 11768

Nihil obstat:
Right Reverend Monsignor Alex Stenson
Censor Deputatus

Cum permissu:
Most Reverend Joseph A. Carroll, D.D.
Diocesan Administrator, Auxiliary Bishop of Dublin

18th September 1987

Design by Eddie McManus

Printed in Ireland by
Mount Salus Press Ltd

Acknowledgements
Extracts from the Psalms in this work are from *The Psalms: A New Translation*,
published by William Collins and Sons Ltd, and are used by permission of A. P.
Watt Ltd on behalf of The Grail, England.
   All other biblical passages are from the Revised Standard Version of the Bible,
copyrighted 1966 by the Division of Christian Education of the National Council
of the Churches of Christ in the USA.

Contents

'My immortality is necessary, if only because God would not do anything unjust to extinguish completely the flame of love for him once kindled in my heart.'

Fyodor Dostoyevsky

Introduction

There is an increasing tendency to deny the reality of death. Witness how undertakers do their utmost to pretty it up, and how preachers try to cover it in soothing phrases and euphemisms. We shouldn't be surprised at this tendency. The very thought of death fills people with anguish. After all, people are afraid to have a tooth out. But in death it isn't a tooth, it's everything, one's whole life on this earth that is being pulled out. It's only natural to recoil from such a fate.

However, in the long run, the denial approach does not help. It is no better than a flare in the night. Death is a reality, an enormous reality. Every attempt at denying this is both dishonest and counter-productive. People must be helped to confront death and to become reconciled with it. Those who do so will find that their lives will become more fruitful as a result.

The thing that best helps us to confront death is, of course, our Christian faith. It's interesting to see that Christ himself was filled with anguish at the thought of death and recoiled from it. In the garden of Gethsemane his sweat fell to the ground like drops of blood as he prayed, 'Father, if you are willing, take this cup away from me.' (Luke 22:42). Nevertheless, he confronted that awful death, went through it, and overcame it. Even though our faith doesn't give us detailed and precise answers as to what happens after death, nevertheless, it does enable us to face it with courage and hope, because we know we can conquer it in Christ.

Hence, in talking about death we can afford to be realistic. We do not have to plaster things up. We do not have to wave a magic wand so as to banish people's grief. People have a right and a need to go through their grief. It would be wrong to deprive them of what can be one of the most enriching experiences of life. 'The deeper that sorrow carves into your being, the more joy you can contain' (Kahlil Gibran). We must, of course, endeavour to provide comfort, not, however, mere 'inspirational' comfort, but the comfort that flows from our faith in Christ.

Sometimes you hear a priest call for joy on the day of a funeral. This I believe is misguided. It is nonsensical to go on about the wonders of spring when snow lies thick on the ground and frost holds everything in a vicelike grip. But it is right to talk about it when the first snowdrops appear. So at the actual time of death one should go easy on joy. Joy may come later, but it is hardly to be expected on the day we lose our loved one. What one can and must do is offer hope.

All this does not mean there should be no music at a funeral. Music can be a great help. As for the colour of the vestments, while purple may better reflect the mood of the mourners, white better reflects the faith of the Church.

Needless to say we must never deepen our hearers' gloom. It would be unpardonable to humiliate the bereaved in the slightest way at such a vulnerable moment. Nor must we pass judgement on the deceased. That is not our job. Even in the bleakest case we must give some glimmer of hope. We should say all the good we can about the deceased. This does not mean we have to canonise him (her). The thing we should never do is tell lies.

PRIMACY OF THE WORD OF GOD

Confronted with the reality and mystery of death, human words are totally inadequate. 'Sorrow makes us all children again. It destroys all differences of intellect. The wisest knows nothing' (Emerson). Our only sure source of light and hope is the Word of God.

What a treasure we have in the Scriptures. They do not offer us a mere snack. They offer us a feast. It is a great pity then that, instead of serving up a rich sampling from this feast to the people of God, we are often content to serve up a miserly portion by way of the same few readings used over and over again. Let us be generous. In this book I offer a wide variety of readings to show what is possible. I think a great enrichment results. For convenience the readings are included in the book itself.

The readings used in the funeral liturgy should be chosen with sensitivity and studied carefully in advance. It is essential that they be read well. I do not think it is a good thing to ask the next of kin to read them, unless they are used to reading in public. These precious words are infinitely more important than the wisest we can conjure up. They must be proclaimed in such a way that the message comes across loud and clear.

Naturally I place special emphasis on the Gospel. The words of Christ are to the bereaved what water is to the desert traveller. At a time of loss one's spirit seems to drink them in, to savour them, and to feel the divine power in them. Christ alone has the words of eternal life, as Peter said. Only his words are adequate to the challenge of death. They are the solid rocks on which we build our hope of an eternal dwelling place. All other words are sand.

If we preach the Gospel confidently and in a way that people can understand, we will find that everybody is listening. The words go straight to the hearts of our hearers. Funerals provide a priceless opportunity for sowing the good seed. It has been claimed that people hear nothing on the day of a funeral. They do.

By 'sowing the good seed' I do not mean indulging in a whole lot of moralising. Moralising is like giving a patient who is in pain a lecture instead of treatment. Death is no time for this. The best kind of 'moralising' is to preach the Good News.

ANNOUNCING THE GOOD NEWS

The minister's one essential task is to announce the Good News. To proclaim God's gift of eternal life through the victory of Christ over death. 'God loved the world so much, that he gave his only Son, that all who believe in him might not perish, but might have eternal life' (John 3:16). Nowhere and at no time is the announcement of the Good News more appropriate and more necessary than at the time of death.

However much we might wish to stress the good the deceased has done, we must be careful lest we convey the impression that eternal life can and must be earned by our own efforts. Eternal life is a gift, always a gift. Witness the example of the man who had misspent his life, for whom Christ opened the door of paradise the very day he died (Luke 23:43). Or the example of the man who has wasted his life begging, and who on dying was carried straight to heaven by the angels (Luke 16:22). People are frightened, rather than encouraged, by the idea of eternal life which must be won by our own efforts.

THE HOMILY

At death, as at birth, the uniqueness of the person stands out. Therefore, each liturgy should, to some degree, be special. Hence it is essential to get to know at least a fragment of the biography of the deceased. Otherwise how can we say anything special? We will fall back on platitudes and generalities which leave people cold. The more we know about the deceased the better. If we take the trouble to enquire, we will find that the next of kin are only too ready to provide us with the information we need. If we sit down with them these things gush out unsolicited. All we have to do is listen.

The homily should be short, simple, personal and not too solemn. Our words have a value only to the degree that they come from the heart of one person and enter the heart of another, bringing forth life. Speak from the heart and to the hearts of the hearers. Even the unrehearsed language of one who speaks from the heart goes straight to the hearts of the listeners. If the heart is full, the words will come out, and the message will be understood.

The homilies as they stand in the book are incomplete. Each one has a gaping hole at its centre. It is up to the preacher to fill this with some material from the life of the deceased. This material is not meant to turn the whole homily into a eulogy, praising the deceased for the good deeds he (she) did through his (her) own efforts. Rather, it is meant to draw attention to what the grace of God accomplished in that person, and it should never overshadow the proclamation of the Good News.

WHOLE LITURGIES

I give not just a homily but a liturgy. Some of the liturgies are written for specific occasions such as the death of a child or an old person. The rest are of a general nature and, with a little tailoring, could be made to suit a wide variety of occasions.

The approach concentrates more on life than on death. We are celebrating not just a burial but a life that has been lived. And of course we are talking to the living, not to the dead. There is a tendency to apply the Gospel only to the world of the sacred. This leads to a great impoverishment. The Gospel has to be applied to the whole of life, not just the religious bits of it, as if they alone mattered, as if they alone guaranteed us entry into eternal life. Hence, in talking about the deceased, we should talk about the whole of his (her) life, of his (her) ordinary life, not just the religious side of it.

I also provide six liturgies under the title 'Remembrance Liturgies'. These are intended for such occasions as the month's mind, anniversaries, and so on. There is also a selection of reflections provided, as well as a number of Prayer Services. The latter are intended for use at the funeral home or at the reception of the remains at church.

REPETITION

Repetition is a big problem especially for priests working in large parishes who have to cope with several funerals each week. One does not want to sound insincere at such a delicate time. But if one always says the same things, and constantly falls back on the same few readings and psalms, this may well be the impression that comes across.

Repetition is a deadly thing first of all for the minister himself. It robs his words of all spontaneity and freshness. He gets into a stifling routine. For him today's funeral is just one more funeral. He becomes a professional in the worst sense of the word. He goes through it without emotion, giving a cold and impersonal performance. Not as much as a breath of the sorrow of the mourners touches him. Such a minister leaves the mourners crying in the wilderness.

No less devastating is the effect of repetition on the listeners. The most pure, the most beautiful concepts lose their meaning and their vigour for being repeated too frequently and too smugly. The Word of God suffers the same fate. People have heard it all, or at least parts of it, so often that it glances off them like the rays of the sun glance off rocks.

One reason why I have provided such a variety of approaches is to combat repetition. I hope that the selection given will help the minister to bring some freshness and originality to each funeral. Indeed I hope it will stimulate him to make the approaches his own and to add to them.

There is no need to try to say everything every time. It should be sufficient to dwell on one aspect of the Christian approach to the mystery of life and death. Besides, every part of a good liturgy speaks. So what is not said in the homily can be said elsewhere, perhaps in a prayer of the faithful, or in a reflection. If we try to cover everything every time we cannot hope to avoid the repetition trap.

VISITING THE BEREAVED

When we set out to visit a bereaved person our first preoccuption is 'What will I say?' Actually we are not asked to say anything at all, but only to listen. By listening we enable the to vent their feelings. Even if we manage to utter some words, they will bereaved always be inadequate.

Deeds matter a lot more than any words we might manage to say. A deed makes words redundant or at least very secondary. What is the most important deed we can perform for the bereaved? It is to be present with them. By being with them we show them that we care, even if we can do nothing to help them.

People want the minister to share their lives, especially their sorrows. He may have no words to say, but he is there. His ministry lies more in powerlessness than in power. However, without genuine love and affection, there can be no true gesture of solidarity. Where these are lacking there will only be formality and coldness which the bereaved will not find helpful.

A Hindu monk who was dying asked a Catholic priest to instruct him in the basics of the Christian faith. When he had done so, the monk said, 'You have filled my mind with beautiful thoughts but you have left my heart empty.'

The minister is a sign of the love of God for his people, and a sign of his presence with them especially in time of sorrow.

'Men travel side by side for years, each locked in his own silence or exchanging words which carry little or no freight, till danger comes. Then they stand shoulder to shoulder. They discover that they belong to the same family' (Antoine de Saint Exupery).

Death and calamity bring people together as nothing else. All differences vanish, all barriers fall down. All those disruptive factors which may have existed between people up to that day, are scorched out of existence on the day of death.

The involvement of the community is most appropriate. After all, as Christians we believe that we have not only a common dignity but also a common destiny. We are members of the people of God, brothers and sisters in Christ, and are destined for the Father's kingdom. Hence, my life and my death are not purely and simply my own business. 'The life and death of each of us has its influence on others' (Romans 14:7).

The presence of the community is also a great support and consolation for the bereaved. Unfortunately this support is often limited to the day of the funeral. To do this is like rescuing a man from the sea but abandoning him the moment we step ashore. There should be a continuing involvement of the community in the weeks and months that follow, when the real grief-work has to be done.

The whole area of death and bereavement offers an enormous challenge and calls for great sensitivity. But it also provides a marvellous pastoral opportunity.

I hope this book will make a small contribution towards meeting this challenge and availing of this opportunity.

FLOR McCARTHY

Liturgies

1. JOURNEY TO THE PROMISED LAND

We are all on a journey – the journey of life. For Christians, the goal of this journey is the promised land of the kingdom of heaven. However, we cannot enter the promised land without passing through death. Our brother (sister) N. has just passed through it.

Christ too had to pass through death in order to enter the land of his risen glory. Let us draw near to him so that he may increase our faith and strengthen our hope. *(Pause)*.

Let us ask forgiveness for our sins which cause us to stumble on the road to the Father's kingdom.

I confess to almighty God ...

Readings on p. 96.

First Reading (Genesis 12:1-4). Every life is a journey into the unknown. But believers embark on this journey firmly believing, as Abraham did, that at the end of it God has a land of promise waiting for them.

Second Reading (Hebrews 11:1-2.8-10.13-16). Faith is the lamp that guides our path as we travel like pilgrims through this world towards our eternal homeland.

Gospel (John 6:44-51). Jesus is the bread of life. All who are nourished with this bread will reach the promised land of eternal life.

Our times have seen many great journeys, the most spectacular being the journeys to the moon. But the greatest journey of all is the journey of life. This is true even for the person who has never left his/her own fireside. We are all travellers on this earth. Every step of our journey is unique and unretraceable.

What is the meaning of life's journey, and where is it leading? For those without faith, it is a journey that leads nowhere. Which is to say that it has no ultimate meaning. But for those with faith, it is a journey that leads not just to another world, but to the other world, or, as Scripture says, to the promised land. What a splendid prospect this entails. This is why faith is the most important thing in life.

When it comes to faith, Abraham is our great model. At the word of God he left everything – home, family, country – and set out for a land he had never seen. The only compass he had was faith in God's promise. His faith was rewarded. God made of him a great people, and it was from his descendants that Christ came.

Christ it is who reveals to us the true nature of the promised land and, therefore, the true goal of our earthly journey. The promised land is not really a country at all, but a special relationship with our heavenly Father. Our final destination is the Father's house. The real journey then is a spiritual journey. This spiritual journey is infinitely more important than any journey to the moon.

The spiritual journey begins on the day of our Baptism. This is the day our life was linked with Christ's. This is the day we discovered that we are children of God, destined to inherit the kingdom of heaven. This is the day we joined a great people, the people of God, which means that we no longer have to travel alone.

Here the preacher could refer the life-journey of the deceased, stressing his/her faith.

The promised land is not a remote country we know nothing about, but which we hope to enter when we die. Those who believe in Christ have already set foot in it, because through him they have entered into a special relationship with the heavenly Father. Nevertheless, we cannot enter the promised land fully and definitively without first passing through death.

Faith alone guarantees the blessings we hope for. As long as we are on earth we are still searching for 'our real homeland'. We journey in hope, sustained by faith in God's promise, and nourished by the food Christ gives us in the Eucharist.

When we die we have to leave everything behind us. It is then, especially, that we have to imitate the faith of Abraham, and set out for a strange land, relying only on God's promise. But if we have lived by faith, the last step in our journey will be no harder than any of the ones that preceded it.

'Every step I take reminds me that, wherever I am going, I am always on the march to eternity'. (Helder Camara).

'The poorest wood-cutter, worker, or miner can have moments of inspiration which give him a feeling of an eternal home to which he is near' (Van Gogh).

PRAYER OF THE FAITHFUL

President: We are the new people of God. With Christ as our leader we are journeying together towards the promised land of the kingdom of heaven. Let us pray to our heavenly Father for N., for ourselves, and for others. *Response*: Hear us, O Lord.

Reader(s): That N. who began his (her) spiritual journey at Baptism may now reach its goal in the kingdom of heaven. Let us pray.

N. was nourished with the bread of life; may he (she) now enjoy the banquet of eternal life. Let us pray.

For those who mourn for N.: that they may be comforted by the faith that he (she) has gone to God, the destination of all of us. Let us pray.

For all who worship here: that they may receive an increase of faith in God and in his great promise. Let us pray.

For those whose lives are empty because they lack spirituality; for those who are going through the desert of suffering. Let us pray.

That God, in his infinite power and great mercy, may bring all the dead into the promised land of the kingdom of heaven. Let us pray.

President: Heavenly Father, we thank you for the hope you give us in Christ, hope of good things beyond all human imagining. Sustain our faith, and grant that we may never allow the urgencies of our human tasks to distract us from the vision of our eternal homeland. We ask this through Christ our Lord.

COMMUNION REFLECTION No. 5 or 11.

2. THE STORY OF A LIFE

INTRODUCTION AND CONFITEOR

The death of someone we love casts a gloom over our lives. As believers, the only thing we can do is to flee to the Gospel for consolation. There we see that when Christ died the apostles felt exactly as we feel now. But the risen Christ joined them, opened their eyes, and turned their sorrow into joy.

Christ is with us as we celebrate this Eucharist, and he will turn our sorrow into joy, if not today, then tomorrow. Let us draw near to him and lay our sorrow before him. *(Pause)*.

Lord Jesus, you speak to us when the Sciptures are read, explaining to us the meaning of our life and death. Lord, have mercy.

You come to us in Communion to nourish the divine life you first shared with us at Baptism. Christ, have mercy.

You comfort us with the assurance that one day you will share with us your victory over death. Lord, have mercy.

Readings on p. 98.

HEADINGS FOR READINGS

First Reading (Isaiah 35:3-6.10). This reading contains a message of hope for all those who are afflicted, weary and afraid.

Second Reading (1 Corinthians 15:51-57). Through his resurrection, Christ has taken the sting out of death for all those who believe in him.

Gospel (Luke 24:13-31 (Shortened Version). The story of two men whose lives had been shattered by the death of Jesus, of how the risen Jesus joined them and showed them that it was by dying that he entered into glory.

HOMILY

Wherever people have lived there is a story to be told. In fact each of us has a unique story to tell – the story of our life. Everybody's story deserves to be listened to and taken seriously because it is his (her) story. To reject a person's story is to reject that person. To know a person's story is to understand a person.

When a person dies we begin to tell that person's story. His (her) life-story passes before the eyes of our mind. It is all laid out before us, with its joys and sorrows, successes and failures.

Here the preacher could tell a little of the story of the deceased.

However, the sad fact is that all our stories end in death. Even when death comes naturally and at the end of a long and full life, we do not like a story that ends like that. We want our stories to end 'and they all lived happily ever afterwards'. Indeed when a story ends badly, no matter what heights it may have taken us to, it can leave us feeling worse off than if we had never heard it. It's darker when the light goes out than if it had never shone.

We can understand then how those two disciples felt as they trudged wearily back home to Emmaus on Easter Day. The story of Jesus, which had filled their lives briefly with hope and meaning, had ended badly, very badly. It ended with the death of their hero. The fact that he died a violent death added to the darkness and emptiness they were now experiencing.

Their story was indeed a sad one. But they were talking about it, which was a good thing. When Jesus joined them he encouraged them to talk about it. He showed such delicacy in joining them as a stranger. We often find it easier to unburden on a stranger. They poured out their whole story to him. They told him the good parts of it, and then its sad ending. For them death signified the end of the story, the end of the dream, the end of everything.

Having listened to them, Jesus took up the story where they had left off. He opened their minds to the fact that the cross, far from being the end of the dream, was paradoxically the very means by which it was realised. 'Was it not necessary that the Christ should suffer and (so) enter into his glory?'

Then he opened their eyes so that they were able to recognise him. The very one who had died was alive and walking by their side! So death did not have the last word in the story after all. 'O death, where is your victory? O death, where is your sting?' The story had, after all, a brighter ending than they could even have imagined.

Every human story is the story of a journey, the journey of life. Christ is with us on this journey, even though we may not recognise him. He is so close to us that our stories merge with his. He shares with us his victory over sin and death.

When all is said and done, it is only Christ's story that makes sense of ours – glory achieved through suffering and death. The resurrection of Christ opens all our stories to the prospect, not only of a good ending, but of a glorious ending.

The last word in each of our stories belongs to God.

PRAYER OF THE FAITHFUL

President: God our Father has given us victory over sin and death through his Son Jesus. He will not refuse us anything we ask him in faith. *Response*: Lord, hear our prayer.

Reader(s): Now that N. has come to the end of his (her) earthly journey, may Christ show himself to him (her), and give him (her) a place at the eternal banquet. Let us pray to the Lord.

That Christ in his mercy may blot out all his (her) sins. Let us pray to the Lord.

For those who mourn N's passing: that they may not be afraid to show their sorrow and to talk about it to God and to other people. Let us pray to the Lord.

That we may see Christ as the companion of our lives, and allow him to draw close to us especially in the dark moments of our journey. Let us pray to the Lord.

For all who are crushed by failure and disappointment and who have no hope left. Let us pray to the Lord.

For all who departed from this life believing in God: that they may find light, happiness and peace in his kingdom. Let us pray to the Lord.

President: Heavenly Father, your Son proved his love for you and for us by undergoing a humiliating death. You rewarded him by raising him from the dead and setting him at your right hand in glory. Help us so to follow him in this life that we may deserve to share his glory in the next. We ask this through the same Christ our Lord.

COMMUNION REFLECTION No. 2 or No. 5

3. THE MARKS OF A DISCIPLE

INTRODUCTION AND CONFITEOR

Death brings a lot of things into perspective. In a flash we see that the only thing that matters in the long run is goodness of life. Let us pause for a moment to look at our lives. *(Pause)*.

In the Beatitudes Christ left a map for his followers. There he indicated the kind of priorities they should have.

Lord, you blessed the poor in spirit, and said that they would inherit the kingdom of God. Lord, have mercy.

You blessed the clean of heart, and said that they would see God. Christ, have mercy.

You blessed the peacemakers, and said that they would be called the children of God. Lord, have mercy.

Readings on p. 100.

HEADINGS FOR READINGS

First Reading (Sirach 2:1-9). Those who serve God must expect to meet many trials. But through them all God will uphold them.

Second Reading (Philippians 4:4-9). Those who live good lives are truly happy and enjoy the priceless gift of peace of mind and heart.

Gospel (Matthew 5:1-10). Jesus tells us the values by which his disciples are to live. Those who live like this are already living in the kingdom of God.

HOMILY

The Beatitudes give us a list of qualities Christ wishes to see in his followers, qualities which were exemplified in his own life. A mere glance at them will convince us that they are a complete reversal of conventional standards and values.

The world says, 'Blessed are the rich, for they can have anything they want'. But Christ says, 'Blessed are the poor in spirit'. By 'poor in spirit' he means those who put their trust not in money but in God; those who realise that it is not the amount of money we possess that make us truly rich but the kind of people we are. To such as these he promises the kingdom of heaven.

The world says, 'Blessed are those who live it up'. But Christ says, 'Blessed are those who mourn'. It is only those who can love who are capable of true mourning. To open one's heart to other human beings is to share their burdens and sorrows. But to open one's heart is to begin to live.

The world says, 'Blessed are the tough and the strong'. But Christ says, 'Blessed are the gentle'. Gentleness is not a form of weakness as many think. It is a form of great strength. Life calls for a lot of gentleness. Think of the gentleness in the hands of a mother or a surgeon.

The world says, 'Blessed are those who hunger for power, status, and fame'. But Christ says, 'Blessed are those who hunger for what is right'. To live rightly is what life is about. Those who rate this as important as eating and drinking will taste real happiness even here.

The world says, 'Blessed are those who show no mercy and who take no prisoners'. But Christ says, 'Blessed are the merciful'. Happy those who make allowance for the sins of others, and whose greatness lies in their ability to forgive. They will receive God's mercy for their own sins.

The world says, 'Happy those who have clean fingernails, clean teeth, and clean skins'. But Christ says, 'Blessed are those who have clean hearts'. It is from the heart that all our thoughts, words and deeds flow. If the heart is clean, then all that flowsfrom it will be clean – like water flowing from an unpolluted spring.

The world says, 'Blessed are the troublemakers and war-mongers'. But Christ says, 'Blessed are the peacemakers'. Happy those who spread understanding among people, those who welcome the stranger, and who work for a more just society. They are true children of God.

The world says, 'Blessed are those who cheat and who get away with it'. But Christ says, 'Blessed are those who make a stand for what is right'. If they suffer for their stand, the wounds they bear will be honorable wounds.

> Here the preacher could refer to the deceased, showing how one or more of the Beatitudes were exemplified in her/his life.

These are the things Christ said were the badges of a true disciple. They are the marks of a child of God. They make us rich in the sight of God. They are also the keys to another world – the world of Christ and his Gospel. They open our minds and hearts to a new way of seeing and judging. They give us a whole new set of bearings.

The things the Beatitude gives us in this life are very beautiful and precious – all those things which make life worthwhile, things such as peace, goodness, joy, love, compassion, mercy, gentleness, integrity, freedom of spirit. But they are only a foretaste of the good things to come.

A person who lives according to the Beatitudes is already living in the kingdom of heaven. Eternal life will merely be the full blossoming of a plant that is green with life and health.

'As I stand before Christ, the honours bestowed on me by others lose all value'. (Carlo Carretto).

PRAYER OF THE FAITHFUL

President: Those who live in the spirit of the Beatitudes have nothing to fear from death. They already belong to the kingdom. Let us pray to the Father who through his Son teaches us how to live as his children. *Response*: Lord, hear our prayer.

Reader(s): For all the followers of Christ: that they may not seek the riches of this world but those things which make them pleasing in the sight of God. Let us pray to the Lord.

That N., who was gentle, sincere, kind and peace-loving, may now come to possess the full happiness of the kingdom of God. Let us pray to the Lord.

That as he (she) bore the marks of a disciple of Christ on earth, Christ may now declare him (her) blessed before his Father in heaven. Let us pray to the Lord.

For those who mourn N's passing: that Christ may bless and comfort them in their sorrow. Let us pray to the Lord.

For all here present: that we may hunger after a life of goodness, so that even here on earth we may taste true happiness and peace of mind. Let us pray to the Lord.

For all our departed relatives and friends, and for all who have died in the peace of Christ: that they may enjoy the fulness of eternal life. Let us pray to the Lord.

President: Heavenly Father, you want to see in us those qualities which you saw and loved in your Son Jesus. Help us to become more like him on earth so that we may share his glory in heaven. We ask this through the same Jesus Christ our Lord.

COMMUNION REFLECTION No. 18 or No. 7.

4. THE SEED MUST DIE

INTRODUCTION AND CONFITEOR

Unlikely as it may seem, from every death new life comes. Unless the seed dies, the flower cannot be born. So, paradoxically, it is by dying that we are born into eternal life. Christ our Brother, who shares his risen life with us, now stands among us to comfort and strengthen us. *(Pause).*

All of life is a process of dying and being born.

Lord, you help us to die to sin so that we can live to holiness. Lord, have mercy.

Lord, you help us to die to selfishness so that we can live a life of love. Christ, have mercy.

Lord, you help us to die to the false self, so that we can live to the true self, made in God's image. Lord, have mercy.

Readings on p. 102.

HEADINGS FOR READINGS

First Reading (Sirach 2:1-9). Those who serve God must expect to meet with many trials. But through them all God upholds them.

Second Reading (Romans 6:3-4.8-11). At Baptism we were given a share in the risen life of Christ, a life that death cannot extinguish.

Gospel (John 12:23-27). We hear Jesus talking about his imminent death. He fears it, yet desires it, for the hour of his shame will in fact turn out to be the hour of his glory.

HOMILY

How beautiful it is to watch shoots of young corn swaying in the wind and dancing in the sun. But how strange is the process through which these shoots come into being. First of all, the grains of wheat have to be buried in the cold, damp soil. Next they have to die. If they didn't die, no new life would come forth. But when they die, then miraculously from the grave of the old grains new shoots of corn spring forth. In time, each of these shoots will produce a whole earful of new grains. What a strange process indeed.

Now the way of salvation is similar to the story of a grain of wheat. It is Christ who tells us this, and he himself has gone this way before us. He knew that if he was to fulfil the mission his Father had given him he would have to undergo a humiliating death. Naturally he recoiled from it. He said, 'Now that the hour has come, my soul is troubled.' The night before he died he was in such agony that his sweat fell to the ground like drops of blood.

He was faced with a very hard decision – to save his life or to lose it, to do his own will or to do the will of his Father. But in a sense the decision had already been made. A long time back he had decided to do his Father's will rather than his own. In a sense, then, he had already died – died to all forms of self-seeking.

When the actual moment of death arrived, he surrendered himself into his Father's hands. And the Father rescued him from the tomb and gave him new life. Thus the hour of his humiliation became the hour of his glory and of his greatest fruitfulness, for it was his death that brought life to all of us.

Christ said that we too must die if we are to come to new life. We begin the process of dying at Baptism when, as Paul says, 'we were buried wsith Christ'. It was then our real death took place – death to sin.

And it was also at Baptism that our real life began. 'Christ was raised from the dead by the glory of the Father, so that we too might walk in newness of life.' At Baptism we let go of the old life of sin, and became a new creature able to live in the freedom of the children of God. We began to sway in the wind and dance in the sun with the new life Christ gave us.

> Here the preacher could refer to the deceased, and maybe point out how this mystery was realised in his/her life through sacrifice and self-giving.

To die to self can be a lot harder than physical death. It is, of course, a life-long process which we can only embark on, and persevere in, with the grace of Christ. But those who die to the old, false, sin-ridden self, and who put on the new, true self, modelled on Christ, will find death easy.

When one's whole life has been orientated towards self-giving and obedience to the will of God, like Christ's was, then at the end one gladly and freely surrenders it back into the hands of God. Then the hour of our humiliation becomes the hour of our glorification. At that moment we are born into the fulness of eternal life.

'Life consists not merely in being but in an unending process of becoming. He who lives his life merely to be, loses it; he who loses his being in order to become, lives for ever.' (Laurens van der Post)

PRAYER OF THE FAITHFUL

President: We believe that those who die with Christ in Baptism, will live with him for ever in heaven. Strengthened by this faith, and comforted by this hope, let us pray to him as we are surrounded by the anguish of death. *Response*: Lord, graciously hear us.

Reader(s): N. died with Christ in Baptism; may he (she) now share the fulness of his risen life in heaven. Lord, hear us.

That all the sufferings and trials he (she) endured during life may win for him (her) full remission of his (her) sins. Lord, hear us.

That he (she) may reap a rich harvest from all his (her) acts of self-denial and generosity. Lord, hear us.

That Christ, who himself knew the anguish of death, may comfort all those who mourn for N., especially his (her) family. Lord, hear us.

For all here present: that we may not be afraid to die to self so that we can live for Christ and for others. Lord, hear us.

For all those who have no hope of a life beyond the grave: that they too may hear and believe the Good News of Christ. Lord, hear us.

President: Father, your Son died so that we might live. Help us so to live in this world that we may come to enjoy the fulness of your life in the kingdom of heaven. We ask this through Christ our Lord.

COMMUNION REFLECTION No. 12 or No. 21.

---

5. WALKING ON WATER

INTRODUCTION AND CONFITEOR

At no time do we feel so helpless as when we stand in the presence of death. And nothing tests our faith as severely as death does. But it is precisely at this time that we must turn to our one sure source of strength and hope, namely, Christ.

Let us place ourselves in the presence of him who is never more than an arm's length away from us. *(Pause)*.

Lord, by your presence you calm our fears. Lord, have mercy.

Lord, by your presence you strengthen our wavering faith. Christ, have mercy.

Lord, by your dying and rising you have robbed our death of its sting. Lord, have mercy.

Readings on p. 104.

HEADINGS FOR READINGS

First Reading (Isaiah 35:3-6.10). A message of hope for all those who are afflicted and afraid.

Second Reading (1 Corinthians 15:51-57). Through his death and resurrection Christ has robbed our death of its sting, and has turned defeat into victory.

Gospel (Matthew 14:22-33). This is a story of faith. At the word of Christ Peter leaves the safety of the boat and sets out across the waters of the sea to walk towards Christ.

HOMILY

At a first glance it might seem that the incident related in the Gospel has no relevance whatsoever for us. To be able to walk on water would be fun, but we could hardly claim that it is a necessity for us. So what has this incident to say to us? Of all the incidents in the Gospel, this is perhaps the most relevant. It touches the life of every single one of us. No one escapes. And its message is a most comforting one.

Like the apostles on the lake, we too are embarked on a voyage – the voyage of life. Sometimes our small boat makes good progress. At other times it runs into strong head-winds and heavy seas. But sooner or later each of us has to leave the earthly 'boat' that has carried us over the waters of life, and set out across the dark waters of death.

At death the old reliables that have supported us all our lives are taken away from us one by one. The solid support vanishes from beneath our feet, and we are on our own. The depths quickly begin to close in around us, and extinction towers over us.

At that moment no human power can save us. Moreover, we are incapable of the slightest act to save ourselves. The only one who can save us is Christ. Only he can snatch us from these depths. It is then that we must imitate Peter. When he grew frightened and began to sink, he had the humility and good sense to cry out to Christ, and Christ reached out his strong hand and rescued him from the depths.

During his life on earth Christ did not resort to magic or choose the way of escapism. He didn't avoid death. He confronted it. On Calvary he set out across its dark waters, relying on his Father to save him. His last words were, 'Father, into your hands I commend my spirit'.

Christ alone succeeded in walking across the waters of death without being swallowed up for ever. Consequently he was able to save Peter. He is able to save us too, if we have faith in him.

Here the preacher could refer to the life of the deceased, stressing her/his faith in Christ.

For a Christian, death is no longer a leap into the unknown. It is a summons to come to Christ. At that moment he will say to us what he said to Peter, 'Come to me.' And if we hesitate he will add, 'It is I. Do not be afraid.'

In a sense the whole life of a Christian is a kind of 'walking on water'. It is a walking in faith, which means living by the word of Christ. He is not a ghost-like figure from the past. He is the Son of God who lives among us and who comes to us when things get too much for us.

Now if during our life we have built up a relationship of trust with Christ, and if we have got used to obeying his voice and to taking risks on his word, then when death comes we will find it easy to obey him. We will find it natural to reach out our hand to him. Then he will take our hand and, with his divine power, haul us onto the shores of eternity.

In death only God can save us.

PRAYER OF THE FAITHFUL

President: As we stand before the mystery of death, Christ stands among us and says to us, 'Courage! Do not be afraid.' Let us ask him to hear our prayers and calm our fears and anxieties. *Response*: Lord, hear our prayer.

Reader(s): That Christ may reach out his hand and rescue our sister (brother) N. from the waters of death and bring her (him) safely to the shores of eternity. Let us pray to the Lord.

That Christ, who knows and understands our weakness, may grant her (him) full pardon for her (his) sins. Let us pray to the Lord.

That those who grieve for N. may be comforted by the faith that assures them that she (he) has gone to a land where there is no more sorrow, lament, or death. Let us pray to the Lord.

For all who worship here: that they may experience the closeness of Christ to them during this celebration and so grow in faith in him. Let us pray to the Lord.

For those who have no faith, and who are at the mercy of the cold winds of anguish and despair. Let us pray to the Lord.

For all the faithful departed: that God may bring them into that land where the reign of death is ended. Let us pray to the Lord.

President: Heavenly Father, strengthen our little faith, so that in the midst of life and death we may keep our eyes fixed on Christ your Son, and so come to the safety of your ever-lasting kingdom. We ask this through the same Christ our Lord.

COMMUNION REFLECTION No. 2.

6. BUILDING ON HIS WORDS

INTRODUCTION AND CONFITEOR

Our hope of eternal life does not rest on mere human words but on the words of God given to us in Christ. Christ said that if we build our lives on his words we are building them on solid rock. No one ever claimed such authority for his words.

So, in the midst of death let us draw comfort and strength from the words of Christ. *(Pause).*

Lord, you alone have the words of eternal life. Lord, have mercy.

Lord, your words are a lamp for our steps and a light for our path. Christ, have mercy.

Lord, though heaven and earth should pass away, your words will never pass away. Lord, have mercy.

Readings on p. 106.

HEADINGS FOR READINGS

First Reading (Isaiah 35:3-6.10). A message of hope for all those who are afflicted, weary and afraid.

Second Readings (1 Corinthians 2:1-6.9). No eye has seen, no ear has heard what God has prepared for those who love him.

Gospel (Matthew 7:24-27). Those who listen to Christ's teaching and who live according to it, are building the house of their life on a rocklike foundation.

HOMILY

Some years ago in Russia a group of dissidents was arrested. On being brought in they were subjected to the usual thorough body-search. One man was found to have a small ball of paper in his mouth. It contained a few pages from a book.

The man knew that long years in some remote prison camp lay ahead of him, and that it was quite possible he would never return to the free world. So what pages was he taking with him to give him the courage and strength to face such a bleak future? The pages came from the Gospel. They contained the Sermon on the Mount, the conclusion of which we just read.

It is reasonable to assume that prior to this the words Christ meant a lot to this man. He was not turning to them merely as a last resort. He was turning to something that had filled his life with meaning and hope, and had thus already proved its worth. Which suggests that he was not just a listener but a doer of the word.

So it was to these marvellous words of Christ that he now fled. He wanted to take them with him as a lamp for his steps. The light of this lamp would illuminate the dark path that stretched out unendingly before him. To those words he would anchor whatever hopes he still had for himself and for his life on earth. On these words he would build his entire future.

Just as arrest stripped that prisoner of everything he owned, so death strips us of everything. We have nothing of our own that we can turn to or rely on, nothing in the world to guide us or give us light. In the face of death, all human words leave us in the dark. We have nothing to sustain us but the word of Christ, nothing but his light to illuminate our dark path. We know nothing of the mystery of the beyond. We have no maps of the other side. All we have is the word of Christ. But this is more than enough. 'Lord, to whom shall we go? You have the words of eternal life.' (John 6:68).

It is not enough, however, to listen to the words of Christ. We must do them. We must try to live by them. Only then will they shed light into our path. To believe in these words, but not to live by them, is to be carrying an unlighted lamp.

> Here the preacher could refer to the life of the deceased, showing how he (she) lived by the words of Christ, even if only in some aspect of his (her) life.

It is only when we do the word of Christ that we are building rather than merely planning or hoping to build. If we really do try to live by his words, then we will find that we have anchored ourselves to something so solid that not even death will be able to wrench us free. We will have anchored ourselves not just to the words of Christ but to Christ himself.

Heaven and earth will pass away, but the words of Christ will never pass away. If we build our lives on his words, when death comes we will find that what we have built will not collapse like sand-castles before the tide. It will last into eternity.

PRAYER OF THE FAITHFUL

President: Surrounded by the sorrows of death, let us turn to

Christ, who alone has the words of eternal life. *Response*: Lord, hear us in your love.

Reader(s): N. was anchored to Christ in Baptism; may she (he) now come to share with him in the prize of everlasting glory. We pray in faith.

That Christ may forgive her (his) sins, and protect her (him) with his loving care. We pray in faith.

For those who are laden with grief, especially the family of N.: that the Lord may grant them courage and strength. We pray in faith.

That the Lord may open the eyes of all those who are blinded by materialism so that they may be able to glimpse the good things God has prepared for those who follow Christ. We pray in faith.

For all the followers of Christ: that they may not merely believe in his words but live by them. We pray in faith.

That all here present may have their faith in Christ and in his Gospel renewed and deepened by their participation in this celebration. We pray in faith.

President: Father, your Son alone has the words of eternal life. He came that we might have life and have it to the full. Help us to listen to his voice, and to act on his words, so that we may come to the glory of his kingdom, where he lives and reigns with you and the Holy Spirit, one God, for ever and ever.

COMMUNION REFLECTION No. 22.

7. HARVEST TIME OF THE SPIRIT

INTRODUCTION AND CONFITEOR

Death is like harvest time – we reap the good we have sown during our life. Harvest time is a time of joy for the reaper. But it is a time of sadness for all those little creatures who feed on the grain.

N. has gone to reap the fruits of all the good he (she) sowed during life. But we are left with a feeling of sadness and emptiness. Nevertheless, death can be a moment of grace for us, because it provides us with an opportunity to look into the field of our life to see what is growing there – wheat or weeds? *(Pause)*

Let us turn to the Lord of the harvest and ask his forgiveness for the weeds of sin that persist in our lives.

I confess to almighty God.

Readings on p. 107.

HEADINGS FOR READINGS

First Reading (Ecclesiastes 3:1-8.11). There is a time and a season for everything.

Second Reading (Galatians 6:7-10). Paul urges us never to tire of doing good, because if we persevere, we will one day reap the harvest of our good deeds.

Gospel (Matthew 13:4-9). God continues to sow the seed of his word in our hearts and minds so that our lives may be fruitful in goodness.

HOMILY

Harvest-day is the supreme day in which there is no room for anything but the truth. On this day the straw is set aside. The chaff is blown away by the wind. The weeds – and there isn't a wheatfield in the world that doesn't produce some – are consigned to the flames. The only thing that matters is grain. Like sacks of gold, it is taken away and stored carefully in the farmer's barn.

Death is the harvest time of the spirit. On the day of death everything suddenly becomes so clear – good and evil become as different as wheat and weeds.

At death it's not the amount of money or possessions that a person has amassed that matters. These, like the straw and chaff, have to be left behind. It is what a person has made of himself (herself) that matters. On this day the essence of a person is revealed. A person's character stands out. Happy for that person if he (she) has forged it well over the years.

But what of the weeds? By weeds I mean a person's faults and sins. Everybody produces some weeds.''In the best of all hearts, there remains an unprooted small corner of evil.' (Solzhenitsyn). On harvest-day any farmer worthy of the name concentrates on the wheat, not on the weeds. Even though the harvest is never a hundred per cent, there is always plenty to be thankful for. Hence it is right that on the day of death we concentrate on a person's good points. As for his (her) sins – let us consign them to the flames of God's mercy.

Here the preacher could refer to the harvest of goodness in the life of the deceased.

We must remember in talking about the harvest that we are not dealing with tangible things. We are dealing with things of the spirit. While it is true that when a person dies the essence of that person is revealed, it is also true to say that when a person dies an unknown world passes away.

Nothing that is truly important about a person is calculable, measurable, or weighable. A person is more than the sum of the materials that went into his making, just as a cathedral is a great deal more than the sum of its stones. What we are is not to be sought in the outward reflection of our deeds, but in the invisible depths of our being. We see only the shell. Each person is a mystery to every other person, and to a large extent to himself. Hence, even when we put all the fragemnts that we know about another person together, we still do not have the complete picture.

Sometimes a farmer reaps only a fraction of what he has sown. Outside forces (birds, bugs, poor soil, drought, etc.), over which he has no control, rob him of part of the harvest. That is why in Christ's story the harvest was only sixty per cent in some cases, and even as low as thirty in others. In death people reap, not only the good they have managed to accomplish, but also those things for which they have striven, but which through no fault of their own they failed to achieve.

However, in the final analysis, what is gathered into the heavenly Father's barn is known only to him.

'Life is only a kind of sowing time; the harvest is not here.' (Van Gogh)

PRAYER OF THE FAITHFUL

President: Even though we may sow in tears, we will reap the harvest in joy, for the Lord works marvels for those who have become his sons and daughters in Christ. Let us pray to the Father with great trust and confidence. *Response*: Hear us, O Lord.

Reader(s): That N. may reap with joy a rich harvest from all the good he (she) did during life. Let us pray.

That he (she) may also reap the fruits of those things for which he (she) strove and which, through no fault of his (her) own, he (she) never attained. Let us pray.

That God may consign to the flames of his mercy the weeds and thorns of his (her) sins. Let us pray.

For those who mourn N.'s death: tha they may find strength in the knowledge that for many days to come they will continue to reap the harvest of goodness he (she) sowed. Let us pray.

For this community: we are like seeds planted by God in the same field; may we help one another to grow. Let us pray.

For each of us: that we may draw inspiration from N.'s example, and so persevere in goodness. Let us pray.

President: Father the soil of our lives is often thin, stony and filled with weeds. But your seed is strong and sturdy. Help us to care for it so that we may produce thirty- or sixty- or even a hundred-fold in the day of the harvest. We ask this through Christ our Lord.

COMMUNION REFLECTION No. 30.

---

8. GOING HOME

INTRODUCTION AND CONFITEOR

Without a home, that is, a place where we belong and are loved, life would be a misery. But without an eternal home life would, in the long run, be absolutely meaningless.

However, Christ assures us that we do have a home to go to when we are uprooted by death. This home is our heavenly Father's house. He even says that he has gone there to prepare a place for us in that house. This should give tremendous hope at a time of death. *(Pause)*.

Our sins cause us to stumble on the road to the Father's house. Let us confess them, asking forgiveness from God and from one another.

I confess to almighty God ...

Readings on p. 109.

HEADINGS FOR READINGS

First Reading (Isaiah 49:8.13-16). Just as a mother cannot forget her child, so God can never forget any of his children. He has our names written on the palm of his hand.

Second Reading (2 Corinthians 5:1.6-10). Paul tells us that, when our earthly life is over, God has an everlasting house built for us in heaven.

Gospel (John 14:1-6). In the eternal house God has prepared for us there is plenty of room for everyone, and Jesus has gone ahead to prepare the way for us.

HOMILY

If you have ever watched the birds you will surely have noticed the following phemomenon. During the day they fly aimlessly about over the fields and plains. But when evening comes on, their wanderings cease and they find a destination. They begin to fly towards something definite. In other words, they fly towards home.

As I sit here writing these lines I cast an occasional glance out of my window to scan the evening sky. Darkness is falling on the fields and streets. In half an hour or so it will be night. In the fading light the rooks are coming in. Now that night is approaching they are heading for the familiar grove of beech trees. They come in ones, twos, and whole batches. After a lot of circling and raucous cawing, they finally settle down for the night. All their journeying, all their labours are over for at least another day. They can rest now. They are home.

All living creatures need a home to go to at the end of the day. We too need a home. To have a home is not just to have a building. It is to have a set of close ties with certain people, people who accept us for what we are and who give us a feeling of belonging. Conversely, to be homeless is not just to have nowhere to go, but to have no close ties with anyone, and to be wanted by nobody.

But we don't only need a home here on earth. We also need an eternal home to go to when death brings down the curtain on the day of our life. Our faith tells us that there is an eternal home waiting for us at the end of our earthly life. This is why faith is the most important thing in life. Without it we would be deprived of the hope of an everlasting home.

> Here the preacher could talk a little about the deceased, especially if he/she was a person of faith and someone to whom the home and the family were very important.

At the Last Supper, Jesus knew that the night of death was coming on. But he had no doubt about the goal of his life. He said, 'I came from the Father and have come into the world; again, I am leaving the world and going to the Father.' (John 16:28). Jesus saw his death as 'going to the Father', and that was not only to go home but to live in the fullest sense possible.

Jesus also said to his apostles, 'I go to prepare a place for you.' For Christians, then, life is an exile. In spite of all the buildings we put up and roots we put down, we do not have here a lasting home. All we have, as Paul says, is a kind of tent. At death the tent is folded up and we depart for that permanent home Christ has promised us.

When death uproots us we are not homeless. We are merely going to our true home. Thus our leaving becomes an arrival; the outward journey turns into a homeward road. While we are here on earth we are in exile, that is, away from the Father's house. To die is to go home to the Father's house.

'You have made us for yourself, O Lord, and our hearts will never rest until they rest in you.' (St Augustine).

'Like a flock of homesick cranes flying night and day back to their mountain nests, let all my life take its voyage to its eternal home.' (Tagore)

PRAYER OF THE FAITHFUL

President: Christ is the way, the truth, and the life. No one can come to the Father except through him. Let us pray with confidence through him who shared our earthly exile so as to bring us to our heavenly home. *Response*: Hear us, O Lord.

Reader(s): N. has departed his (her) earthly home; may he (she) reach the joy and peace of the Father's house. Let us pray.

That Christ may have mercy on him (her), forgive his (her) sins, and bring him (her) to everlasting life. Let us pray.

For those who mourn his (her) passing: that they may be comforted by the hope that he (she) has gone to his (her) everlasting home. Let us pray.

For all here: that nothing in this life may cause us to forget our eternal home. Let us pray.

For all our deceased relatives and friends: that the Lord may bring these and all the departed into the light of his presence. Let us pray.

President: Father, you made us for yourself, and our hearts will never rest until they rest in you. Grant that amidst the uncertainties of this changing world our hearts may be set on our eternal home where true joys are to be found. We ask this through Christ our Lord.

COMMUNION REFLECTION No. 24 .

9. THE GREAT LOSS

INTRODUCTION AND CONFITEOR

We, and especially the family of N., have suffered a great loss. In our sorrow we turn to Christ, the Good Shepherd. He understands our pain, and he alone can give us comfort, hope and strength. *(Pause)*.

Lord, you go looking for us when we get lost on the paths of life. Lord, have mercy.

You are happy when we find our way back to the arms of our heavenly Father. Christ, have mercy.

At death, when all seems lost, you give us the bright hope of gaining eternal life with you. Lord, have mercy.

Readings on p. 111.

HEADINGS FOR READINGS

First Reading (Ezekiel 34:11-12.15-16). Just as a faithful shepherd takes care of all the sheep in his flock, especially those that are in danger, so the Lord takes care of all his people.

Second Reading (1 Thessalonians 4:13-18). Like everyone else, Christians grieve over the loss of a loved one. But the grief of Christians is lit up with hope.

Gospel (John 10:14-15.27-30).Christ is the good shepherd *par excellence*. He gives his sheep life not only here but also hereafter.

HOMILY

It is a well-known fact that anything we lose assumes an exaggerated value. It seems less dispensable than the sum-total of all the things we still possess. For instance, you lose the key to your house. Suddenly that key becomes the most important object you own. Without it you are cut off from everything in the house. It seems as if you will not be able to live without it.

How much more true this is when it is not an object that we lose but a person, and when the loss is irretrievable as it is in death. It is impossible to describe the feeling that comes over one at such a time. The feeling that somehow, in an instant of time, everything is changed and nothing will ever be quite the same again. Tomorrow will never again be like yesterday. The very trees, the grass, the flowers, the sky are no longer the same. The world is empty. We feel like orphans.

> Here the preacher could dwell a little on the life of the deceased, and on the loss felt at her/his death.

The loss of someone we love, someone on whom we greatly depended, is a shattering experience. It seems to empty the whole future of happiness, and even of meaning. Only one who believes in a God guiding us can bear such a loss as this. Faced with such a loss the only thing we can do is flee to the Gospel.

In the Gospel we meet the Good Shepherd. We see his knowledge of, and concern for, his sheep. He would rather lose his own life than allow the wolf or thief to snatch one of those sheep. His sheep, knowing his love for them, listen to his voice and follow him.

Christ is that Good Shepherd. We are his people, the sheep of his flock. To him every single one of us is important and precious. He gave his life to save us from eternal death. Those who belong to him and who follow him will never be lost. He will give them eternal life. And all this he does to show us how precious we are to the heavenly Father.

'God so loved the world that he gave his only Son, that whoever believes in him should not perish but have eternal life.' (John 3:16). This is the Gospel. This is the Good News.

Our loved ones, who died believing in Christ, are not lost. We have Christ's word for this. They are still part of his Body (the Communion of Saints) to which we belong. It's just that they belong to the heavenly part of it, while we still belong to the earthly part of it.

One day we shall find them again when we too, God willing, will enter into the fulness of eternal life. This hope will not fill the emptiness we feel at this moment but it will help us to cope with our loss.

'And the stately ships go on
To their haven under the hill;
But O for the touch of a vanished hand
And the sound of a voice that is still.' (Tennyson).

PRAYER OF THE FAITHFUL

President: Christ is the Good Shepherd who gave his life to save his sheep. In our loss, let us turn to God and with confidence make our needs known to him. *Response*: Lord, hear us in your love.

Reader(s): N. experienced the love of Christ the Good Shepherd in this life; may she (he) now enjoy the fulness of eternal life in the kingdom of the Father. We pray in faith.

That Christ the Good Shepherd may heal in her (him) the wounds caused by her (his) own sins and the sins of others. We pray in faith.

May those who grieve over her (his) loss be comforted by the hope that the Good Shepherd will take care of her (him). We pray in faith.

For ourselves: that we may listen attentively to the voice of the Good Shepherd so that he may lead us along the path of eternal life. We pray in faith.

For all the faithful departed, especially our relatives and friends: that they may dwell in the house of the Lord for ever. We pray in faith.

For those who do not follow Christ because they do not hear his voice or know him. We pray in faith.

President: Father, you sent your Son to us to ensure that none of your daughters or sons might be lost but might have eternal life. Help us to trust him and to follow him so that we may find eternal life at the end of our earthly journey. Through Christ our Lord.

COMMUNION REFLECTION No. 24 or No. 23.

---

10. PARTING TIME

INTRODUCTION AND CONFITEOR

Death is a time of parting. The more we love someone the harder parting is. The only thing that makes death tolerable is the hope our faith gives us that we shall meet our loved ones again in God.

As we pray for our brother (sister) N. during this Mass, may we experience a strengthening of our faith. *(Pause)*.

Lord, you are the hope of all who turn to you. Lord, have mercy.

You are the way that leads to the Father's kingdom. Christ, have mercy.

You are the unbreakable bond that binds us to the Father and to one another. Lord, have mercy.

Readings on p. 113.

HEADINGS FOR READINGS

First Reading (Wisdom 3:1-6.9). Those who live a good life may have a difficult time here on earth, but when they die God will reward them with immortality.

Second Reading (1 Thessalonians 4:13-18). Our faith doesn't prevent us from grieving for the dead, but it gives us the priceless gift of hope – hope that we shall see them again.

Gospel (John 16:16-22). Jesus is about to die, that is, to go to the Father. He assures his disciples that they will see him again.

HOMILY

Life is full of partings. No matter how close our relationships with our loved ones are, we still cannot have them with us twenty four hours of every day. We still have to part with them from time to time.

Partings are always painful. The closer the bond we have with someone, and the longer the period of separation is likely to be, the more we feel the pain of parting. It is only when we have to part with somebody that we realise how much he (she) means to us. 'Love knows not its own depth until the hour of separation' (Kahlil Gibran). In fact, the real worth of our friend may not become apparent to us until he (she) has actually gone from us. 'What we most love in our friend may be clearer in his absence, as the mountain is clearer to the climber from the plain' (Gibran).

Now what is is true of the ordinary partings of life is, of course, even more true of the parting we call 'death'. Death is the most irrevocable parting of all. We know (though in the newness of grief, mercifully, we cannot yet take it in) that our loved one will not be returning.

In the case of sudden death we are not even given a chance to say a proper good-bye. We would dearly love to take leave of our loved one warmly and tenderly, in a manner befitting a final farewell. Now we will never get a chance to say all that was in our heart. We will never get another opportunity to tell the loved one how much we valued and loved him (her).

However, not all partings are devoid of joy. Sometimes, though saddened at the thought that a friend is going from us, we are happy that he (she) is going to better things. But it may take a little time for this joy to break through.

> Here the preacher could refer to the life of the deceased, and perhaps also to the manner in which he (she) departed the earthly scene.

In our sadness at the departure of N., the Gospel comes to our aid. The night before Jesus died, his disciples were plunged into gloom at the thought of his leaving them. But he said to them, 'You have sorrow now, but I will see you again and your hearts will rejoice.' In other words, death would not be an everlasting parting.

Our faith tells us that our loved ones have not gone from us for ever. They have not disappeared into nothingness. They have not ceased to exist. They have merely departed for that farther shore on the other side of life, that shore which is the final destination of all of us.

Our loved ones have gone before us to see, to worship, to love, and to intercede for us. When we reach that farther shore, we will meet them again. Meanwhile, we see them off, going with them as far as we are allowed. We bid them farewell with our prayers. They have gone to better things. As Paul puts it, they are now with the Lord for ever. Those who die in grace go no further from us than God, and God is very near to us.

'Death is not so bad; it is only a farewell' (Hermann Hesse).

'So live here that you may pass wiith ease to that other shore' (Tagore).

PRAYER OF THE FAITHFUL

President: God is our beginning and our end. At birth we come from him. At death we return to him. Comforted by this faith, we pray with confidence for N., for others and for ourselves. *Response*: Father, hear us in your love.

Reader(s): That N. who has departed from us may reach the safety of eternity's shore. We pray in faith.

That God in his mercy may blot out the sins he (she) committed through human weakness. We pray in faith.

For those who mourn for him (her): that the Lord may turn their sorrow into joy. We pray in faith.

That the Lord may grant eternal life to all those whom we loved in this life but whom death has taken from us. We pray in faith.

For ourselves: that we may so live here on earth that when death comes we may pass with ease to that other shore. We pray in faith.

President: Father, into your hands we commend the soul of N. May no torment touch him (her). May he (she) reach a place of refreshment, light and peace. We ask this through Christ our Lord.

COMMUNION REFLECTION No. 32 or No. 31.

---

11. ENCOUNTER WITH CHRIST

INTRODUCTION AND CONFITEOR

When the people of Naim were caught up in the sorrows of death, God visited them in the person of Christ. God visits us too in the midst of our sorrow, for as we begin this celebration Christ stands among us as the Lord of life and death.

Let us turn to him in our sorrow and need. *(Pause)*

Lord Jesus, you give comfort to all who mourn. Lord, have mercy.

You give hope to all who stand in the shadow of death. Christ have mercy.

You brighten the horizon of all our tomorrows with the promise of eternal life. Lord, have mercy.

Readings on p. 115.

HEADINGS FOR READINGS

First Reading (Isaiah 25:6-9). Faced with death, God is our only source of hope and salvation. He will destroy death and wipe away all tears.

Second Reading (1 Corinthians 13:8-12). Here on earth we see God dimly; in the next life we shall see him face to face.

Gospel (Luke 7:11-17). At Naim Jesus shows that he is Lord over death, and shows the people that God cares about them.

HOMILY 1   *For someone who was a life-long, committed Christian*

We all have some hero or heroine whom we admire and long to meet. I know someone who has a great unfulfilled ambition. It is to meet the Russian writer, Alexander Solzhenitsyn. Why? Because Solzhenitsyn's life has inspired him, and his writings have enriched him in a way, and to a degree, he could not possibly put into words.

Thus, if one day he does succeed in meeting him, it will be the climax of a relationship he has built up with him over the years. He will not be meeting a stranger. He will be meeting a dear friend. If he does not meet him, he will still be grateful for having had him as an invisible spiritual and moral companion for at least part of his earthly journey.

We are all embarked on this earthly journey. Many of us are beset by fears. However, our fear of death is our deepest fear and lies at the root of most of our other fears. But our Christian faith ought to make a big difference to the way we see death. The story of every Christian's life is the story of a friendship with Christ. This friendship begins with an encounter with Christ (at baptism). It also ends with an encounter with Christ (at death).

For those with faith, death ceases to be an encounter with the unknown. Instead, it becomes an encounter with Christ. To someone who has made Christ the invisible companion of the journey of life, and whose life has been inspired by Christ's teaching, death becomes a meeting with a dear friend, in fact, with an older brother. When death comes, Christ comes also, bringing the everlasting life which he won for us with his own death.

> Here the preacher could refer to the deceased, stressing especially the quality of her/his Christian faith.

What each of us must do is very clear. We must strive to ensure that the Christ who linked his life with ours at Baptism, making us children of God and heirs to eternal life, does not remain a shadowy figure on the margins of our lives, but becomes a friend in whom we are learning to confide more and more.

This relationship with Christ is at the very heart of the Christian life. However, it is something we must work at. While we are on earth, as Paul says, 'we see in a mirror dimly'. Our knowledge of God, and of the things of God, is limited and easily gets clouded over. Besides this, our path is strewn with difficulties, puzzles and temptations.

If our relationship with Christ is the most important thing in our life, then death will lose its power over us, and we will be able to live in the joy and freedom of the children of God. Those who have developed a close and warm relationship with Christ during life will find it easier to recognise and trust him when he comes at death.

Christ comes to us many times during life, summoning us to a deeper and fuller life, a life more in keeping with our dignity as children of the Father. When he comes to us at death, he will do for us what he did for the little boy at Naim. He will awaken us to life, not however to this earthly life which must one day cease, but to eternal life which will never cease.

HOMILY 2 *For someone who was away from the faith*

We are all embarked on the journey of life. Many of us are beset by fears. However, our fear of death is our deepest fear and lies at the root of many of our other fears. But it is especially here that our Christian faith comes to our aid.

The story of a Christian's life is the story of a relationship with Christ. This relationship begins at Baptism. Christ meets us at the start of our earthly journey. He links his life to ours. Through him we become children of God and heirs to eternal life.

But he does not leave us to struggle through life on our own. He offers himself to us as the invisible companion of our journey. He also makes available to us the support of the Christian community.

He also comes to meet us at the hour of our death. He comes to accompany us through the dark valley towards the Father's kingdom, where he will share with us the everlasting life he won for us with his own death. For those with faith in Christ, death ceases to be an encounter with the unknown. Instead it becomes an encounter with Christ, who in Baptism, not only made himself our friend, but our elder brother.

It all sounds so simple and so wonderful. And it really is. Yet complications can arise. Our knowledge of God, and the things of God, is so limited. Our vision is so clouded. As St Paul says, 'here we see in a mirror dimly'. As well as this, each of us is plagued with weaknesses, and our path is strewn with difficulties of one kind or another.

Here the preacher could refer to the deceased, stressing the good she/he did, and the difficulties she/he encountered.

Little wonder then that we sometimes make mistakes. We go down roads that lead nowhere. Above all, we forget the Christ who came to meet us at the start of our lives. However, we must not lose heart or hope. Christ understands us better than we understand ourselves. Even though we may forget him, he does not forget us.

Salvation is always a gift from God. It is given most freely to those who know that before him they are poor, and who are not too proud to ask for it. Christ did not come to be our judge but our saviour. Like the first encounter with Christ at Baptism, the last one (at death) is not something we can merit with any good works. It is a spontaneous act of compassion on the part of Christ, as it was for the widow's son at Naim, (and the thief on the cross).

People may lose Christ for a period of life, perhaps even for the whole of it, and still encounter him at the end, and for them too death is transformed into life. At the hour of death it is Christ's image that will rise before us. It is to him that we have to justify our life and to no one else. But he is a friend, always a friend.

PRAYER OF THE FAITHFUL

President: When the people of Naim saw the great deed which Jesus had done they knew that in him God had visited them. God still visits us his people, especially when are in the midst of sorrow., Let us pray to him through Christ, the Lord of life and death.
Response: Lord, graciously hear us.

Reader(s): At Baptism Christ awakened N. to the life of God; may he now awaken her (him) to the fulness of eternal life. Lord, hear us.

N. lived believing in Christ as the hope of her (his) life; may Christ now lead her (him) safely home to the Father's house. Lord, hear us.

That Christ may visit the family of N. with comfort, hope and peace. Lord, hear us.

That Christ may visit the community assembled here, and keep it rooted in faith and love. Lord, hear us.

That Christ may visit our world, which is dominated by death, and kindle in it the hope of eternal life. Lord, hear us.

That Christ may visit all our departed relatives and friends and bring them into the light of his presence. Lord, hear us.

President: Heavenly Father, visit us your people during this Eucharist which we celebrate in memory of Christ your Son. Help us to experience your loving and merciful presence among us, and to know that life is stronger than death. We ask this through Christ our Lord.

COMMUNION REFLECTION No. 3 or No. 4.

12. THE LIGHT OF LIFE

INTRODUCTION AND CONFITEOR

We gather in darkness because, with N's death, a light has gone out in our midst. But for the light of Christ the darkness would over-whelm us *(Draw attention to the paschal candle, symbol of the risen Christ, the light of the world.)*

Our sins darken our lives. Let us now call them to mind. *(Pause)*

Lord, in you a new light has dawned upon our world of sadness and shadows. Lord, have mercy.

Lord, with this light to guide us, we will walk confidently along the path that leads to eternal life. Christ, have mercy.

Lord, with you as our guide, even the darkness of death will hold no terrors for us. Lord, have mercy.

Readings on p. 118.

HEADINGS FOR READINGS

First Reading (Isaiah 9:2-6). The prophet foretells the coming of a great light through the birth of a special child.

Second Reading (1 Corinthians 13:8-12). In this life we see God and his kingdom dimly, as in a mirror; but in the next life we shall see everything clearly.

Gospel (Mark 10:46-51). Christ opens the eyes of Bartimaeus, who immediately begins to follow him. Through the gift of faith, our eyes are opened and we too become followers of Christ.

HOMILY

The world can be a very bewildering place. There is so much darkness about, so many paths that one can follow, so many voices that one has to listen to. Little wonder that many people become confused and get lost on the highways and byways of life.

We need a special kind of sight, a special kind of vision. Here is where the Christian faith comes in. Dostoyevsky said, 'While on earth we grope along in the dark and, but for the precious image of Christ before us, we would lose our way completely and perish.' He himself did a fair amount of groping and searching before arriving at this conclusion.

Faith helps us to find our way in the dark. It is the most important thing in life. It is the light of our lives. It is to us what a compass is to a sailor in a storm. The smallest child with faith 'sees' more than the greatest scientist who has no faith. Christ, the light of the world, enlightens all those who believe in him. Those who follow his light make things very simple for themselves.

Even the tiniest light helps to dispel some darkness and enables us to inch our way forward. How much more does the light of Christ help us to walk with confidence through the darkness of this world until we reach the land of everlasting day. Christ's light is a blazing torch that is able to light up even pitch-black paths. It is so sure and steady that no darkness, not even that of death, can extinguish it.

The light of Christ was first kindled in our hearts at Baptism. On the day of our Baptism our parents received a candle on our behalf. This candle was lit from the Paschal or Easter Candle (now burning in our midst) which stands for Christ, risen from the dead. As we received this candle the priest prayed, 'Receive the light of Christ. See that it is kept burning brightly ... until the Lord comes.'

Our brother (sister) N. was enlightened by the light of Christ.

Here the preacher might show how the life of the deceased was lit up by faith in Christ and could point to some of the ways in which he/she shed light into the lives of others.

Bartimaeus was in darkness until the day he met Christ. On that happy day he not only got his ordinary sight back, but got the gift of faith too, and immediately became a follower of Christ. To bè a Christian is to have one's eyes opened by Christ, and to be a follower of his.

The light of faith guides every step of a Christian's life on earth. Even though we never see fully, but only, as Paul says, 'in a mirror dimly', nevertheless we need no longer be afraid of the dark. Even the darkness of death need hold no terrors for us. Christ, our brother, has passed through the dark valley ahead of us.

Thanks to our Baptism we are linked to our brothers and sisters in the Christian community. We are members of a community on which the light of Christ has dawned.

'Why fear the dark? It is the dark that brings the stars to us' (Helder Camara).

'Death is not extinguishing the light; it is putting out the lamp because the dawn has come' (Tagore).

THE PRAYER OF THE FAITHFUL

President: Christ said, 'I am the light of the world; he who follows me will not walk in darkness but will have the light of life.' With Christ's light shining on us, we pray in hope. *Response*: Lord, graciously hear us.

Reader(s): That N. who was enlightened by Christ in Baptism, may now enjoy the full vision of God. Lord, hear us.

That the darkness of his (her) sins may be banished by the light of God's mercy. Lord, hear us.

The light of Christ guided N. through this life; may this light now shine gently on those who mourn his (her) death. Lord, hear us.

That God's eternal light may shine on all our departed relatives and friends. Lord, hear us.

That the light of Christ may guide all of us safely through the shadows of this world until we reach our homeland of everlasting life. Lord, hear us.

President: Father, lead us from the faith by which we know you in this life to the vision of your glory in the life to come. We ask this through Jesus Christ our Lord.

COMMUNION REFLECTION No. 1 or No. 2.

---

13. THE HUNGER FOR ETERNAL LIFE

INTRODUCTION AND CONFITEOR

We hunger for happiness; we long for a life without end. But death seems to rob us, not only of what we possess, but of our hopes and dreams too.

Only one person promised what we are all crying for. That person was Christ. He promised the bread of eternal life to those who believe in him. Let us turn to him now. *(Pause)*

Lord, like a deer that yearns for running streams, my soul is yearning for you, my God. Lord, have mercy.

My spirit is thirsting for you, the God of my life. Christ, have mercy.

Even though my soul is cast down by sorrow, I will go on hoping in you and praising you. Lord, have mercy

Readings on p. 119.

HEADINGS FOR READINGS

First Reading (1 Kings 19:4-8). The great prophet Elijah is so beset by troubles that he wants to die. But God sends him a mysterious food which helps him to go forward once more.

Second Reading (1 Corinthians 2:1-6.9). To all the humble and simple ones, God provides the hope of unending happiness.

Gospel (John 6:44-51). Christ is the bread of eternal life. On the strength of this bread we can walk all the way to eternal life.

HOMILY

Those who live in First World countries have an incredible abundance and variety of bread. (In what follows I am using the word 'bread' to mean, not just bread, but material things in general). Yet, despite this glut of bread, people are still not happy. Why is this?

It is because people are hungering for something more vital and necessary than bread. Our hunger goes deeper than it seems. Man is not just an animal, a body. He is also a spirit. His body might be well-fed, yet his spirit could be starving, with the result that he as a person is languishing in a half-life. People do not die only for want of food. They also die for want of such things as meaning, hope, love, and faith in God. They die, not just from a hunger of the body, but also from a hunger of the heart and the spirit.

Furthermore, most people at some stage of their lives, encounter the desert – the desert of loneliness, or illness, or depression, or failure, or ... But the desert from which most people shrink is the desert within themselves – that feeling of emptiness and poverty we all experience at one time or another, even though we may be living in an oasis of comfort and pleasure.

Hence, I think that today people are beginning to glimpse the truth of the words of Christ, 'Man does not live on bread alone.' Those who live on bread alone (material things alone) will never be fully nourished and, therefore, never fully satisfied.

It is especially when we encounter the desert that we feel the need of another kind of bread. Ordinary bread will not do by itself. Like the Israelites of old, we need manna from heaven. We need the kind of bread only God can give. And God really does give it to his children. He gives it to us in abundance in and through Christ, his Son.

> Here the preacher could refer to the deceased, drawing attention to whatever desert he/she may have endured, and stressing how he/she found nourishment and strength through faith in Christ, and perhaps specifically in the Eucharist.

Our deepest hunger of all is our hunger for eternal life. People want not only a full stomach but immortality. This is our most insistent yearning. The bread of eternal life, which only Christ can give, is the only bread that will fully satisfy this yearning, this hunger. This bread makes all other bread seem tasteless. This is the bread for which each of us, often unknown to our conscious self, is secretly crying.

Only God can satisfy the hunger of the human heart and the

human spirit. In Christ God provides us with the bread of eternal life. It was for this very reason that Christ came down from heaven. He gives us this bread abundantly in the Eucharist. This is the bread that sustained all the saints and martyrs.

Even apart from our experience of the desert, we need this special bread if we are to live the life of the spirit, a life worthy of a child of God. Without it we will always be spiritually hungry. Whereas physical hunger is a plague, spiritual hunger is a blessing. It makes us turn to Christ who said, 'Blessed are those who hunger ... they will be satisfied.'

PRAYER OF THE FAITHFUL

President: Anyone who belives in Christ has eternal life, for Christ is the bread sent down from heaven by the Father so that his children may not die but may have eternal life. Let us pray to him who gives life to the world. *Response*: Lord, hear us in your love.

Reader(s): N. ate the bread of eternal life on earth; may he (she) now enjoy the eternal banquet of which this is a foretaste. We pray in faith.

That Christ may raise him (her) up to the fulness of that divine life he came on earth to share with us. We pray in faith.

For N's family, relatives and friends, whose spirits are cast down by sorrow: that they may find strength through their faith. We pray in faith.

Strengthened by the bread of angels, Elijah walked all the way to the mountain of God; strengthened by the bread Christ gives, may we walk all the way to the kingdom of heaven. We pray in faith.

For those who are without faith: that Christ may open their ears to the Good News which tells of the unimaginable good things God has prepared for those who love him. We pray in faith.

For all the faithful departed: that they may enter into the full possession of the promised land of heaven. We pray in faith.

President: Father in heaven, inspire us to yearn for you always, like the deer for running streams, until you satisfy all our longings in heaven. We ask this through Christ our Lord.

COMMUNION REFLECTION No. 19 or No. 21.

14. THE RESURRECTION AND THE LIFE

INTRODUCTION AND CONFITEOR

There are many things which cause tears to fall, but without doubt death is the greatest offender. Death brought tears to the eyes of Christ himself. But as the Son of God, he is the one who gives hope and consolation to all those who mourn. Let us pause to make an act of faith in his presence with us in our sorrow. *(Pause)*

The only death a Christian need fear is the death of sin. Let us confess our sins, and ask Christ to raise us up from them.

I confess to almighty God.

Readings on p. 121.

HEADINGS FOR READINGS

First Reading (Lamentations 3:17-26). Those who are overcome with anguish and pain, but who hope in God, will experience relief.

Second Reading (1 Corinthians 15:51-57). Thanks to Christ's resurrection, death has lost its sting and will not have the final say in our lives.

Gospel (John 11:17-27). By raising Lazarus from the tomb Jesus shows that he is Lord over death as well as Lord over life.

HOMILY

We live in a world where death is more talked about than life. The news headlines are dominated, day in and day out, by death. Today we ourselves stand in darkness and in the shadow of death. But we are not without light and hope. We are not without a friend.

Our brother (sister) N. has died. But he (she) was a believer in Christ. This means that, like Lazarus, he (she) was a friend of Christ. More than this. In Baptism he (she) became a brother (sister) of Christ. So, in our grief, we can imitate Martha and Mary who, in their grief, had recourse to Christ.

Like them we can say to him, 'Lord, your friend has died.' And Christ will come to us as he came to them. In fact, we know that he is already with us. He understands our loss. He does not dry our tears, for they are right, proper and necessary. But he shares our grief and gives us hope.

Here the preacher could refer to deceased and to the sense of loss felt at his/her death.

Christ says, 'I am the resurrection and the life; he who believes in me, though he die (physically), yet shall he live.' This is a most revolutionary statement. Christ declares that he, in his own person, is the victory over death. He is eternal life. In him what was once a hope in a far-distant future has become a present reality.

This is the greatness of our faith. Eternal life is not something that happens to us when we die. Those who believe in Christ, and who are linked to him through Baptism, already have eternal life within them. The seed is well and truly planted, though its full blossoming only comes after death. How is this? It is because in Christ we have already touched the very life of God which is immortal. In Baptism we are grafted onto Christ, the true vine, and begin to live with his life – the life of God.

We feel sad at the onset of winter because the earth turns brown and everything begins to die. Nevertheless, we are not too despondent, for we know that spring will return and renew everything once more. In the same way, we are plunged into sadness when the winter of death claims the life of a loved one. But we are not overwhelmed. What sustains us is our faith in Christ which assures us that life will prevail over death. Through his death and resurrection Christ has taken the sting out of death.

Thanks to our Baptism and faith in Christ, we are already living the life of God. Thus, even in the midst of the winter of death, we know that spring is already quietly at work within us and among us.

PRAYER OF THE FAITHFUL

President: Christ is the resurrection and the life. Let us pray that we may be rooted in a love which overcomes death and casts out all fear. *Response*: Lord, hear our prayer.

Reader(s): That N. may enjoy the full flowering of that life Christ shared with him (her) at Baptism. Let us pray to the Lord.

Christ called Lazarus from the tomb; may he call our brother (sister) N. forth from this land of shadows to the land of eternal light. Let us pray to the Lord.

That Christ may free him (her) from the bonds of his (her) sins. Let us pray to the Lord.

As Christ comforted Martha and Mary, may he comfort all of us who mourn N's passing, and especially N's family. Let us pray to the Lord.

For all here present: that we may have the faith in Christ that Martha and Mary had. Let us pray to the Lord.

For those who die without hope: that they too may hear the words of Christ and live. Let us pray to the Lord.

President: Heavenly Father, you sent your Son into our world, a world dominated by death, to plant within our hearts the hope of eternal life. Grant that we who are linked to lhim through faith may one day see him face to face in that land where death will be no more. We ask this through Christ our Lord.

COMMUNION REFLECTION No. 26.

---

15. THE PEARL OF GREAT PRICE

INTRODUCTION AND CONFITEOR

The most precious thing in life is not silver or gold, but wisdom. Wisdom helps us to know God's purpose for us in this life. Death helps us to see what is important in life. So, though it is a time of sorrow, it is also a time of grace. It opens our eyes to the vision of the eternal. *(Pause)*

Let us confess our sins to God, who is all-wise and all-forgiving.

I confess to almighty God.

Readings on p. 123.

HEADINGS FOR READINGS

First Reading (Wisdom 7:7-11). This talks about the importance of wisdom. Those who possess wisdom will not go wrong, because they have God's light to guide them.

Second Reading (1 Corinthians 2:1-6.9). Mere human wisdom ultimately leaves us in the wilderness. But God's wisdom leads to life, and to good things beyond all human imagining.

Gospel (Matthew 13:44-46). Those who find the kingdom of God find something which is rarer than the most priceless pearl.

HOMILY

Since the dawn of time people have been searching for buried treasure. In the olden days they searched for it in the fields, hills and sea. If only they could find gold or diamonds or pearls, they would be happy. Today people look for treasure in the lottery, the casino and the stock exchange. If only they could hit the jackpot, then their joy would brim over.

One way or another we are all treasure-hunters. We are all looking for 'the pearl of great price', that is, something that will make us completely happy. There is nothing wrong with this. Christ encouraged it. The fact is, we are incomplete, and therefore dissatisfied. The only pity is that many don't know where to look for the pearl or even what it consists in.

Christ tells us what the pearl is and shows us where it can be found. This was the very reason he came down on earth. He says that the kingdom God is the pearl of great price. It alone is worth everything. Those who find it are truly fortunate. Even if in the eyes of the world they are poor, in the eyes of God they are rich.

The kingdom is a very simple concept. It means to know that one is a child of God, with an eternal dignity and destiny. It means to know the meaning of life and how we should live it. The treasure is hidden, yes, but only from the wise. It is revealed to the simple, those to whom God gives the gift of wisdom. Wisdom has nothing to do with being smart or even intelligent. It means to know God's purpose for us and to live according to it.

Our chief task in life is not to be successful or fulfilled. It is to live well. Spirituality is our real vocation. Unfortunately, many things, good in themselves, can block all roads to the one thing that distinguishes us from the animals, namely, spiritual activity. 'People exhaust themselves in the senseless pursuit of material things and die without realising their spiritual wealth' (Solzhenitsyn).

Here the preacher could refer to the deceased, showing how he/she knew what life was about, thus giving expression in his/her life to the wisdom of the Gospel.

No one can be happy who ignores or misses the main purpose of our life on earth. Hence, the only question that really matters is how best to live in this world. Those who find the answer to this question have found the pearl. And those who have found the pearl will know real joy even here on earth. But this joy is only a foretaste of what they will experience hereafter, when they will come into full possession of the kingdom.

Deep down, however vaguely, everybody experiences a desire for the kingdom of God. If we lose God, we lose all. If we find God, we find all.

'The luckiest thing that ever happened to me in my life was getting to know God' (Carlo Carretto).

'What the world lacks today is not so much knowledge of the first things of life as experience of them' (Laurens van der Post).

PRAYER OF THE FAITHFUL

President: In his great love for us God the Father has not left us without wisdom. He has sent his Son to teach us and to help us find our way into his kingdom. *Response*: Hear us, O Lord.

Reader(s): For the Church: that through an effective preaching of the Gospel it may provide a lamp for a world darkened by doubt and unbelief. Let us pray.

For world leaders: that they may govern with wisdom so that the world may enjoy justice and peace. Let us pray.

N. Was enlightened by the wisdom of the Gospel in this life; may he (she) now find his (her) way into the eternal kingdom. Let us pray.

That he (she) may be released from his (her) sins, and blessed with eternal light and peace. Let us pray.

For the sorrowing family, relatives, and friends of N.: that they may find strength and consolation in their faith and in the love and support of the community. Let us pray.

For all here present: that we may never exchange what is lasting and priceless for what is passing and cheap. Let us pray.

President: Father, with Christ as our shepherd and teacher, may we so live in this passing world as to attain to the glory you have promised. We ask this through the same Christ our Lord.

COMMUNION REFLECTION No. 19 or No. 29.

---

16. BEARING ONE'S OWN PARTICULAR FRUIT

INTRODUCTION AND CONFITEOR

Life is a great challenge and also a great opportunity. We have all been given gifts by God which we have to discover, develop, and use. N. is a good example of someone who used his (her) talents well.

Let us look briefly at our attitude to life and to the gifts God has given us. *(Pause)*.

Few of us would be so bold as to claim that we have made full use of God's gifts. So let us ask his forgiveness for our slackness and sins.

I confess to almighty God.

Readings on p. 125.

HEADINGS FOR READINGS

First Reading (Sirach 2:1-9). Those who serve God must expect to meet with many trials. But through them all God upholds them.

Second Reading (1 Corinthians 12:31-13:1-7). Without love all gifts are empty.

Gospel (Matthew 25:14-15.19-23). The story of a man who was given a sum of money, and who made good use of it, thereby earning the praise of his master.

HOMILY

Each of us is special to God. No two of us are alike. Each of us is born to bear our own particular fruit. This is why God blessed each of us with different talents. However, while God has seen to it that all of his children are endowed with some talents, it's obvious that he gives special talents to some. N. is a case in point.

> Here the preacher could dwell a little on N's special talent.

Though we all have been given some talents, nothing is delivered into our hands ready-made and fit for use. In fact, the first thing we have to do is *discover* our talents. The second thing is to *develop* them. There is an eternity between what we are given and what we acquire through the use of what we are given. It is one thing to be given a special talent. It is quite another thing to make full use of that talent. A talent is like a seed. It needs careful nurturing in order to grow, ripen and bear fruit. Those born with special talents have to work hard at developing the skills without which these talents would remain buried treasure.

> Here the preacher could dwell a little on how N. worked at developing his/her talent.

Talents are given to us, not just for our own enrichment, but for the enrichment of others too. But talents such as music, sport, and so on, are not, in the first place, the talents Christ is talking about in the parable we read. It is *we* who are the talents. Therefore ultimately it is what we make of ourselves that matters. Of what use would it be for me to become the greatest musician in the world if I left myself undeveloped?

> Here the preacher could refer to the kind of person N. was. The job is easy if it can truthfully be said that he/she was a good human being. It is easier still if he/she was an active Christian.

Let us take courage from N's example to develop and use the gifts of nature and grace God has given us. We all know that we could *do* more and *be* more. As Emerson said: 'Every man believes that he has a greater possibility. He believes that there is a last chamber, a last chest, that has never been opened.' Let us not wait until the day of death to open this chest.

We must not judge success in the way the world judges it, but in the way Christ judges it. For Christ what matters is the quality of our lives. In the parable he praised the servant for two qualities in particular. He said, 'Well done, *good* and *faithful* servant.' Those two qualities, goodness and faithfulness, are two of the most important qualities in life. They are within the reach of all of us.

Life is a great opportunity, but it is given to us only once. It is God's gift to us. What we do with it is our gift to God. God has given us the stones with which to build a cathedral, or prison, or nothing at all.

PRAYER OF THE FAITHFUL

President: We are children of the Father. He loves us and has showered many gifts and graces on us through his Son Jesus. He wants us to use these gifts so that we can live full lives here and then come to share eternal life with the blessed hereafter. *Response*: Lord, graciously hear us.

Reader(s): For the Church: that it may encourage its members to develop and use all their gifts of grace and nature. Lord, hear us.

For N.: that for all the efforts he (she) made, and the work he (she) did, he (she) may hear words of praise from Christ to whom we must all one day give account of our lives. Lord, hear us.

That God in his great mercy may overlook his (her) sins and give him (her) a merciful judgement. Lord, hear us.

For those who mourn for N., and who are now deprived of the benefits of his (her) talents: that God may turn their darkness into light. Lord, hear us.

For ourselves: that we may not envy those who are more talented than we are, and that we may not be satisfied with ourselves until we have made full use of our own talents. Lord, hear us.

For all those whose talents lie idle either through laziness, cowardice, or simply through lack of opportunity. Lord, hear us.

President: Father, we are the talents. Grant that we may not bury any part of ourselves. Help us to become the kind of sons and daughters you can be proud of. We ask this through Christ our Lord. Amen.

COMMUNION REFLECTION No. 20 or No. 29.

---

17. THE FALL OF A SPARROW
Death of an Infant

Nowadays parents are encouraged to see and hold their dead baby. This will be difficult for them at the time, but later on they will be glad they did it. They might also like to take a photograph. This will help them build up a small store of memories on which to focus their grief. It is also advised to give a still-born infant a name. The full rites of Christian burial can, if so desired, be used even for an unbaptized infant.

INTRODUCTION AND CONFITEOR

We don't like to see anyone pluck a tiny flower that has just appeared over the ground. It somehow doesn't seem fair or right. We feel it ought to be given a chance to grow and bloom.

This is even more true when the 'flower' in question is a little human being. Hence we are deeply saddened that little N. has been plucked from life so soon. Nevertheless, as believers, we have one great consolation. The hand in which this little flower ends up is the hand of God.

It is to God that we turn in our sorrow. *(Pause).*

They are happy whose strength lies in you. Lord, have mercy.

They are happy who dwell in your house. Christ, have mercy.

They are happy who walk without blame. Lord, have mercy.

Readings on p. 127.

HEADINGS FOR READINGS

First Reading (Isaiah 49:8.14-16). God never forgets any of his children. He consoles us in our afflictions, because we are the fruit of his love.

Second Reading (1 John 3:1-2). God shows his love for us in this life by making us his children. He will show his love for us in the next life by letting us see him as he is.

Gospel (Matthew 10:28-31). God's care for his creation extends right down to the very smallest of his creatures.

HOMILY

Of all birds, sparrows are the most insignificant. They are small in size and dull in colour. They undertake no great flights. They live in bushes rather than in trees. Though they are found in vast numbers the world over, we take them completely for granted. In fact, we hardly notice them.

When Christ wanted to give us an idea of how far-reaching and all-embracing is the knowledge and care of our heavenly Father he spoke about the sparrows. 'Can you not buy two sparrows for a penny?' he said. 'Yet not one falls to the ground without your Father knowing.'

By this he means that everything that happens to any of his creatures, even the least and most insignificant, is seen by the

Father and is important to him – yes, even the fall of a single sparrow. The fact that he doesn't prevent this fall, doesn't mean that he is indifferent to it. God is never indifferent. He sees and records it.

Christ goes on to draw the conclusion: 'So there is no need to be afraid; you are worth more (to the heavenly Father) than hundreds of sparrows.' If God is concerned about the sparrows, we can be sure that he is far more concerned about us, who are his sons and daughters.

Today, if you'll pardon the expression, we are burying a human sparrow. We are laying to rest a tiny infant who never did anything significant. In fact, who never did anything at all. Who fell to earth before it had a chance to get properly airborne. But we have Christ's word for it that the heavenly Father has seen and recorded the fall of this little infant.

No matter how small an infant might be we must not underestimate his/her value. It is said that all the ocean is contained in a single drop of water, and that there is a giant oak tree hidden in every acorn. So, in a sense, the fulness of human life was contained in this little infant. Furthermore, our faith tells us that there was kindled within him (her) a spark of the life of God himself, which death cannot extinguish.

Let us have no fear for N. N. is worth more to the heavenly Father than a million sparrows. We can be sure that he will take good care of him (her).

Here on earth N. died as a bud on the first day of spring. May he (she) grow and ripen in the soil of eternity.

PRAYER OF THE FAITHFUL

President: Let us not be afraid. Let us stop being anxious, for God, our Redeemer and Saviour, is with us. He will help us. Let us pray to him with the trust of a child. *Response*: Lord, hear us in your love.

Reader(s): That we may let go of N. with confidence, knowing that he (she) is going into the hands of the heavenly Father. We pray in faith.

Small though he (she) was, there was in him (her) a divine spark which death cannot extinguish. May he (she) now see the face of God in heaven, and intercede for us there. We pray in faith.

For all who grieve because N. was plucked from life so soon: that they may find comfort in the faith that they will see him (her) again when we shall all meet in Christ's everlasting kingdom. We pray in faith.

For doctors, nurses and all who care for life at its weakest moments. We pray in faith.

That everywhere and in all circumstances human life may be respected. We pray in faith.

For all of us here present: that we may remember at all times, but especially at times of trouble and anxiety, that we are precious to God and that he will take care of us. We pray in faith.

President: Father, from whom we come and to whom we go, into your strong but gentle hands we commend this little infant N., whose stay among us was so brief. Receive him (her) into the kingdom of the little ones who constantly see your face. May he (she) shine on us and remind us that we are your children and that you always care for us. We ask this through Christ our Lord.

COMMUNION REFLECTION No. 6 or No. 28.

---

18. LET THE LITTLE ONES COME TO ME 1
Death of a child or youth through illness

INTRODUCTION AND CONFITEOR

Christ said to his disciples, 'Come to me, you who labour and are heavy laden, and I will give you rest.'

This same invitation is extended to us who are laden with sorrow at the death of N. So let us draw close to Christ for he is our only source of hope and consolation. *(Pause)*

Lord, you console the broken-hearted. Lord, have mercy.

You bring rest to those who are crushed by life's burdens. Christ, have mercy.

You bless the little ones who place all their hope in you. Lord, have mercy.

Readings on p. 129.

HEADINGS FOR READINGS

First Reading (Wisdom 4:7-15). It is not the length of a person's life that matters but the quality of it.

Second Reading (Romans 8:14-18). In and through Christ we have become children of God, and therefore heirs to eternal life.

Gospel (Matthew 11:25-30). The Father in his love and mercy reveals the kingdom to those who are simple and humble of heart like children.

HOMILY

When a child (youth) dies we are inclined to say, 'What a pity he (she) was taken before he (she) was ripe and able to bear fruit.' In other words, we speak of promise rather than actual achievement. This is unfair to the child. We don't speak thus of the new blade of wheat. We appreciate it for what it is – a blade of young wheat. Every child, no matter how brief his (her) stay among us, has already borne some fruit, in some cases considerable fruit.

Jean Vanier, who has spent years working with the handicapped, tells a story about a six-year-old boy who died. He was only three years old when he was struck down with a paralysis which, little by little, invaded his whole body. Towards the end he lost his sight also. A few months before he died his mother was sitting by his bedside, weeping, when suddenly the little boy said to her, 'Don't cry, Mummy. I still have a heart to love my Mummy.' That little boy had attained to a high degree of maturity.

> Here the preacher could refer to the deceased, to what he (she) suffered and the 'fruit' he (she) bore as a result of that suffering. The above is an example of the kind of fruit to which one might be able to point.

To live as N. lived, to endure what he (she) endured, and then to die so calmly and bravely, is in fact equivalent to having lived to a ripe old age. It shows that it is not length of life that matters but the intensity and quality of it. It confirms what Scripture says, 'A blameless life is ripe old age' (First Reading).

We do not know why innocent children have to suffer so much and die so early. It is not true to say that God wills it. That would be unthinkable. One thing we do know for sure, for we have seen it with our own eyes. It is this: God does not allow his little ones to suffer alone. He surrounds them with love – of their parents, family, and friends. He strengthens and upholds them so that the mighty waves of suffering do not engulf them.

Then, out of their pain, God reaps a rich harvest. He sees to it that not one drop, not one grain, of it is lost or wasted. Their pain becomes a source of redemption for all of us. They, above all, share in the redemptive sufferings of Christ, the Innocent One, the sinless Lamb who died to redeem us sinners.

If God surrounded N. with so much love during his (her) brief earthly life, we can be sure that he will take good care of him (her) now that he (she) has gone hom to him.

'It is one of the most unjustifiable pretensions of our age that it measures time and experience by the clock. There are a host of considerations and values which a clock cannot possibly measure' (Laurens van der Post).

PRAYER OF THE FAITHFUL

President: Let us have recourse to God our Father in prayer with the confidence and trust of a child. *Response*: Hear us, O Lord.

Reader(s): That Christ who loved the little ones may reveal to N. the joy and peace of the Father's kingdom. Let us pray.

That what N. suffered may be a source of blessings for us and for many others. Let us pray.

That from his (her) place in the kingdom of God, he (she) may intercede for us. Let us pray.

For his (her) parents, family and friends: that God may comfort them with the assurance that they will see him (her) again when we will all meet in Christ's everlasting kingdom. Let us pray.

For all those who loved and cared for N. during his (her) illness. Let us pray.

That we who, are still children of God, no matter what our age, may be convinced that if we share Christ's sufferings in this life we will also share his glory in the next. Let us pray.

President: Father, we now commend our little brother (sister) N. to your care. Give him (her) a place of honour in your kingdom for he (she) shared in the cross of your Son on earth. We ask this through Christ our Lord.

COMMUNION REFLECTION No. 6 or No. 28.

---

19. LET THE LITTLE ONES COME TO ME 2
Death of a child or youth through tragedy

INTRODUCTION AND CONFITEOR

We gather to celebrate the funeral Mass of N., who was only a child (youth) when his (her) life was tragically cut short. We begin by calling to mind what our faith teaches, namely, that in Christ we have all become children of God and heirs to eternal glory. *(Pause)*.

Lord, you keep on reminding us of the great dignity you conferred on us when you made us children of the Father. Lord, have mercy.

You call us back to the house of the Father's love and forgiveness when, through pride and selfishness, we stray from him. Christ, have mercy.

You show us that the Father loves us and that he has an eternal home prepared for us. Lord, have mercy.

Readings on p. 130.

HEADINGS FOR READINGS

First Reading (Isaiah 49:8.14-16). Just as a mother cannot forget her child, so God cannot forget any of his children.

Second Reading (Romans 8:14-18). In and through Christ we have become children of God, and therefore heirs with him to eternal glory.

Gospel (Matthew 18:1-4;19:13-15). This shows the love and regard Christ has for the little ones of the Father's kingdom.

HOMILY

When the life of a child (youth) ends prematurely, we are inclined to speak as if everything was in the future for the child in question, as if nothing had been lived or achieved during the brief time he (she) had been among us. This is a mistake. The fact is, N. lived a life, though it was cut short by tragedy at the tenth [*or whatever*] milestone.

True, in a sense, N's life had scarcely started. But the fact is, it had started. Nevertheless, we are tempted to say, 'I'd love to know what the future held for this child.' What the future held for this child is not the point.

We judge an experience not simply by the duration of it, but by the intensity of it. Children, as every parent knows, can pack an awful lot of living into a single day.

If you have ever observed children on a beach you will have noticed how they are full of eyes and ears. Every object they find is picked up and examined closely. Even the most ordinary object, which we adults wouldn't even notice, becomes an object of wonder to them and gets their undivided attention. How dedicated they are to their tasks. No artist was ever as engrossed in his painting as they are in their explorations. For them time has ceased to exist.

And what an out-pouring of effort, what a deluge of energy you witness. How much work those tiny hands can get through. How much ground those tiny feet can cover. What an incredible amount of energy is contained within a child, when that child is fully alive. Are they happy? The question is superfluous. They are in ecstacy.

How alive children are. There is something beautiful about every child, though he (she) is unfinished. Children teach us how to live. They are always themselves. This is what makes them so charming and unique. They continually interrupt us, and indeed often disturb us with their questions. They have a habit of asking all the important questions: questions about life, death, and God.

Here the preacher could refer a little to the deceased child.

We don't know why tragedies such as this happen. But we are

certain they are not the will of God. We know that the little ones are especially dear to him. Christ said, 'Let the children come to me, for to such belongs the Kingdom of heaven.'

We are grateful for what this child has taught us and given us. We are grateful for him (her). Any parent worthy of the name will take special care of a child that gets hurt. Hence we can confidently surrender N. into the hands of our heavenly Father, knowing that he will take special care of him (her).

'In my youth, before I lost any of my senses, I can remember that I was all alive' (Thoreau).

PRAYER OF THE FAITHFUL

President: Let us now pray in trust for Christ who shows in word and deed that the little ones are precious to him and to the Father.
Response: Lord, hear our prayer.

Reader(s): That Christ may take N. gently by the hand and lead him (her) into that kingdom which he said belongs to all those who are little. Let us pray to the Lord.

As a child N. thirsted for life here on earth; may he (she) now enjoy the fulness of life in the kingdom of God. Let us pray to the Lord.

For the parents of N.: that they may be consoled in the knowledge that as they cherished him (her) in life, God will cherish him (her) in death. Let us pray to the Lord.

For all the children of world: that we may never be a stumbling block to them, but rather that we may open the doors of life to them. Let us pray to the Lord.

That we may be conscious of, and strive to live up to, our great dignity as children of God. Let us pray to the Lord.

That we may be convinced that all those who share Christ's sufferings in this life will share his glory in the next. Let us pray to Lord.

President: Father, in Christ you have shown us how much you love the little ones of this earth. Write the name of N. on the palm of your hand, and grant him (her) a place of honour in your kingdom of light and peace. We ask this through Christ our Lord.

COMMUNION REFLECTION No. 28 or No. 15.

---

20. A TIME OF RIPENING
Death of an elderly person   1

INTRODUCTION AND CONFITEOR

We are bidding farewell to someone who was granted the grace of a long and full life. We are naturally saddened by his (her) death, but we are grateful for all the blessings God has given us through him (her). Let us now pause briefly to call to mind some of these blessings. *(Pause)*.

Lord, you bless all those who trust in you. Lord, have mercy.

They are like a tree that never withers because it is planted by the waterside. Christ, have mercy.

Even when they are old, they are still able to bear fruit. Lord, have mercy.

Readings on p. 132.

HEADINGS FOR READINGS

First Reading (Ecclesiastes 3:1-8.11). There is a time and a season for everything.

Second Reading (2 Corinthians 4:14-5:1). Paul tells us of the home God has prepared for us when death forces us to fold up the earthly tent we live in at present.

Gospel (Luke 12:22-31). Christ urges us to avoid useless worrying and fretting about material things. Instead, we are to place unlimited trust in our heavenly Father, to whom each of us is important and precious.

HOMILY

Old age, like any other stage of life, has its own joys and sorrows, pleasures and pains.

Old age brings infirmity. As the years go by one has to make sacrifices and renunciations. One hasn't the same strength or energy. There are inevitable disabilities and, most likely, illnesses too. All this is a bitter reality.

But old age has its good side also. It has its advantages, comforts and joys. After all the hustle and bustle of life, comes a time of calm and relaxation. It's amazing how placid a once turbulent river can become as it nears the ocean. In the garden of old age flowers, which once we hardly gave a thought to, can blossom — flowers such as patience, serenity, consideration, tolerance, understanding and, above all, compassion.

> Here the preacher might dwell a little on the 'flowers' that bloomed in the life, and especially in the old age, of the deceased.

The thing that is most desirable in old age is peace of mind. To find beauty and meaning in old age one must say Yes to it and everything it brings with it. Without this Yes, the worth and meaning of one's last years may be lost. But to find serenity one must be reconciled, not just with those years, but with one's entire life. We must be able to look back on our life and accept it in its totality. We must not allow the inevitable dark parts to depress us. When we look back over our lives in faith, we will find that it was precisely at our weak moments that we discovered God's love and mercy, that loving providence Jesus spoke about. We possess of our past only what we love.

If we are reconciled with our life, then old age will be littered with enriching memories. We will be filled with gratitude for the past and hope for the future. Then no matter what our material circumstances may be, we will be very rich. We will already be in possession of the kingdom of heaven. Varnish makes old things shine and appear new. A smile makes an old person beautiful, and shows that he (she) has learnt how to grow old.

People who grow old well, can attain a quality of life, a state of maturity and ripeness, which may have eluded them all their lives. 'All leaves, even grasses and mosses, acquire brighter colours just before they fall' (Thoreau).

If one is reconciled with one's life, then it shouldn't be too difficult to become reconciled with one's death, since they both come from the same hand — the hand of our heavenly Father. If he takes care of the flowers and birds he will take care of us who are his children.

Blessed are those who care for the old and who make them feel wanted. They help the old to live in the light and sweeten their memories.

'I love to look at a hundred-year-old tree, loaded with shoots as though it were a stripling. It teaches me the secret of growing old, open to life, to youth, to dreams, and makes me aware that youth and age are steps towards eternity' (Helder Camara).

PRAYER OF THE FAITHFUL

President: If we trust in God, and have as our top priority to live a life pleasing to him, he will take care of us in life and in death. Let us pray with confidence to our Father in our hour of need. *Response*: Lord, graciously hear us.

Reader(s): N. lived a long life; may he (she) obtain rest from his (her) labours, and the reward of all his (her) goodness. Lord, hear us.

That Christ may pardon his (her) sins, and bring him (her) to a place of light, happiness and peace. Lord, hear us.

That Christ may look with love on those who mourn N.'s passing. Lord, hear us.

For those who looked after N.: that their generosity may be rewarded with abundant blessings. Lord, hear us.

That all of us who have known him (her), and who take part in this celebration, may receive an increase of faith and hope. Lord, hear us.

That all the dead, especially our relatives and friends, may find light, happiness and peace in the kingdom of heaven. Lord, hear us.

President: Lord, may you support us all day long, till the shadows lengthen and evening falls, and the busy world is hushed, and the fever of life is over, and our work is done; then in your mercy, Lord, grant us a safe lodging, a holy rest, and peace at last. We ask this through Christ our Lord.

COMMUNION REFLECTION No. 32.

21. MISSION ACCOMPLISHED
Death of an elderly person 2

INTRODUCTION AND CONFITEOR

God gives each of us many gifts during the course of life. But his greatest gifts to us are the people who are dear to us and good to us. In N. God gave us a great gift. Even though we are sad now that the gift has been withdrawn, we should be grateful for all God has given us through N. Gratitude will help us cope with our loss.

Let us call to mind the fact that we do not always fully appreciate our friends until they have left us. *(Pause)*

Let us now ask the Lord's forgiveness for this and for all our other sins.

I confess to almighty God.

Readings on p. 134.

HEADINGS FOR READINGS

First Reading (Lamentations 3:17-26). God's kindness and faithfulness help all those who trust in him to cope with anguish and affliction.

Second Reading (2 Timothy 4:6-8). Thanks to the grace of God, Paul is able to say that he has been faithful to the end; he is now confidant that God will reward him for his faithfulness.

Gospel (John 17:1-5). Because Christ has done the work his Father gave him to do, the hour of his death is transformed into an hour of glory.

HOMILY

A human life goes forward like a wave rolling towards the shore.

Imagine you are standing on the seashore, watching the waves come in. At a certain point you fix your eyes on one particular wave which is as yet a long way out. Tall and majestic, it stands out from the others by reason of its frothing mane. It is full of power and beauty. Yet it is intimidating too. It is capable of carrying enormous weights on its crested back.

You watch it roll forward, driven on by the wind, pulled by the invisible force of the moon. As it moves forward bits of it begin to spill off. However, as it nears the shore, it gathers all its resources together and raises itself to its full height. Then it touches the bottom and topples over, spilling out its contents down to the very last drop. These rush forward towards you with much hissing and seething. It delivers the last drop right at your feet.

It has exhausted itself completely. It has given itself away totally. It has spent itself utterly. Then, having gently caressed the sand at your feet, it immediately begins to withdraw. Its work done, slowly and without fuss, it ebbs away. It slips back to join the great ocean whence it came. There it will be re-assembled in some new combination of molecules and droplets, and on another day it will be washed up on a new shore.

So it is when an old person dies. Once they were strong and healthy, laden with human freight. But then at some point they went over the top and a decline set in. Finally, the shore of death loomed up ahead. But that is all right, for their work is done. They have given themselves away completely. They have nothing left. They withdraw gently from us, to return to the Source of their being, there to be re-assembled in a new and permanent manner when death delivers them onto eternity's shore.

> Here the preacher could refer to the life of the deceased, stressing the work he/she did, the sacrifices he/she made, the 'freight' he/she carried before old age robbed him/her of strength. In many cases all this may be so far in the past as to be unknown to most of those present. It cries out to be recalled.

If the old are weak and feeble and a little troublesome at times, it is because they have given away their all.

Even though Christ was only thirty-three when he died, he was able to say, 'Father, I have finished the work which you gave me to do.' It is a very great blessing to be able to say that one has finished one's life's work, to be able to say with Paul, 'I have fought the good fight, I have finished the race, I have kept the faith.'

Such people do not so much die as wear out. But of what they have done and achieved, nothing will be lost. Everything is stored away and will go to make up that 'crown of righteousness' Paul also talks about, a crown reserved for them by the Lord, the righteous judge of all.

PRAYER OF THE FAITHFUL

President: For those who live a sincere and good life, the hour of death is transformed into an hour of glory, because Christ gives them the crown of eternal life. Let us pray in our hour of loss.
Response: Lord, graciously hear us.
Reader(s): N. has finally reached the shore of eternity; now that all his (her) earthly tasks are completed, may he (she) enjoy rest from all his (her) labours. Lord, hear us.

N. fought the good fight; he (she) finished the race; he (she) kept the faith; may he (she) now receive from Christ the crown of eternal glory which he won for us with his death and resurrection. Lord, hear us.

That the hardships and sufferings N. endured in this life may gain for him (her) full remission of all his (her) sins. Lord, hear us.

For those who grieve over his (her) death: that through their faith in Christ their sorrow may soon be changed into joy. Lord, hear us.

For all those who cared for N. in his (her) old age: that the Lord may reward them for their kindness and patience. Lord, hear us.

For all who knew and loved N: that they may draw inspiration from his (her) life. Lord, hear us.

President: Lord, may you support us all day long, till the shadows lengthen, and evening falls, and the busy world is hushed, and the fever of life is over, and our work is done; then in your mercy, Lord, grant us a safe lodging, a holy rest, and peace at last. We ask this through Christ our Lord.

COMMUNION REFLECTION No. 30.

---

22. SHARING HIS SUFFERINGS
For someone who bore a lot of suffering and/or illness

INTRODUCTION AND CONFITEOR

Many people are severely tested during their lives. N. is a case in point. He (she) was very severely tested by illness (or great hardship). But, thanks to the grace of God, he (she) bore it with patience and fortitude.

Let us reflect for a moment on the fact that all followers of Christ have to undergo trials and tribulations before entering into his risen glory. *(Pause)*

Lord Jesus, you are the sinless one who suffered the shame and agony of the cross to save us sinners. Lord, have mercy.

Lord Jesus, you died so that we might die to sin and live to holiness. Christ, have mercy.

Lord Jesus, you underwent death so that you might open for us the gate to eternal life. Lord, have mercy.

Readings on p. 136.

HEADINGS FOR READINGS

First Reading (Wisdom 3:1-6.9). The souls of those who have been tested and purified by suffering in life, are in the safe keeping of God's hands in death.

Second Reading (Romans 8:14-18). If we share Christ's sufferings here we will share his glory hereafter.

Gospel (John 12:23-27). Christ tells us that, just as a seed must die in order to bear fruit, we must die in order to live fully here and hereafter.

HOMILY   *For someone who suffered a lot through illness*

No one escapes the clutches of suffering. Everybody has some trial to undergo or cross to bear. However, for some people the trial can be very severe and the cross very heavy. N. is a case in point.

Here the preacher could dwell briefly on the sufferings of the deceased.

There's no point in being sentimental about suffering. An illness which prevents a person from working makes him (her) feel useless. It deprives one of the pride one gets from earning one's own passage in life. It also robs one of one's independence, making one feel a burden on one's loved ones. On top of all this there is the illness itself and the pain it involves. Suffering can destroy a person. It can make a person feel that the whole meaning of life has perished. To die would be easier than to go on living.

Yet, properly borne, suffering can be a great opportunity, even a blessing in disguise. Our pain can bear fruit. The value of suffering does not lie in the pain of it, but in what the sufferer makes of it. The real tragedy is not that we suffer, but that we sometimes waste suffering. We waste an opportunity to grow. The soul is purified, and the character transformed, through suffering.

Here the preacher could refer to the way the deceased bore his/her pain.

A Christian must not only accept suffering but also make it holy. However, nothing so easily becomes unholy as suffering. Suffering that is merely endured does nothing for our souls except harden them. Suffering is useless unless borne with love. But how can one bear pain with love?

Firstly, we must not see suffering as a punishment from God. God punishes no one. He allows us to suffer, yes, but only because good can come from it. Just as a mother will shower more love and care on her sick child than on her healthy child, so God loves us more when we are in pain. Thus, our pain can bring us closer to him.

Secondly, we have to find a meaning in our suffering. It has been proved over and over again that people are able to bear great pain provided it has a meaning for them. Think of the pain long-distance runners endure. Suffering ceases to be suffering in some way the moment we find meaning in it. Indeed it can even become easy and joyful.

Now the highest meaning a Christian can give to his/her suffering is to see it as an opportunity to share in the sufferings of Christ. Christ did not choose the way of ease and evasion. He chose the way of suffering. It was through his suffering that he attained to his glory. It was through his suffering that he redeemed the world.

The great secret then is to link our sufferings to those of Christ. If we suffer with him on earth we will be crowned with him in heaven. He is with us in the midst of our sufferings. He gives us strength to bear them with love so that they will become redemptive, not only for ourselves, but for others too. A person who links his (her) sufferings to those of Christ becomes a source of blessings for the entire community.

'I trust in God even when my faith is put to the test and I understand nothing' (Carlo Carretto).

'If our trials sometimes get us down we mustn't be deterred by melancholy on the path that leads to immortal glory' (Van Gogh).

HOMILY 2   *For someone who had a particularly hard life*

If we had a choice, most of us would (without hesitation) choose what is commonly known as 'the good life', that is, a life of ease, comfort and pleasure. We would avoid like a plague things such as hardship, suffering and pain. Yet we need hardship too. Those who cannot suffer can never grow up.

Hardship saves us from a life of mediocrity and superficiality. Vincent van Gogh had a very difficult life. He knew loneliness, poverty, hunger, failure, and mental illness. Yet, in spite of all this, he said, 'If at times I feel the desire for a life of ease, I go back fondly to a life of hardship, convinced that I learn more from it. This is not the road on which one perishes.'

> Here the preacher could refer to the hardship suffered by the deceased, and to what he/she reaped from it.

Our attitude to suffering depends very much on our attitude to life. If we see the meaning of our earthly existence in prospering materially, then we will try to keep well clear of suffering. But if we see the meaning of life in growing as human beings and children of God, then we will not shy away from it.

We derive more benefit from a life of hardship than from a life of comfort. But this is not an easy lesson to learn. So many voices tell us that it is not so. It's not easy to appreciate the benefits of suffering when we are actually going through them. The biggest benefits usually come later on.

Through suffering people acquire spiritual depth. If we did not suffer we would blunder through life without understanding anything. Those who bear trials and difficulties have a better chance of attaining human and divine maturity. The only real pity would be if we wasted our suffering.

Christ said that those who follow the hard road and who strive to enter the Kingdom of heaven through the narrow gate, are the lucky ones. Though the road may be strewn with difficulties it leads to life here and hereafter.

If we have a hard life we shouldn't feel that God has it in for us. Rather, we should feel a certain sense of privilege. This is the road Christ himself took – the road that led to Calvary. But it didn't end with Calvary. It ended with Easter. Christ supports all those who follow him down this road, and he promises to share his Easter victory with them.

If we share Christ's sufferings on earth, we will share his glory in heaven. Struggle makes victory taste all the sweeter.

'We must bear hardship in order to ripen' (Van Gogh).

'It was only when as a prisoner I lay on rotten straw that I began to feel within me the first stirrings of good' (Solzhenitsyn).

PRAYER OF THE FAITHFUL

President: We are children of the Father and co-heirs with Christ his Son. If we share Christ's sufferings in this life, we will share his glory in the next. With this hope let us pray in confidence to our Father. *Response*: Lord, hear our prayer.

Reader(s): N. shared in the passion of Christ; may he (she) now share in his risen glory. Let us pray to the Lord.

May the suffering by which N. was tested, purify him (her) from
all stain of sin. Let us pray to the Lord.

For those who mourn N's death: that they may be comforted by
the knowledge that, after all his (her) pain, he (she) is now at peace.
Let us pray to the Lord.

For all who suffer: that they may bear their pain with Christ-like
love and patience. Let us pray to the Lord.

For those who work for the sick and suffering: that they may have
a kind heart and gentle hands. Let us pray to the Lord.

For all here present: that we may remember that what we suffer in
this life can never be compared to the glory which is waiting for us in
the next. Let us pray to the Lord.

President: Father, your Son proved his love for you and for us by
undergoing a humiliating death. You rewarded him by raising him
from the dead and setting him at your right hand in glory. Help us to
follow him with courage in this life so that we may share his glory in
the next. We ask this through the same Christ our Lord.

COMMUNION REFLECTION No. 3 or No. 18.

---

23. WHEN THE LIGHTS GO OUT
Tragic Death   1

INTRODUCTION AND CONFITEOR

We stand in the darkness of death. The darkness is all the more
oppressive because it came upon us suddenly and tragically. But
God has not left us without light. He has sent his Son to enlighten
us, and to give us hope. Let us flee to him now. *Pause.*

Lord Jesus, you reveal to us the mystery of the Father's love for
us. Lord, have mercy.

Lord Jesus, you open for us the gates of salvation by forgiving all
our sins. Christ, have mercy.

Lord Jesus, you give light to us as we stand in darkness and in the
shadow of death. Lord, have mercy.

Readings on p. 138.

HEADINGS FOR READINGS

First Reading (Isaiah 25:6-9). Death is the cause of much sorrow
and many tears. But for those who put their hope in God the time
will come when all tears will be wiped away.

Second Reading (Romans 8:31-35.37-39). Because God loves us and always takes our side, we are able to overcome every kind of trial and suffering.

Gospel (Luke 23:35-37.44-48). As Christ died the world went dark. Even so, as he died, he entrusted his spirit into the hands of his heavenly Father. In this way he showed us how to die.

HOMILY

At some time or other we have all experienced an occasion when the electricity is suddenly and unexpectedly cut off. Everything stops. The television goes blank. The radio goes silent. The cooker goes cold. The lift jerks to a halt. And, worst of all, the lights go out.

We are caught in a blackout. We are plunged into darkness. For a while at least we feel lost, helpless, and maybe even frightened. Most likely we are angry too because of the disruption of our work and plans. We want to know why this has happened. We want to blame somebody.

Tragic death, which is almost always sudden too, is like a blackout. One minute the sun is shining. Next minute it is dark night. Without the slightest warning, or the slightest chance to prepare ourselves, we are plunged into an impenetrable darkness. In the space of a minute our whole world is turned upside down.

> Here the preacher might refer to the deceased, whose light has been so suddenly and tragically extinguished.

Nothing can prepare us for something like this. Neither our education, nor our upbringing, nor our experience can save us from the devastating effects of such a blow.

Naturally, we ask why it happened. There is a tendency to say, 'It is the will of God.' Let us be perfectly clear: God did not will this tragedy to happen. No earthly father would willl such a death on one of his children. Neither would God. But if God can do all things, why did he not prevent it? God can do all things except take away our freedom. One thing we can be sure of: it concerns God even more than it concerns us, for it is one of his children that has died tragically.

There is only one thing we can do. Just as when a blackout occurs we rush for a light, any light, even that of a humble candle, so now we rush to the only light that can penetrate this awful darkness, namely, the light of Christ.

As Christ died St Matthew tells us that 'from the sixth hour there was darkness all over the land until the ninth hour' (27:45). In other words, the apostles and friends of Jesus experienced a blackout similar to what we are experiencing right now. They were lost and disorientated. All their hopes and dreams crumbled. But what they did not know at the time was that the darkness would not have the last say. Christ's light would shine again.

How marvellous it is when after a blackout the lights come on again. How wonderful then it must have been for the apostles when on Easter Day they bathed once more in the light of Christ. It was not quite the old light. It was a new light. It was the light of their risen Lord who broke the chains of death and rose in triumph from the grave.

Our risen Lord is with us at this moment. His light shines on us who are in darkness and in the shadow of death. St Paul says that nothing, neither suffering, nor tragedy, nor death can separate us from the love of God in Christ. This tragedy will strengthen our faith and deepen our conviction in the love of God for us.

N. was a believer in Christ. We are confident that Christ will not only take care of him (her), but will take special care of him (her) precisely because of the kind of death he (she) suffered. He will lead him (her) safely home to the Father's eternal kingdom, where sorrow and tears will be no more.

'Darkness makes us look even harder for the light' (Carlo Carretto).

'A lonely death, a tragic death, may yet have more to say of the peace and mercy of Christ than many another comfortable death' (Thomas Merton).

PRAYER OF THE FAITHFUL

President: God the Father brought his Son through the darkness of Calvary to the glory of the resurrection. We are confident that he will bring us too through the darkness of death to his kingdom of light and peace. Let us now turn to him with our petitions. *Response*: Hear us, O Lord.

Reader(s): That Christ, to whom N. was united in Baptism, may welcome him (her) into heaven and give him (her) a share in his glory. Let us pray.

As death surprised N. with its suddenness, may Christ now surprise him (her) with his mercy and kindness. Let us pray.

For the family, relatives and friends of N.: that they may find comfort in their faith in God, and strength through the support of the community. Let us pray.

For all here: that we may grow in faith so that we can stand firm even when hardship, misfortune, or even tragedy visits us. Let us pray.

For all those who have left this world in God's friendship, especially those who were dear to us. Let us pray.

President: Heavenly Father, give us the certainty that beyond death there is a life where broken things are mended and lost things are found; where there is rest for the weary and joy for the sad; where all that we have loved and willed of good exists, and where we will meet again our loved ones. We ask this through Christ our Lord.

COMMUNION REFLECTION No. 16 or No. 2.

---

24. OUT OF THE DEPTHS WE CRY
Tragic death   2

INTRODUCTION AND CONFITEOR

The tragic death of N. has shocked and saddened us all. But we are not without hope. We are not without help. God is with us. It is one of his children that has died. With God on our side, we will triumph over suffering, tragedy and even death. Let us pause to call to mind his love for us. (Pause).

Let us turn to Christ our Brother, in whom the love of the Father is made visible.

Lord Jesus, you underwent a tragic and painful death in order to open for us the gate to eternal life. Lord, have mercy.

In the midst of the pain and uncertainties of life you help us to go on trusting in the Father and in you. Christ, have mercy.

At the right hand of your Father, you plead for us who are now in the grip of sorrow. Lord, have mercy.

Readings on p. 141.

HEADINGS FOR READINGS

First Reading (Isaiah 25:6-9). Death is the cause of much sorrow and many tears. But, for those who put their trust in God, the time will come when their tears will be wiped away.

Second Reading (Romans 8:31-35.37-39). Because God loves us and always takes our side, we are able to overcome every kind of trial and suffering.

Gospel (Luke 24:13-31, abbreviated). The story of two people whose lives had been shattered when Jesus died, how the risen Jesus joined them and revived their hopes.

HOMILY

Each of us has a unique story to tell. It is the story of our life.

Everybody's story deserves to be listened to with respect, precisely because it is his (her) story.

The sad thing about all our stories is that they invariably end in death. It is not so bad when death comes naturally, and at the end of a long and full life. But sometimes it comes when the story is scarcely halfway through, and brings what has been a good story, or at least a promising one, to an abrupt, painful and tragic end.

> Here the preacher could refer briefly to the circumstances of the deceased person's death.

The day a person dies we begin to tell that person's story. His (her) life story passes before the eyes of our mind. It is all laid out before us, with its ups and downs, joys and sorrows, successes and failures. It is like a book, hitherto closed, which is suddenly thrown open for all to read.

> Here the preacher could tell a little of the deceased person's story.

A death such as this shocks and saddens us all. We have all suffered a great loss, but especially N's family. We know now how those two disciples on the road to Emmaus felt on Easter Day. They, like us, were plunged into gloom because someone they loved had died tragically. What were they talking about? What else but the death of their friend. Here was someone who was not only a good man, but a great prophet, as he had proved by the things he had done and said. Yet now he was dead and buried. It was hard to believe it. Their hopes, which a short time ago had been so bright, were now reduced to rubble.

Just when things were at their darkest, light came from a most unexpected source. The very one they thought was dead joined them, only they did not recognise him at first. Slowly, Jesus opened their minds to a great mystery. The tragic death which they looked upon as the end of their dream was the very means by which that dream became a reality. The one they had seen die had passed through death and was now crowned with glory by his Father. 'Was it not necessary that the Christ should suffer and (so) enter into his glory?'

Jesus joins us in our hour of sorrow. He listens to our sad story, which is the story of N's death. He opens our minds and hearts to understand that beyond death there is a life, a life of glory which he won for us with his own painful death.

Strengthened by this faith, like the two apostles, we too will live again. Our hopes and dreams will be given back to us. The great thing is that Christ has overcome death for all of us. Meanwhile, we can with the utmost confidence, commend our brother (sister) to Christ's care.

It certainly was not God's will that N. should die tragically. But from this tragedy God will draw good. It is one of those trials which St Paul says will serve to bring us closer to God and make us more convinced than ever of his love for us.

PRAYER OF THE FAITHFUL

President: With God on our side who can be against us? Since he did not spare his own Son but gave him up to benefit us all, we may be certain that he will not refuse us anything he can give. Let us therefore turn to him in our hour of need, and pray to him with unlimited confidence. *Response*: Father, hear us in your love.

Reader(s): That N. whose life was so cruelly cut short by tragedy, may now enter into the fulness of that life Christ won for us with his own death. We pray in faith.

That the shock and pain we are suffering may win for him (her) a speedy and full pardon of his (her) sins. We pray in faith.

That the Lord may show compassion on those who mourn for him (her), and turn their darkness into light. We pray in faith.

For ourselves: that in the midst of all the trials and uncertainties of life we may set our hearts on pleasing God and seeking his kingdom. We pray in faith.

For all the faithful departed, especially those who were dear to us: that, freed from every shadow of death, they may take their place in the new creation where all tears are wiped away. We pray in faith.

President: Father, give us the cetainty that beyond death there is a life – where broken things are mended and lost things are found; where there is rest for the weary and joy for the sad; where all that we have loved and willed of good exists, and where we will meet again our loved ones. We ask this through Christ our Lord.

COMMUNION REFLECTION No. 17 or No. 1.

---

25. A WITNESS TO CHRIST

INTRODUCTION AND CONFITEOR

One of the things which robs us of life and prevents us from giving ourselves more generously to Christ is fear. We are afraid of many things ... of sacrifice, of what others will say, and, above all, of death. N. gave us a great example of courageous and generous following of Christ.

Christ will help us too to follow him more whole-heartedly. Let us turn to him now, asking him to forgive our sins of cowardice and selfishness. *(Pause)*.

I confess to almighty God.

Readings on p. 143.

HEADINGS FOR READINGS

First Reading (Job 19:23-27). God vindicates all those who put their trust in him.

Second Reading (1 Peter 1:3-4.6-9). The trials which the followers of Christ have to endure are short-lived, but will win for them praise, honour and glory in heaven.

Gospel (Matthew 10:26-32). Christ exhorts his followers to bear witness to the Gospel openly and fearlessly. If they do so then he will claim them as his own in the tribunal of his heavenly Father.

HOMILY

In every court-case witnesses have a crucial role to play. Without the presence of at least one credible witness, the case will surely be lost. The task of the witness is simple. He or she has to provide evidence. Without solid evidence the most important and urgent case will fizzle out. A witness needs many qualities, but the most important ones are courage and truthfulness.

Christ said that he too needs witnesses. 'You will be my witnesses,' he said to his apostles just before he left them. The task of witnesssing to Christ has been handed down the ages to our own times. The need for witnesses is just as crucial today as ever before. perhaps even more so. 'Of what good is the word of Christ without an example?' (Dostoyevsky).

What is meant by a witness in this case? A Christian witness is someone who by his (her) life bears testimony to the Gospel of Christ. We need people who witness in word, but above all in deed. One of the things that deters people from witnessing is fear. In the gospel we have just read, three times Christ tells his witnesses that they should not be afraid.

The case for Christianity depends on the presence of witnesses, that is, real Christians. How can people come to know and encounter Christ unless they meet him in the lives of his followers? When the early Christians were no longer required to become martyrs, that is, witnesses to Christ with their blood, many of them became 'confessors', that is, witnesses to him through their lives of prayer and service. One does not have to die in order to witness faithfully, One has only to live – which may be harder.

Many Christians seem to think that it is enough to confess Christ in church on Sunday. But this is not enough. It is out there in the world, a world that is indifferent, sceptical, and sometimes hostile, that we have to witness. It is in the middle of the market-place that we have to stand up and be counted. It is not good enough to be secret disciples of Christ. We have to give public witness to Christ's love and truth.

> The preacher could now dwell a little on the Christian witness given by the deceased.

To live the way he (she) did in a world that denied everything he (she) stood for was no easy task. However, the correctness of one's cause gives a person enormous strength.

Followers of Christ have to keep their eyes on Christ who is continually calling them to a life of faithful and courageous witness. At some stage of their lives, his followers have to begin to live in a clear and truthful way that speaks to others of the values of the Gospel.

It is not given to everyone to suffer for the Gospel. It is only given to a chosen few. To be chosen by God is, of course, a great privilege. However, far from ensuring a life of ease and comfort, it ensures suffering for the faith at the hands of an ungodly world.

What a wonderful promise Christ makes to those who bear witness to him. He says, 'Everyone who acknowledges me before men, I also will acknowledge before my Father who is in heaven.'

N. witnessed to Christ on earth. May Christ now claim him (her) as his own in heaven.

PRAYER OF THE FAITHFUL

President: God our Father raised Jesus from the dead so that we might have the sure hope of an inheritance that will never fade. This is our great consolation in our sorrow. Let us pray to God whose children we are. *Response*: Lord, graciously hear us.

Reader(s): For all Christians: that they may bear open and fearless witness to Christ through lives of prayer and service. Lord, hear us.

For the pope and the bishops: that they may lead the people of God with courage and wisdom. Lord, hear us.

N. bore witness to Christ on earth; may he (she) now be crowned by him with honour and glory in heaven. Lord, hear us.

For those who mourn N's death: that they may be consoled in

their loss by their gratitude to God for the kind of witness he (she) gave. Lord, hear us.

For all those who are suffering for their belief in Christ. Lord, hear us.

For all here present: that we may be inspired by the example of N. to witness to Christ in our daily lives with courage and generosity. Lord, hear us.

Christ, through his divine power, has broken the power of death; may he lead all our departed relatives and friends into the joyful vision of his presence. Lord, hear us.

President: Heavenly Father, give us the grace to witness to your Son on earth so that he may be proud to claim us as his followers when we appear before you in death. We ask this through Christ our Lord.

COMMUNIION REFLECTION No. 11.

---

26. A WITNESS TO LOVE

INTRODUCTION AND CONFITEOR

Of all the commandments Christ gave us, the commandment to love is the most important. Indeed, it sums up all the others. We are celebrating the funeral of N. who showed us, in a most practical way, how this commandment can be lived.

In a sense the only failure in the life of a Christian is the failure to love. Let us think about our failure to love. *(Pause)*.

Let us confess our sins to God, especially those against his commandment of love.

I confess to almighty God.

Readings on p. 145.

HEADINGS FOR READINGS

First Reading (Isaiah 58:6-9.11). Those who show love for others, especially for the poor, will always have a light to guide them, and will be very close to God.

Second Reading (1 John 4:7-12.17). Those who love others will be able to face the day of judgement without fear.

Gospel (Matthew 25:31-40). To love others is to love Christ; to love Christ is to gain admittance to the Father's kingdom.

HOMILY

Without love the world would be a very bleak place. Hence we should not be surprised to find that love occupies the central place in the Gospel of Christ. He said that his followers would be recognised by the love they showed towards one another. He went even further. He said they would be judged on love. St John of the Cross was only echoing the words of Christ when he said, 'In the evening of life we shall be examined on love.'

To those who are sensitive to the needs of others, life offers innumerable opportunities to practise Christ's commandment of love. It is not a question of doing big things. Nor is it a question of giving *things*. Rather, it is a question of giving *of oneself* in little ways, of one's energy, of one's time, of one's love.

'Learning to love is hard and we pay dearly for it' (Dostoyevsky). Imaginary love yearns for an immediate heroic act that is achieved quickly and seen by everybody. Real love, on the other hand, requires hard work and patience, and often goes unseen and unrecognised. It is not a sporadic thing. It is more a way of life. True love seeks nothing at all except the good of the other person. To love means to share the burdens of others.

Not all are capable of this kind of love. A few kind gestures, a commitment or two, and people have a good conscience. Love calls for deeds. It is not enough to say, 'I love you' or 'I care about you' and then do nothing. Most people find it easier to love those who are far away than those with whom they rub shoulders every day.

Here the preacher could refer to the love shown by the deceased.

N. has shown us what love is and how we can practise it in ordinary, everyday ways. He (she) was one of those generous people who find their deepest satisfaction in life in devoting themselves to the welfare of others.

When we love unselfishly we become agents of God's love and providence. We also become witnesses to Christ's continuing love for, and presence among, his adopted brothers and sisters. And there is nothing better in this world than to be a witness to the love of Christ.

Christ not only gave his followers the commandment to love, but he lived it himself. Throughout his public ministry he took on the role of servant, giving himself unselfishly to all his brothers and sisters, especially to the poorest and lowliest. Finally, he gave his life for them. Calvary is the greatest act of love the world has known. It was the love of Christ that saved the world.

To close one's heart is to begin to die. To open one's heart is to begin to live. 'We know that we have passed out of death into life, because we love the brethren' (1 John 3:14). Those who love are already saved. To them Christ will say, 'Come, O blessed of my Father, inherit the kingdom prepared for you from the foundation of the world.'

May our brother (sister) N. hear those words now.

'Do people weigh you down? Don't carry them on your shoulders. Take them into your heart' (Helder Camara).

'Dying is not ceasing to live, but ceasing to love' (Michel Quoist).

PRAYER OF THE FAITHFUL

President: My friends, since God has loved us so much, we too must love one another. No one has seen God, but as long as we love one another God will live in us and his love will be complete in us, and we know that love is stronger than death. So let us pray to the God who first loved us. *Response*: Lord, hear us in your love.

Reader(s): N. lived Christ's commandment of love; may he (she) now hear those words, 'Come, O blessed of my Father, inherit the kingdom prepared for you from the foundation of the world.' We pray in faith.

N. showed much love for others in this life; may he (she) now experience the loving mercy of God for his (her) sins and failings. We pray in faith.

That from his (her) place in the kingdom of the Father, he (she) may intercede for us and continue to help us. We pray in faith.

For those who mourn for N.: that they may find strength through reaping the fruits of what N. sowed with love. We pray in faith.

For all here present: that we may draw inspiration from the example of N. and so strive to live out in our own lives Christ's great commandment of love. We pray in faith.

For all those who have died, who during their lives on earth loved and helped us. We pray in faith.

President: Father, all those who love others after the example of Christ your Son are truly blessed by you in this life, but what they receive here is only a shadow compared with the good things you have prepared for them in the next life. We make all our prayers through Jesus Christ, our Lord.

COMMUNION REFLECTION No. 27 or No. 9.

27. A DEDICATED PERSON

INTRODUCTION AND CONFITEOR

One of the greatest treasures in life is to have a work into which we can put our heart and soul. Such a work will make our life both happy and fruitful. N. was blessed in this way.

Refer very briefly to his/her dedication.

Let us pause to look at our lives to see what is it that gives them meaning. *(Pause)*
Our lives are impoverished in many ways, but especially by sin. Let us ask God's pardon now.
I confess to almighty God.

Readings on p. 148.

HEADINGS FOR READINGS

First Reading (Sirach 2:1-9). Those who serve God faithfully must expect to meet many trials. But through them all God upholds them.
Second Reading (1 Corinthians 9:24-27). Dedication makes great demands on a person but it also promises great rewards.
Gospel (John 10:11-15.17-18). The truly dedicated are those who work with love. Christ gives a lovely example of this.

HOMILY

We invest an enormous amount of our lives in work. Hence, the way we see our work is of the greatest importance. If we can find a meaning in our work, it becomes an ascending path, and a source of great enrichment for ourselves and others. But if we can find no meaning in our work, it becomes a descending path, impoverishes us, and does little for anyone else.

The worst kind of work of all is compulsory work. The penal quality of such work lies not so much in the fact that it is hard as in the fact that it is forced, and done under threat of punishment. Such work is always done slowly and badly, and does little to enhance the dignity of the worker.

But when work is done freely, then even when it is hard and there is no advantage to the worker, he exerts his utmost efforts to perform it as quickly and as well as possible. It ceases to be a chore. It becomes almost a pleasure and brings its own rewards.

Vincent van Gogh struggled for many years trying to find out what he wanted to do with his life. Finally, after much searching and groping, he discovered at twenty-seven that he wanted to be a painter. From that day on, his life changed. It was not that it became a picnic. The opposite would be nearer the truth. It was just that from then on he no longer doubted himself, and however difficult or burdensome his life became, the inner serenity, the conviction of his own particular calling never deserted him. He said, 'I am as rich as Croesus, not in money, however. I am rich because I have found in my work some thing to which I can devote myself heart and soul, and which gives meaning and inspiration to my life.'

> Here the preacher could refer to the deceased, stressing how he/she brought a sense of 'vocation' to his/her work, and the benefits he/she and others reaped as a result.

People like N. are very lucky people. They have found a real treasure. They have found a 'vocation' in life. Even though their work may still be difficult and extremely demanding, it ceases to be a mere job. It becomes a task freely chosen and done with love. It glows with meaning. We must never equate a happy life with an easy one.

Happy those who have found a worthwhile work in life. They are lucky because they have something into which they can put at least part of their soul, something through which their true spirit shines. It does not matter how humble this work is, so long as it does for them something of what Van Gogh's (or N's) work did for him.

Often death comes before its due time, with the result that our life's work is left unfinished. This is something over which we have no control. What is in our power is to invest our work with meaning. The highest meaning we can give to our work is to see it as a service to God and to others. In this case, it is no exaggeration to say that it opens for us the gate to salvation.

People who give their lives to labours of love go straight to one's heart. I am quite sure that they go straight to the heart of God too.

It is not so much death that frightens people as a life without meaning.

'Work is love made visible' (Kahlil Gibran).

PRAYER OF THE FAITHFUL

President: Those who are dedicated are truly blessed by God and their lives overflow with meaning and fruitfulness. In our loss we make our needs known to God. *Response*: Hear us, O Lord.

Reader(s): That N. may now reap the fruit of all his (her) years of hard work and unselfish dedication (to the needs of others). Let us pray.

That all the fruits that he (she) has borne in this life may gain forgiveness for his (her) sins now. Let us pray.

We have all lost a great example in N.; that the Lord may comfort us, and especially N's family, in this loss. Let us pray.

That each of us may be inspired by N's example. Let us pray.

For all those who work unselfishly for others, and who often are not recognised or thanked in this life. Let us pray.

That the Lord may grant eternal life to all the faithful departed. Let us pray.

President: Father, fill our hearts with your love, so that we can share it with our brothers and sisters. Thus our lives will be filled with meaning and we will be laying up treasure for ourselves in heaven. We make our prayer through Christ our Lord.

COMMUNION REFLECTION No 7 or No. 30.

---

28. A FAITHFUL SERVANT

INTRODUCTION AND CONFITEOR

We are celebrating the funeral Mass of one who could truly be called 'a good and faithful servant'. To be faithful is not easy. It demands a lot of sacrifice.

We are all unfaithful in many ways. One alone is fully faithful, namely, God. Though we may abandon him, he does not abandon us. So let us have recourse to him with confidence, and confess our infidelities. *(Pause).*

Lord, you are compassionate and loving, slow to anger and rich in mercy. Lord, have mercy.

Lord, you forgive all our sins; you heal every one of our ills. Christ, have mercy.

As a father has compassion on his children, so you have pity on those who fear you. Lord, have mercy.

Readings on p. 150.

HEADINGS FOR READINGS

First Reading (Sirach 2:1-9). Those who serve God must expect to meet with many trials. But through them all God will uphold them.

Second Reading (2 Timothy 4:6-8). Thanks to the grace of God, Paul is able to say that he has been faithful right to the end, and is

now confidently awaiting the crown of glory God has reserved for
his faithful servants.

Gospel (Luke 12:35-40.42-44). This contains the parable of the
waiting servants. It urges a constant watchfulness and faithfulness.

HOMILY

Faithfulness is one of the greatest and most important things in life.
It is as precious as a gem, and almost as rare. 'To be a human being is
precisely to be faithful' (Antoine de Saint Exupery). Everybody has
some responsibilities. In a very real sense we are responsible, not
only for ourselves, but for each other.

While faithfulness is precious it is also costly. It is not an easy
road. It is a hard road. If one wishes to be faithful one must be
prepared to put oneself, together with one's pleasures, comforts
and interests, in second place.

Faithfulness is the ability to stick with one's choice, the will to
struggle for it, and to turn the inevitable obstacles and setbacks into
positive elements on one's chosen path. It requires not so much
physical strength as strength of character, of soul, and of spirit.
Though it is costly, even here on earth it brings great rewards in its
wake. It brings joy, peace and growth. There can be no happiness,
no growth, except in the fulfilment of one's obligations. A person's
moral greatness consists in being faithful.

Here the preacher could refer to the faithfulness shown by the
deceased.

If we are at our task, if we are faithful, then death, even sudden
death, is not likely to hold any terrors for us. (Cf. Gospel.) People
who are caught up in an absorbing undertaking cease to be afraid
even when surrounded by danger. The person who is at his post,
doing his task faithfully, need not be afraid of the sudden arrival of
the overseer. He will not even be unduly bothered should the
overseer arrive before the task is finished. He knows that the latter
will understand that he did not have sufficient time. He knows that
for the overseer it is enough that he should find his servant at his
job, like a reliable sentry at his post. He will not be on edge, fearful
lest the overseer might arrive and catch him idling, or with the job
hardly started. No, he will calmly open the door at the first knock.

Christ is the one who was totally faithful. He was faithful to his
Father, faithful to the task his Father gave him to do. The night
before he died he said, 'Father, I have finished the work you gave
me to do.' But his fidelity cost him his life.

Paul too was able to say that his work was done. 'I have fought the
good fight, I have finished the race.' However, this is a grace not

given to everyone. Death often comes as a disrupter of our work
and plans. There is nothing we can do about this. The future is in
God's hands. The present alone is ours. We must go on being
faithful to our present tasks and responsibilities.

A certain cleaning lady in a hospital was told that she was dying.
On being asked, 'What will you do?' she replied, 'I will go on
cleaning the corridors.' That is the spirit of the Gospel. For a
Christian, death heralds the arrival, not of an exacting overseer, but
of Christ our Saviour and Brother. Happy those servants whom he
finds at their post. He will sit them down at the table of the Father's
Kingdom and wait on them.

PRAYER OF THE FAITHFUL

President: Let us pray to God our Father, who alone is totally
faithful, and who, in spite of our many infidelities, does not abandon us, but through Christ continues to love us and draw us towards
himself. *Response*: Father, hear us in your love.

Reader(s): For all Christians: that they may follow Christ with
constancy and generosity. We pray in faith.

For all our political and civil leaders: that they may be faithful to
their promises and commitments. We pray in faith.

That N., who proved himself (herself) a good and faithful servant
in this life, may now hear those wonderful words from Christ, 'Well
done, good and faithful servant, enter into the joy of your Master.'
We pray in faith.

That the Lord may turn a merciful eye on his (her) sins and
infidelities. We pray in faith.

For those who mourn N., especially his (her) family: that they
may find inspiration and comfort in his (her) example. We pray in
faith.

For the grace of fidelity for all here present. We pray in faith.

That the Lord may reward with eternal life all the faithful departed. We pray in faith.

President: Teach us, good Lord, to serve you as you deserve; to
give and not to count the cost; to fight and not to heed the wounds;
to toil and not to seek for rest; to labour and not to ask for any
reward save that of knowing that we do your holy will. We ask this
through Christ our Lord.

COMMUNION REFLECTION No. 10.

29. COME TO ME, ALL YOU WHO LABOUR
For an ordinary worker

INTRODUCTION AND CONFITEOR

Christ said, 'Come to me, all who labour and are heavy laden, and I will give you rest.' During this Eucharist he invites us to approach him. Weighed down with the burden of sorrow, let us not be afraid to accept his invitation. *(Pause)*

The first burden Christ lightens for us is that of our sins. Let us confess them with humility so that he may remove them from us.

I confess to almighty God.

Readings on p. 152.

HEADINGS FOR READINGS

First Reading (Genesis 1:27-31). God made us in his own image, and gave us responsibility for the world. Through work we fulfil this responsibility.

Second Reading (Colossians 3:14-15.17.23-24). In all that they do, Christians must remember that it is for the Lord they are working. Then the Lord will reward them for all their labours.

Gospel (Matthew 11:28-30). Christ gives rest to all the over-worked and weary ones who come to him.

HOMILY

Most of us invest an enormous chunk of our lives in work. Our ordinary work or job gobbles up at least a third of our lives, often leaving us exhausted and drained. For many people work is unspectacular, monotonous, tiring and insignificant.

Many people spend their entire lives like this. Apart from the odd break from the routine, nothing great ever happens. And yet a kind of greatness is still open to them. To perform one's ordinary tasks cheerfully, day in and day out, presents no small challenge. In fact it calls for a kind of heroism. When done faithfully, one's ordinary work gives a person great dignity and helps him (her) attain a high degree of maturity.

> Here the preacher could refer to the life of the deceased, and especially to that occupation for which he (she) was best known.

It is interesting that when Christ came on earth he did not come as a king or a great political leader. He came as an ordinary workman. For most of his relatively short life he worked as a carpenter in a small village. There was nothing spectacular about his work. By and large, it was routine and insignificant. No doubt it often left him exhausted and perhaps frustrated too. Yet he did it faithfully until the day he heard another call.

There is a tendency to write off these years of Christ's life (the so-called hidden years), or at least to rate them of little account, as if Christ was merely marking time, merely waiting for his real work to begin. Nothing could be further from the truth. These years were of immense importance for him. During them he was growing in wisdom and grace. He was showing us that the most important thing in life is not the work we do but what we make of ourselves.

Faith in Christ gives us a sense of our dignity as human beings and children of God. 'Ever since Christ came on earth, gods and nations have ceased to be, and man came into being – man the carpenter, man the ploughman, man the shepherd with his flock of sheep at sunset, man who does not sound in the least proud, man thankfully celebrated in all the cradle songs of mothers and in picture galleries the world over' (Pasternak).

Faith invests not only our work but the whole of our lives with meaning, with eternal value and significance. We must not underestimate anything we do, or write off any part of our lives as of little or no value. Everything gives us an opportunity to grow, to mature, to ripen as human beings and children of God.

Hence, for each of us, working out our salvation, taking up the cross of Christ means no more and no less than taking up each day's tasks, work and suffering. If we see it like this, then no matter how dull or tedious those tasks may be, we invest them with enormous meaning. They become for us a means to the very highest goal – eternal life.

'To do the duty of the moment – that's what the Gospel means to me' (Catherine de Hueck Doherty).

'In the long run, the only thing that ripens is the meagre work of every day' (Van Gogh).

PRAYER OF THE FAITHFUL

President: We turn to Christ who gives rest to the weary, joy to the sad, and eternal life to all who believe in him. *Response*: Lord, hear our prayer.

Reader(s): N. worked hard all his (her) life and died believing in Christ; may Christ now give him (her) rest from all his (her) labours. Let us pray to the Lord.

That Christ may forgive N. his (her) sins, and give him (her) the reward of his (her) good deeds. Let us pray to the Lord.

For those who bear the heavy burden of grief, especially N's family: that Christ may lighten their burden through the love and support of this community. Let us pray to the Lord.

For all those who are crushed with the burdens of life; that Christ may give them strength, hope and dignity. Let us pray to the Lord.

For all here present: that we may never lose sight of our great dignity as children of God and co-heirs with Christ to eternal glory. Let us pray to the Lord.

That all who have died in the peace of Christ may find rest in his kingdom of light and peace. Let us pray to the Lord.

President: Lord, may you support us all day long, till the shadows lengthen and evening falls, and the busy world is hushed, and the fever of life is over, and our work is done; then in your mercy, Lord, grant us a safe lodging, a holy rest, and peace at last. We ask this through Christ our Lord.

COMMUNION REFLECTION No. 8.

---

30. THE EXPRESS STOPS AT A SMALL STATION
For one of the 'little ones' of the earth

INTRODUCTION AND CONFITEOR

We are celebrating the funeral of someone who made no ripples in the pond of world affairs. But God sees and rewards the efforts of all, especially those of the poor and lowly.

Let us turn to God, for in him we live and move and have our being. *(Pause)*

God is generous with his forgiveness and mercy. Let us confess our sins with humility and sincerity.

I confess to almighty God.

Readings on p. 154.

HEADINGS FOR READINGS

First Reading (Sirach 35:6-11). The offering of the upright and generous person is acceptable to God and abundantly rewarded by him.

Second Reading (1 Corinthians 2:1-6.9). No eye has seen, no ear has heard the good things that God has prepared for those who love him.

Gospel (Mark 12:41-44). In the eyes of Christ, it is not the size of the offering that counts, but the spirit in which it is made.

HOMILY

An express train, bearing important people on important business to important destinations would never dream of stopping at a small station in the middle of nowhere. However, there is one great exception – the express train of life. For many this seems for ever to pass them by. Yet one day it will stop at the station where you and I stand. This is the day of our death.

On this day, no matter how lowly and obscurely we have lived, we will be summoned in from the shadows and given the central place in the community. The hitherto invisible stagehand, whose work, however important, has gone unseen and unrecognised, will take his (her) stand at the centre of the stage, under the full glare of the spotlights. All the stars will move to the wings. The little person will take over the star role for that day at least.

(In industrialised societies, it frequently happens that the ordinary citizen dies and is buried mostly unnoticed. This does not tend to happen in rural societies, for instance, in rural Ireland. No one could die, even in the smallest village, without public funeral rites and sorrow being felt and expressed by the community.)

Today television has turned certain people (mostly from the world of sport and entertainment) into 'stars', with the result that the ordinary person is driven into the shadows. This is a great injustice. The humblest little pond in the depths of the woods reflects some of the glory of the sky. It brings down to earth a little bit of heaven. The life of each one, no matter how insignificant it may appear in the eyes of the world, is made up of sacrifices and is sprinkled with heroism.

Today N. has become the central character in the life of this community. He (she) was never interviewed for radio or the newspapers. He (she) never appeared on television. Yet in his (her) own quiet way he (she) made an important contribution to the lives of all who knew him (her).

> Here the preacher could dwell a little on the deceased, stressing his (her) goodness and achievements.

Let us turn briefly to the Gospel. Who but Christ would have noticed the widow's offering? He did not just notice it, he held it up as a shining example to his disciples.

In the world we live in, prizes and awards are given, not for trying, or for spirit, or effort, but for one thing only – results. What matters is the size of the offering and who makes it. But Christ does not judge like this. For him what matters is the spirit shown and the effort made. This is why in his eyes the widow's offering was so great.

This is no transitory moment of importance for the deceased. The Christian sees death as an encounter with Christ. When the train stops, Christ alights and takes us on board. Our loved ones who have died do not vanish into the void, leaving no echo behind them. They are bound for eternity, where Christ will give them a seat of honour at the banquet of the Father's kingdom.

One small honour bestowed on us by Christ is worth more than all the honours the world could heap on us.

'When hard work soaks the shirts of humble folk, look about you and you will see angels gathering drops of sweat as though gathering diamonds' (Helder Camara).

PRAYER OF THE FAITHFUL

President: God regards the poor and lowly of the earth. We ask him to look in love on us, his children, and especially on our brother (sister) N. whom we commend to his mercy today. *Response*: Lord, hear our prayer.

Reader(s): That the Lord who saw and praised the widow's offering, may reward N. for his (her) quiet acts of courage and generosity. Let us pray.

N. lived an obscure life on earth; may he (she) now be given a place of honour by Christ at the banquet of the kingdom of God. Let us pray.

That those who mourn over him (her) may be comforted by their faith in Christ. Let us pray.

That we may never forget that Christ will not judge us on results, but on the efforts we have made and the spirit we have shown. Let us pray.

For all those who have died in the peace of Christ, and all the dead: that Christ may bring them into the joy and peace of his everlasting kingdom. Let us pray.

President: Father, in your kingdom the last will be first, and the little ones will be the greatest. Help us not to seek honour and glory in this life but to strive to please you in all things. We ask this through Christ our Lord.

COMMUNION REFLECTION No. 13 or No. 14.

Remembrance Liturgies

Introduction
Reflections on grieving

GRIEF IS GOOD

Sooner or later everybody has to face the loss of a loved one. Many people are still embarrassed about expressing their grief in public. They feel they must 'bear up'. This is reinforced by the remarks of sympathetic but misguided friends, remarks such as, 'Aren't you great!', 'You're so strong!', and so on.

It is now generally accepted that to suppress grief is not only bad but dangerous, and may lead to serious emotional problems. Unless people are allowed to express their grief, and in their own way, there will be a build-up of resentment because they are prevented from expressing the strongest emotions they will ever experience.

To live fruitfully after the death of a loved one, people must go through a period of mourning. If they go through it fully, they will emerge greatly enriched as persons. 'There are truths which only sorrow can teach, and it is the source of the most important discoveries about life. It is in sorrow that we discover ourselves' (Mary Craig in *Blessings,* Hodder and Stoughton, London).

The way to deal with grief is not to run away from it, or pretend it is not there, but to face it and work through it with as much honesty and love as one can. The lesson of the centuries is that suffering must be borne; there is no way out. If we try to be strong, and seek to put up impregnable defences to keep it out, we will end up emotionally damaged and hardened as persons. We must not keep it out. We must let it in. Nor must we fight it. If we fight it, it will destroy us. A storm breaks trees whereas it only bends grass.

Neither should we use faith as a barrier against grief. Sometimes people say about someone who does not grieve, 'What great faith he (she) has!' But Christ grieved. 'To use faith to suppress legitimate tears is a sort of crime against one's humanity' (Michel Quoist in *With Open Heart,* Gill and Macmillan, Dublin).

Hence, to grieve over the loss of a loved one is a truly good and necessary thing.

THE GRIEF PROCESS

It is common nowadays to talk about 'stages' of grief. These go more or less like this: denial, shock, numbness, emptiness, anger, guilt, depression and finally acceptance. But these emotions do not come in a neat order, and nothing stays fixed. One keeps on emerging from a phase, but it always recurs. And people grieve in different ways. When you are dealing with someone who is in deep grief you can expect anything from abnormal behaviour to total apathy.

People cannot fully appreciate their loss on the day of the funeral. They are too close to the event to be able to take in all its implications. 'On the day of burial there is no perspective. Your dead friend is still a fragmentary being. The day you bury him is a day of chores and crowds, of hands false or true to be shaken, of the immediate cares of mourning. The dead friend will not really die until tomorrow, when silence is round you again. Then he will show himself complete, only to tear himself away again. Only then will you cry because of him who is leaving and whom you cannot detain' (Antoine de Saint Exupery in *Flight to Arras,* Pan Books, London).

The real grief then comes not on the day of the funeral, but in the days, weeks, months and perhaps years that follow. 'It is only after we get home that we really go over the mountain' (Thoreau).

In the newness of grief a person is deaf to consolation. During that stage there is an intense desire on the part of the bereaved to do whatever they can for the deceased. They want to keep in touch with him (her) in any way they can, and to remember. Hence they should be encouraged to talk about the person who died, to remember him (her), yes, even to talk to him (her). Then there is the desire or need to visit the grave, to keep anniversaries, and so on. This is good. It is part of remembering.

In the early stages too there is a tendency on the part of the bereaved to cut themselves off from other people. Those close to them often misinterpret this as lack of sociability and perhaps lack of gratitude as well. But it must be put down to grief and loss of spirit. When we are down in spirit we do not wish to meet people. We simply want to be left alone. Their friends and relatives may avoid them because they do not want to 'stir it all up again', or because they do not want to listen once again to their story. They cannot bear to see the bereaved so full of self-pity. Here is where a little understanding helps. Those who have cut themselves off are more than ever in need of people to call on them.

RECOVERY

Some losses are greater than others. The loss of an aunt or uncle in old age can hardly be compared to the loss of a child or a spouse. It probably takes longer to get over a child's death than any other. We do not expect our children to die before us. We look after them; so we feel it is our fault, we have failed, if they die.

At first you cannot believe that you will ever feel better, or recover from the blow. As a matter of fact, one's loss can even grow larger as time goes on. Nevertheless, relief can and does come with the passage of time. 'Time heals what reason cannot' (Seneca).

We talk about 'getting over it' as if grief was a kind of obstacle that we have to surmount. What we have to do is come to terms with our loss, that is, finally accept it. Recovery is a kind of healing, and we may not be aware of it until it has actually happened. The day you see the first flowers of spring is not the day on which growth begins. Those flowers have been growing quietly under the soil and the snow. Then one day they break through the surface and suddenly you become aware of their presence. It is the same with recovery from grief.

More will be said about grief and recovery in the homilies that follow.

ABOUT THESE LITURGIES

Finally, a brief word about these Liturgies which I have called 'Remembrance Liturgies'. The first thing that should be said is that they are very important. Unfortunately, they are not always encouraged and do not get the thought they deserve.

Once again, the main emphasis is placed on announcing the good news of eternal life won for us by the death and resurrection of Christ. Then the deceased is remembered and prayed for. After this we address ourselves to the grieving. There are lots of things mourners cannot hear on the day of the funeral. Perhaps they are ripe for them now.

The Masses address various aspects of the grief process. Hence, in selecting one of them, care should be taken to see where the bereaved are at in this process. In this way the Mass will be of immense help to them. It will assure them that their loved one is in the safe hands of God, thus strengthening their faith and affirming their hope. It will also help them to work through their grief with courage and hope.

It might be appropriate to celebrate at least one Mass in the home of the deceased.

31. THE DEAD ARE ALIVE

INTRODUCTION AND CONFITEOR

We are gathered to remember N. who died ... ago today. But we must be clear about one thing: we are not remembering someone who is dead and gone. We are remembering someone who died to this life, but who lives with the risen life of Christ in the kingdom of God. This is the Easter message. This is the Good News.

Let us draw close to Christ who as our risen Lord stands among us to strengthen our hope. *(Pause).*

Lord, through your death you help us to die to our sins and to live to holiness. Lord, have mercy.

Lord, through your resurrection you opened for us the gate to eternal life. Christ, have mercy.

Lord, now seated in glory at the right hand of the Father, you continue to intercede for us, your adopted brothers and sisters. Lord, have mercy.

Readings on p. 156.

HEADINGS FOR READINGS

First Reading (2 Maccabees 12:43-45). It is a good thing to offer prayers for our departed loved ones so that they may be purified from their sins and come to the fulness of life in God.

Second Reading (1 Corinthians 15:12-20). Christ has been raised from the dead. He will share his victory over death with us.

Gospel (Luke 24:1-8). This tells how on Easter morning the women received the wonderful news that Jesus was risen from the dead.

HOMILY

In the early stages of grief there is a desperate desire to be near our departed loved one. We feel a need to maintain a link with the one who has died. We want to keep his (her) memory alive. We cannot accept that he (she) is gone from us for ever.

One of the ways we try to meet this need is through visits to the grave. This is good – up to a point. It gives expression to the desire for closeness but, far from easing the pain of our loss, it may well exacerbate it. It tends to make the dead even more dead. Nowhere do we become so sure that our loved one is dead as at the grave.

Early on Easter morning the women were doing what we do – they were going to visit the tomb where the body of their beloved Master had been buried. True, they had a task to perform – to complete the embalming of his body. But this task was not the only reason they were going to the tomb. They were going because they wanted to be near the one who had filled their lives and their hearts, and whose death had left them grief-stricken and empty.

If things had gone as expected they would have embalmed the body of Jesus, closed the tomb again, and come away more convinced than ever that what happened on Friday was not a bad dream. It was a reality. Their Master was dead, dead and gone for ever. But because of what happened at that tomb on Easter morning we can never see a tomb, never see death in the same light again. They were met by two angels who said to them, 'Why do you seek the living among the dead? He is not here, but has risen.'

It was to these dear, faithful women disciples that the Easter message was first given. Christ is not dead. He is alive. So they must not waste their time looking for him at the tomb.

Through the voice of the Church, the same message is given to us: 'Do not look for your loved one in the grave. He (she) is not there.' Jesus overcame death not just for himself but for all of us. He is the first to rise, but we will follow him. For a Christian, then, there is no such thing as death in the sense of final extinction. 'Anyone who believes in me, though he die (physically) will live' (John 11:26).

Our dead are not dead. They are alive. They live in a new and changed way, thanks to the victory Christ gained over death. Let us continue to pray for them in case they still need our help. And let us continue to visit the cemetery if it helps to keep alive the memory of our loved ones. But let us not look for them there. Let us look for them instead in the risen Christ.

If we want to be close to them, to maintain and even deepen our links with them, let us do so by trying to get closer to Christ. The closer we are to our risen Lord, the closer we are to our departed loved ones.

Those who die in grace go no further from us than God, and God is very near.

Note: Perhaps we could give concrete expression to this faith by getting a member of the family to bring up a candle in the offertory procession, light it from the Paschal Candle, and place it on the altar during the Mass.

PRAYER OF THE FAITHFUL

President: Our Lord Jesus Christ passed from death to life. We are confident that our brother (sister) N., who believed in Christ, has done the same. In this hope, we pray. *Response*: Hear us, O Lord.

Reader(s): That, through the merits of Christ's passion, N. may be released from his (her) sins. Let us pray.

That, through Christ's victory over death, N. may overcome death and so enter into the fulness of everlasting life in heaven. Let us pray.

For all who still grieve over him (her): that they may not look among the dead for someone who is alive. Let us pray.

That through our faith in the resurrection of Christ we may overcome our fear of death, and so live in the joy and freedom of the children of God. Let us pray.

For all those who have no faith and who are therefore without hope. Let us pray.

President: Father, your Son was the first to rise from the dead. Grant that we who now share his risen life through baptism, may one day come to share the fulness of that life in your kingdom, where there is no more suffering, tears or death. We ask this through the same Christ our Lord.

COMMUNION REFLECTION No. 23 or No. 28.

---

32. REMEMBERING

INTRODUCTION AND CONFITEOR

We are gathered here because we want to remember N. who died ... years (months) ago today. When we remember someone, that person becomes present to us.

Every time we celebrate the Eucharist we are remembering. We are obeying Christ's command, 'Do this in memory of me.' The risen Christ stands among us to turn our sorrow into joy, and our despair into hope. *(Pause)*.

Lord, you speak to us when the Scriptures are read. Lord, have mercy.

We recognise you when we break the bread of the Eucharist. Christ, have mercy.

You help us to go forth from here to bring joy and hope to others. Lord, have mercy.

Readings on p. 158.

HEADINGS FOR READINGS

First Reading (Isaiah 49:8.13-16). Even if a mother should forget her own child, God will never forget us because we are the fruit of his love.

Second Reading (1 Corinthians 15:20-26). Christ, the first to be raised from the dead, will bring to life all those who belong to him.

Gospel (Luke 22:14-20). Every time we celebrate the Eucharist we are remembering the death and resurrection of Jesus, and are re-enacting the mystery of our salvation.

HOMILY

Memory is a precious faculty. It connects us with people and events which are no longer present to us. When someone we love dies we feel a desperate need to connect our lives with that of the deceased. Here is where memory comes to our aid. As soon as the loved one dies, memory begins to work overtime.

But, of course, as soon as the loved one dies a cloud of grief descends on us. Grief is not a bad thing. In fact it is a good and necessary thing. Nevertheless, it can be very painful, especially when the loss is great. So we may be tempted to suppress it.

However, memory makes this almost impossible. It continually confronts us with our loss. It insists on stirrring things up. So we may be tempted also to suppress our memories of the deceased. But to forget a loved one is to do him (her) a great injustice. We all long to be remembered. To be forgotten is to be treated as if we never existed. What people fear is not so much death as being forgotten.

Jesus also wanted to be remembered. In his love for us he left us a special way of remembering him, namely, the Eucharist. 'Do this,' he said, 'in memory of me.' The wonderful thing is that when we remember him in this way he actually becomes present to us. Not physically present, but nevertheless really present. And through the Eucharist a spiritual bond is forged between us, with the result that we are able to enter into a deeper intimacy with him than if he were physically present.

If we have loved someone, there is no reason why his (her) memory should rise up like a ghost to haunt us. Rather it should be like the visit of a friend who comes to us with gifts. Memory fills our life with the presence of our departed loved one. In fact memory can bring us closer to each other than can physical presence. Absence can help us to see each other in a new and better light. In memory we are in touch with one another's spirits. When we remember with love we evoke each other's spirits, and are thus able to enter into greater intimacy.

When we finally accept that our loved one is gone, we are able to express gratitude to God for his (her) presence with us over so many years. This helps us to let go of such negative feelings as anger and guilt. In their place comes a flood of fond memories to cherish. Memories are like good wine – they improve with time.

One of the ways of repaying the debt we owe the deceased is not to forget. And by remembering him (her), we continue to reap a harvest from what he (she) sowed while with us. There are people whose impact is almost greater in death than in life.

Yet we must not cling to the deceased. We must let him (her) go, go to be with God where we hope one day to join him (her).

'All that we love deeply becomes a part of us' (Helen Keller).

'There is nothing nobler, stronger, healthier, and more beneficial than a good memory' (Dostoyevsky).

PRAYER OF THE FAITHFUL

President: Christ having been raised from the dead will never die again. Death has no more power over him. Let us pray that it will have no power over us or our loved ones either. *Response*: Lord, hear our prayer.

Reader(s): That all who celebrate the Eucharist may be enlightened by the Word of God and nourished by the Bread of life. Let us pray to the Lord.

As we recall N's memory with love, we pray that he (she) may now enjoy the fulness of life with Christ in heaven. Let us pray to the Lord.

For those who still grieve for N.: that they may know that God loves them and will never abandon them. Let us pray to the Lord.

For ourselves: that our remembrance of N. may be a source of comfort and strength to us. Let us pray to the Lord.

That each of us may believe we are precious to God and that he has our names written on the palm of his hand. Let us pray to the Lord.

President: Father, we believe that those we love and who have died are now alive and living in your kingdom. May their memory be for us a source of continuing strength and inspiration. We ask this through Christ our Lord.

COMMUNION REFLECTION No. 25 or No. 28.

33. RESTORING BROKEN RELATIONSHIPS

INTRODUCTION AND CONFITEOR

One of the things those who are grieving tend to do is cut themselves off from other people and sometimes even from life. While this is understandable, it is a mistake and slows down recovery.

Through the voice of the liturgy God says to us this day, 'Courage! Do not be afraid. I am coming to save you.' So let us throw our minds and our hearts open to receive his help and consolation. *(Pause)*.

Now let us humbly acknowledge our sins in order to receive his merciful forgiveness.

I confess to almighty God.

Readings on p. 160.

HEADINGS FOR READINGS

First Reading (Isaiah 35:3-6.10). A message of hope for all those who are weary, afflicted and afraid.

Second Reading (2 Corinthians 5:1.6-10). Paul tells us that when our earthly life is over, God has an everlasting house built for us in heaven.

Gospel (John 20:19-20.24-29). The risen Jesus breaks through to his disheartened disciples, restores their faith, and brings them peace.

HOMILY

Grief is a very painful experience. It hurts badly. Now, when we are hurting we do not want anyone to come near us. This is why people who are grieving tend to cut themselves off. Sorrow cuts us off. We feel so alone, estranged from everything and everybody. Loneliness is one of the biggest problems in grief.

Sometimes neighbours and relatives misunderstand this. They think that the grieving wish to be left alone. So they leave them alone. But this is a mistake. The one thing the grieving need is company and support.

The apostles went through a similar experience after the death of Christ. In the Gospel we find them behind closed doors, cut off from the world. No doubt one reason for this was the fact that they were afraid of the Jewish leaders. But they were also in a state of deep grief. They wanted to be alone. Thomas went one step further. Initially at least he chose to be completely alone in his grief.

It is interesting to note that it was Christ who took the first step towards the apostles. He took the initiative. He broke through the barriers they had erected between themselves and the world, and by coming to them brought them peace.

Contact with others is a great help in dealing with grief. While the desire to isolate ourselves is understandable, it is a mistake. We must try to open ourselves to those who are trying to reach out to us, and we ourselves must make some effort to reach out to others, even if we feel like children learning to walk.

Faith is another marvellous help. Jesus said to Thomas, 'Have you believed because you have seen me? Blessed are those who have not seen and yet believe.' At a time of grief, faith is a priceless asset. Faith is a beacon of light in our darkness. It is an anchor in the midst of the storm. It is a staff to support us as we struggle to carry on with our lives. Above all, it gives us hope, and hope is a primary factor in survival and recovery. Faith assures us that the risen Christ is present with us, and it opens us to receive the gifts he gives us through other people.

Faith does even more than this. It assures us that our loved ones are not dead and gone for ever. They are alive, alive in our risen Lord. Therefore, we can 'touch' them even though we cannot see them. The body after all does not matter all that much. It is relationships that matter, and these transcend death. The sacred bond which love has forged between us and the departed is not broken by death. Rather it is sealed for ever.

Eventually, then, we are reintegrated into the community and the loss of our loved one is accepted, though not forgotten.

PRAYER OF THE FAITHFUL

President: Jesus said to Thomas, 'Thomas, you believe because you can see. Happy are those who have not seen and yet believe.' We are among those who believe without seeing. May Christ come to us this day to banish our doubts and strengthen our faith. *Response*: Lord, hear our prayer.

Reader(s): For the Church: that it may be a community of brothers and sisters who help and support one another. Let us pray to the Lord.

For N.: that he (she) may enter that everlasting house which God has built for his children in heaven. Let us pray to the Lord.

For those who are grieving over N's loss; that God may console them, and restore them to full fellowship with their friends and the community. Let us pray to the Lord.

That we may see the face of Christ in the faces of those who are in pain or need. Let us pray to the Lord.

For all the faithful departed, and especially for our departed relatives and friends: that God may grant them eternal life. Let us pray to the Lord.

President: Father, through faith in your Son and fellowship with one another, may we all come finally to that land of joy and gladness where separation, sorrow and lament will be ended. We ask this through Christ our Lord.

COMMUNION REFLECTION No. 24.

---

34. HEALING THE WOUNDS OF GRIEF

INTRODUCTION AND CONFITEOR

We are here to remember N. Every time we remember we become conscious of our loss and of our grief. Grief causes a wound, sometimes a very deep wound. Like all wounds it hurts. But this is one wound we need not be ashamed of, for it is caused by love.

Christ blessed those who mourn and said they would be comforted. As we recall his words, let us renew our faith in his presence among us. *(Pause)*.

Lord you come to us with the good news of eternal life. Lord, have mercy.

You bind up hearts that are broken with grief. Christ, have mercy.

You lead us from the dungeon of sadness and despair to the freedom and joy of the children of God. Lord, have mercy.

Readings on p. 162.

HEADINGS FOR READINGS

First Reading (Isaiah 61:1-3). God sends his servant to bring good news to the poorest and neediest of his children.

Second Reading (Revelation 21:1-4). When the fulness of God's kingdom will be revealed, there will be no more sadness or mourning or death.

Gospel (Luke 24:36-48). Christ appears to his frightened and disheartened disciples, shows them his wounds, and explains to them the meaning of his death.

HOMILY

One of the deepest and most painful wounds anyone can suffer is that of grief. When we suffer the loss of a loved one we are deeply wounded, especially in that most sensitive and delicate part of us – the heart. Our heart is not just wounded. It is broken.

You sometimes hear people say to a bereaved person, 'Oh, aren't you great! You're so strong!' There is a tendency to praise those who suppress their grief and who manage to hide their sorrow. But this is foolish. Whether we admit it or not, grief wounds us. Now to hide these wounds is not only bad; it is dangerous. But why should we hide them? Christ didn't hide his wounds.

When he appeared to his disciples after his resurrection, the first thing he did was show them his wounds. Now why did he keep those wounds on his risen body? No doubt they helped the apostles to identify him. But the reason is deeper. Those wounds were the signs and proof of his love for them and for us. They were the mortal wounds the Good Shepherd suffered in defending his sheep from the wolf. Far from being things to be ashamed of, they were, like hard-won trophies, things to be proud of.

So there is no need for us to hide the wounds of grief. These wounds are not things we should be ashamed of. Rather they are the signs and proof of our love for our lost dear one. It is precisely because we loved him (her) that we are now wounded by his (her) loss.

They say that one never fully recovers from deep grief. There are always some scars left. But this shouldn't depress us. The main thing is not to be ashamed of these scars. Where there is love there is always pain too. However, though the mark of the wounds may remain, the poison is no longer present once we have come to terms with our loss.

The thing that helps to take the poison out of our wounds is faith. Christ broke the chains of death and rose in triumph from the grave. He shares the fruits of his great victory with all those who believe in him. So our departed ones are not dead. They are alive and living in that land where mourning is no more.

Christ also opened the eyes of the apostles to the value of suffering. 'It was written that the Christ should suffer and on the third day rise from the dead.' It was because he suffered that he was glorified. In the same way, our pain, if borne with love, can bear immense fruit for us.

PRAYER OF THE FAITHFUL

President: God makes his home among his people. We are his people. Let us pray to him, confident that he will wipe the tears from our eyes and restore us to joy. *Response*: Lord, hear us in your love.

Reader(s): For N.: that Christ may forgive his (her) sins, and lead him (her) to the joy of the Father's kingdom. We pray in faith.

For those who mourn for him (her): that Christ may heal the wounds of their grief and change their sorrow into joy. We pray in faith.

That we may never be ashamed to show our grief, knowing that our tears are precious in the eyes of God and he will comfort us. We pray in faith.

For all the dead, especially those who were close to us and good to us: that they may enter the new and eternal Jerusalem where death is no more. We pray in faith.

For those who are in pain and who have no one to comfort them or to tend their wounds. We pray in faith.

President: Heavenly Father, you loved the world so much that you sent your only Son to us. Grant that all who believe in him may not be lost but may have eternal life. We ask this through the same Christ our Lord.

COMMUNION REFLECTION No. 26

35. REBUILDING OUR LIVES

INTRODUCTION AND CONFITEOR

The death of a loved one such as N. shatters our world. It seems as if we have nothing to live for because everything is gone or has lost its meaning.

The only thing that helps us to keep going is our faith in God. God sustains us, consoles us, and helps us to rebuild our lives. In time he even turns our sorrow into joy. Our risen Saviour is with us in our grief. Let us draw close to him now. *(Pause)*.

Lord Jesus, you speak to us when the Scriptures are read, explaining to us the meaning of our life and death. Lord, have mercy.

You come to us in Communion to nourish within us the divine life you first shared with us at Baptism. Christ, have mercy.

You comfort us with the assurance that you will share your victory over death with us, your adopted brothers and sisters. Lord, have mercy.

Readings on p. 164.

HEADINGS FOR READINGS

First Reading (Isaiah 52:7-10). This passage contains the glad message that God consoles and comforts his people.

Second Reading (1 Corinthians 15:51-57). Through his death and resurrection Christ has robbed our death of its sting, and has turned defeat into victory.

Gospel (Luke 24:13-35. Shortened version). The story of two disciples whose world had been shattered by the death of Jesus, and how they found hope again.

HOMILY

The Korean war was raging. A little village came under heavy artillery fire. In the village stood a church. Outside the church, mounted on a pedestal, was a fine statue of Christ. However, when the smoke of battle cleared away, the statue had disappeared. It had been blown off its pedestal and lay in fragments on the ground.

A group of American soldiers helped the priest to collect up the pieces. Carefully they put the statue back together again. They found all the pieces except the hands. They offered to have it flown to the U.S.A. and have hands made for it. But the priest refused.

'I have a better idea,' he said. 'Let's leave it without hands, and let us put on the pedestal, for all passersby to see, the message: "Friend, lend me your hands." '

The death of someone we love shatters our lives. Life comes to a standstill on the day our loved one dies. We stay fixed there, without plans or interests. We find it so difficult to resume life. We can even feel guilty about living, especially about enjoying ourselves.

It is interesting to note that after the death of Christ his disciples felt like this too. In the Gospel we saw two of them going back home. The death of Christ had shattered their world, reducing their dreams to rubble. What are they talking about? About the death of Christ. They are fixed there. For them life came to a halt on Good Friday afternoon.

Then Christ appears to them. The first thing he does is to open their minds to understand that his death, far from being the end of the dream, was the very means by which it became a reality. Then he opens their eyes so that they recognise him. By now it is dark. And what happens? They are so filled with joy that they run all the way back to Jerusalem to tell the others.

It was the experience of Christ's risen presence that helped the apostles to pick up the pieces. Without this they would never have managed. They were too deeply wounded. They had lost too much.

We too have heard the Easter message. Christ is alive! Therefore, our loved one is alive too. Death is swallowed up in victory. Death has been robbed of its sting. Strengthened by this faith, we too will succeed in picking up the pieces and putting them together again. We know, of course, that things will never be quite the same. There will always be a pair of hands missing. But our faith will help us to become reconciled to this.

Of course, the help of others is vital too. We are extremely fortunate if we have people around us who are willing to lend us their hands to help us find and re-assemble the scattered pieces of our former life.

Thus we will begin to move forward and to live once more. What saves a person is to take a step, then another step. Eventually our loss is integrated into our life, and from grief comes growth.

PRAYER OF THE FAITHFUL

President: Christ says to us, 'Come to me, all you who labour and are overburdened, and I will give you rest.' Let us come to Christ with our prayers, confident that he will listen to them. *Response*: Lord, graciously hear us.

Reader(s): During his (her) earthly life N. was nourished with the bread of life; may Christ now give him (her) a seat at the banquet of eternal life. Lord, hear us.

For those who still mourn for him (her): that, with faith in Christ and the help of their friends, they may have the strength to pick up the pieces and go on with life. Lord, hear us.

That as Christians we may always see Christ as the companion of our lives, lightening our burdens, and keeping us firm in faith and serene in hope. Lord, hear us.

For all the dead, especially those who were close to us and good to us: that they may achieve that victory over death Christ won for us through his own death and resurrection. Lord, hear us.

For all those who are struggling under the burdens of pain, sadness, and despair: that we may be sensitive to their needs and help them in any way we can. Lord, hear us.

President: Lord, may you support us all day long, till the shadows lengthen and evening falls, and the busy world is hushed, and the fever of life is over, and our work is done. Then, in your mercy, grant us a safe lodging, a holy rest, and peace at last. We ask this through Christ our Lord.

COMMUNION REFLECTION No. 21

36. THE COMING OF THE SPIRIT

INTRODUCTION AND CONFITEOR

As we gather to celebrate this Mass we know that there is someone missing. N. is missing. We still feel his (her) loss. But we are not without consolation. God consoles us his children.

Let us approach him with humility and trust. *(Pause)*

Lord, you are close to the broken-hearted. Lord, have mercy.

You give light to those who are surrounded by the shadows of death. Christ, have mercy.

Though father and mother should forsake us, you will never forsake us. Lord, have mercy.

Readings on p. 166.

HEADINGS FOR READINGS

First Reading (Lamentations 3:17-26). Those who are overcome with anguish and pain, but who hope in God, will experience relief.

Second Reading (1 Thessalonians 4:13-18). It is natural that we should grieve when we lose a loved one, but as Christians we should not grieve as those who have no hope.

Gospel (John 16:1-7). The apostles were overcome with sorrow at Jesus' impending death. But Jesus consoled them with the promise that he would send them the Holy Spirit.

HOMILY

The sun is going down, filling the world, as it does so, with its golden light. Meanwhile, the moon is high in the sky. But it is so weak and pale that you have to look very carefully to see it. It doesn't appear to be contributing anything whatsoever to the earth.

As the sun goes down it appears to be taking the whole world with it. As it goes, however, a curious and beautiful thing happens. The lower the sun dips in the sky, the brighter the moon becomes. So that by the time the sun has finally departed the scene, the moon has undergone a complete transformation. It is now, far and away, the brightest object in the sky. And as you look around you, you notice to your surprise and delight that the old world has not only been completely restored to you, but has been made new, bright and exciting.

When we lose someone who has meant a lot to us, it is as if the sun

goes down on our life. Everything seems to vanish with the depart-
ing one. We are plunged into gloom, and experience a terrible
feeling of emptiness. We miss our loved one as much as we miss the
light. The void seems to get even greater as time gradually brings
home to us just how much we have lost.

But our faith assures us that all is not lost. We are not in total
darkness. A new light shines on us, or rather the old light under a
new form. Just as the sun, though it has departed the earthly scene,
is still able to reflect its light on the earth, so our loved ones, though
out of sight, have not vanished into nothingness. They still live.
Now enjoying the light of eternity, they are able to reflect some of
this light on us. They are still shining on us, still influencing us.
Death is not absence. It is a new kind of presence.

The apostles were plunged into gloom when Christ died. But
when, from his place in glory at the right hand of his Father, he sent
the Holy Spirit to them as he had promised, they were filled with
hope and joy. They became new people, people who were able to
shine in their own right.

All loved ones who die leave us a parting gift – the gift of their
spirit. This spirit comforts us and maintains the link between us and
them. But the spirit also summons us to life. We are challenged to
grow, to shine in our own right. And what happens? We discover
resources within us we never suspected existed. Thus, though we
lose something, we gain something too; though we are impoverished, we are enriched too. The world is restored to us, bathed in a
new and gentler light.

Those who have a task to do (looking after a family or whatever)
recover more quickly. But recovery can happen for everyone. All
we have to do is believe. Christ too sends us his very own Spirit, the
Holy Spirit, the consoler and upholder of all those who grieve.

PRAYER OF THE FAITHFUL

President: Jesus does not leave us to grieve without hope or help.
He sends his Spirit to us, the Holy Spirit, who makes us firm in faith
and serene in hope. *Response*: Lord, hear us in your love.

Reader(s): That Christ's eternal light may shine brightly on our
brother (sister) N. We pray in faith.

That all of us who mourn his (her) leaving, may realise that we
have gained an intercessor in heaven. We pray in faith.

That we may realise that his (her) spirit continues to shine on us,
helping us to find our way and giving us strength to go on living. We
pray in faith.

For all our departed relatives and friends: that they may come to a
place of refreshment, light and peace. We pray in faith.

That wherever the followers of Christ are found, they may give an example to the world of how to grieve with hope. We pray in faith.

President: Father, give us the certainty that beyond death there is a life where broken things are mended, and lost things are found; where there is rest for the weary and joy for the sad; where all that we have loved and willed of good will exist; and where we will meet again our loved ones. We ask this through Christ our Lord.

COMMUNION REFLECTION No. 29.

Readings

1. JOURNEY TO THE PROMISED LAND

A reading from the Book of Genesis   12:1-4

The Lord said to Abram, 'Go from your country and your kindred and your father's house to the land that I will show you. And I will make of you a great nation, and I will bless you, and make your name great, so that you will be a blessing. I will bless those who bless you, and him who curses you I will curse; and by you all the families of the earth shall bless themselves.'

So Abram went, as the Lord had told him.

This is the word the Lord.

Responsorial Psalm   Ps. 22(23)

Response:
The Lord is my shepherd;
there is nothing I shall want.

The Lord is my shepherd;
there is nothing I shall want.
Fresh and green are the pastures
where he gives me repose.
Near restful waters he leads me,
to revive my drooping spirit.   **R**.

He guides me along the right path;
he is true to his name.
If I should walk in the valley of darkness
no evil would I fear.
You are there with your crook and your staff;
with these you give me comfort.   **R**.

You have prepared a banquet for me
in the sight of my foes.
My head you have anointed with oil;
my cup is overflowing.   **R**.

Surely goodness and kindness shall follow me
all the days of my life.

In the Lord's own house shall I dwell
for ever and ever. **R.**

SECOND READING

A reading from the Letter to the Hebrews   11:1-2.8-10.13-16
Now faith is the assurance of things hoped for, the conviction of
things not seen. For by it the men of old received divine approval.
By faith Abraham obeyed when he was called to go out to a place
which he was to receive as an inheritance; and he went out, not
knowing where he was to go. By faith he sojourned in the land of
promise, as in a foreign land, living in tents with Isaac and Jacob,
heirs with him to the same promise. For he looked forward to the
city which has foundations, whose builder and maker is God.

These all died in faith, not having received what was promised,
but having seen it and greeted it from afar, and having acknowledg-
ed that they were strangers and exiles on the earth. For people who
speak thus make it clear that they are seeking a homeland. If they
had been thinking of that land from which they had gone out, they
would have had opportunity to return. But as it is, they desire a
better country, that is, a heavenly one.

This is the word of the Lord.

Gospel Acclamation   John 6:27
   Alleluia, alleluia! [*Lent*: Praise to you, Lord Jesus Christ!]
   Do not labour for the food which perishes,
   but for the food which endures to eternal life,
   which the Son of man will give to you.
   Alleluia! [*Lent*: Praise to you, Lord Jesus Christ!]

GOSPEL

A reading from the holy Gospel according to John   6:44-51
Jesus said: 'No one can come to me unless the Father who sent me
draw him; and I will raise him up at the last day. It is written in the
prophets, "And they shall all be taught by God." Every one who
has heard and learned from the Father comes to me. Not that any
one has seen the Father except him who is from God; he has seen
the Father.

'Truly, truly, I say to you, he who believes has eternal life. I am
the bread of life. Your fathers ate the manna in the wilderness, and
they died. This is the bread which comes down from heaven, that a
man may eat of it and not die. I am the living bread which came

down from heaven; if any one eats of this bread, he will live for
ever.'
This is the Gospel of the Lord.

---

2. THE STORY OF A LIFE

A reading from the prophet Isaiah   35:3-6.10
Strengthen the weak hands, and make firm the feeble knees. Say to
those who are of a fearful heart, 'Be strong, fear not! Behold, your
God will come with vengeance, with the recompense of God. He
will come and save you.'

Then the eyes of the blind will be opened, and the ears of the deaf
unstopped; then will the lame man leap like a hart, and the tongue
of the dumb sing for joy.

And the ransomed of the Lord will return, and come to Zion with
singing; everlasting joy shall be upon their heads; they shall obtain
joy and gladness, and sorrow and sighing shall flee away.
This is the word of the Lord.

Responsorial Psalm   Ps 138(139):7-12.23-24
  Response:
  O Lord, you search me and you know me.

  O where can I go from your spirit,
  or where can I flee from your face?
  If I climb the heavens, you are there.
  If I lie in the grave, you are there.   **R.**

  If I take the wings of the dawn
  and dwell at the sea's furthest end,
  even there your hand would lead me,
  your right hand would hold me fast.   **R.**

  If I say: 'Let the darkness hide me
  and the light around me be night,'
  even darkness is not dark for you
  and the night is as clear as the day.   **R**

  O search me, God, and know my heart.
  O test me and know my thoughts.

See that I follow not the wrong path
and lead me in the path of life eternal. **R.**

A reading from the first letter of St Paul to the Corinthians 15:51-57

Lo! I tell you a mystery. We shall not all sleep, but we shall all be changed, in a moment, in the twinkling of an eye, at the last trumpet. For the trumpet will sound, and the dead will be raised imperishable, and we shall be changed.

For this perishable nature must put on the imperishable, and this mortal nature must put on immortality. When the perishable puts on the imperishable, and the mortal puts on immortality, then shall come to pass the saying that is written: 'Death is swallowed up in victory. O death, where is thy victory? O death, where is thy sting?'

The sting of death is sin, and the power of sin is the law. But thanks be to God, who gives us the victory through our Lord Jesus Christ.

This is the word of the Lord.

Gospel Acclamation   Luke 24:26

Alleluia, alleluia! [*Lent*: Praise to you, Lord Jesus Christ]
Was it not necessary that the Christ
should suffer these things
and enter into his glory?
Alleluia! [*Lent*: Praise to you, Lord Jesus Christ]

A reading from the holy Gospel according to Luke 24:13-17.19-31

That very day [*Easter Day*] two of Jesus' disciples were going to a village named Emmaus, about seven miles from Jerusalem, and talking about these things that had happened. While they were talking, Jesus himself drew near. But their eyes were kept from recognising him. And he said to them, 'What is this conversation which you are holding as you walk?' And they stood still, looking sad.

Then they said to him, 'Concerning Jesus of Nazareth, who was a prophet mighty in deed and word before God and all the people, and how our chief priests and rulers delivered him up and crucified him. But we had hoped that he was the one to redeem Israel. It is now the third day since this happened. Moreover, some women of our company amazed us. They were at the tomb early in the morning and did not find his body; and they came back saying that they had even seen a vision of angels, who said he was alive.'

And he said to them, 'O foolish men, and slow of heart to believe all that the prophets have spoken! Was it not necessary that the

Christ should suffer these things and enter into his glory?' And
beginning with Moses and all the prophets, he interpreted to them
in all the scriptures the things concerning himself.

So they drew near to the village to which they were going. He
appeared to be going further, but they said, 'Stay with us, for the
day is far spent.' So he went in to stay with them. When he was at
table with them, he took the bread and blessed, and broke it, and
gave it to them. And their eyes were opened and they recognised
him; and he vanished out of their sight.

This is the Gospel of the Lord.

3. THE MARKS OF A DISCIPLE

FIRST READING

A reading from the book of Sirach   2:1-9

If you come forward to serve the Lord, prepare yourself for temptation. Set your heart right and be steadfast, and do not be hasty in
time of calamity. Cleave to him and do not depart, that you may be
honoured at the end of your life.

Accept whatever is brought upon you, and in changes that
humble you be patient. For gold is tested in the fire, and acceptable
men in the furnace of humiliation. Trust in him, and he will help
you; make your ways straignt, and hope in him.

You who fear the Lord, wait for his mercy; and turn not aside, lest
you fall. You who fear the Lord, trust in him, and your reward will
not fail; you who fear the Lord, hope for good things, for everlasting
joy and mercy.

This is the word of the Lord.

Responsorial Psalm   Ps 23(24):1-6

Response:
The Lord's is the earth and its fulness.

The Lord's is the earth and its fulness,
the world and all its peoples.
It is he who set it on the seas;
on the waters he made it firm.   **R.**

Who shall climb the mountain of the Lord?
Who shall stand in his holy place?

Those with clean hands and pure heart,
who desire not worthless things.   **R.**

They shall receive blessings from the Lord
and reward from the God who saves them.
Such are the people who seek him,
seek the face of the God of Jacob.   **R.**

SECOND READING

A reading from the letter of St Paul to the Philippians   4:4-9

Rejoice in the Lord always; again I say, Rejoice. Let all men know your forbearance. The Lord is at hand. Have no anxiety about anything, but in everything by prayer and supplication with thanksgiving let your requests be made known to God. And the peace of God, which passes all understanding, will keep your hearts and your minds in Christ Jesus.

Finally, brethren, whatever is true, whatever is honourable, whatever is just, whatever is pure, whatever is lovely, whatever is gracious, if there is any excellence, if there is anything worthy of praise, think about these things. What you have learned and heard and seen in me, do; and the God of peace will be with you.

This is the word of the Lord.

Gospel Acclamation   Matt 5:3

Alleluia, alleluia! [*Lent*: Praise to you, Lord Jesus Christ]
Blessed are the poor in spirit,
for theirs is the kingdom of heaven.
Alleluia! [*Lent*: Praise to you, Lord Jesus Christ]

GOSPEL

A reading from the holy Gospel according to Matthew   5:1-10

Seeing the crowds, Jesus went up on the mountain, and when he sat down his disciples came to him. And he opened his mouth and taught them, saying:

'Blessed are the poor in spirit, for theirs is the kingdom of heaven.
'Blessed are those who mourn, for they shall be comforted.
'Blessed are the meek, for they shall inherit the earth.
'Blessed are those who hunger and thirst for righteousness, for they shall be satisfied.
'Blessed are the merciful, for they shall obtain mercy.
'Blessed are the pure in heart, for they shall see God.
'Blessed are the peacemakers, for they shall be called sons of God.

'Blessed are those who are persecuted for righteousness' sake, for theirs is the kingdom of heaven.'
This is the Gospel of the Lord.

---

4. THE SEED MUST DIE

A reading from the book of Sirach   2:1-9

If you come forward to serve the Lord, prepare yourself for temptation. Set your heart right and be steadfast, and do not be hasty in time of calamity. Cleave to him and do not depart, that you may be honoured at the end of your life.

Accept whatever is brought upon you, and in changes that humble you be patient. For gold is tested in the fire, and acceptable men in the furnace of humiliation. Trust in him, and he will help you; make your ways straight, and hope in him.

You who fear the Lord, wait for his mercy; and turn not aside, lest you fall. You who fear the Lord, trust in him, and your reward will not fail; you who fear the Lord, hope for good things, for everlasting joy and mercy.

This is the word of the Lord.

Responsorial Psalm   Ps 15(16):5-11

Response:
Preserve me, God, I take refuge in you.

Lord, it is you who are my portion and cup;
it is you yourself who are my prize.
The lot marked out for me is my delight:
welcome indeed the heritage that falls to me.   **R.**

I will bless the Lord who gives me counsel,
who even at night directs my heart.
I keep the Lord ever in my sight:
since he is at my right hand,
I shall stand firm.   **R.**

And so my heart rejoices, my soul is glad;
even my body shall rest in safety.
For you will not leave my soul among the dead,
nor let your beloved know decay.   **R**

You will show me the path of life,
the fulness of joy in your presence,
at your right hand happiness for ever. **R**.

A reading from the letter of St Paul to the Romans   6:3-4.8-11

Do you not know that all of us who have been baptized into Christ Jesus were baptized into his death? We were buried therefore with him by baptism into death, so that as Christ was raised from the dead by the glory of the Father, we too might walk in newness of life.

If we have died with Christ, we believe that we shall also live with him. For we know that Christ being raised from the dead will never die again; death no longer has dominion over him. The death he died he died to sin, once for all, but the life he lives he lives to God.

So you must consider yourselves dead to sin and alive to God in Christ Jesus.

This is the word of the Lord.

Gospel Acclamation   John 12:24

Alleluia, alleluia! [*Lent*: Praise to you, Lord Jesus Christ]
Unless a grain of wheat falls into the earth and dies, it remains alone;
but if it dies, it bears much fruit.
Alleluia! [*Lent*: Praise to you, Lord Jesus Christ]

A reading from the holy Gospel according to John   12:23-27

Jesus said:

'The hour has come for the Son of man to be glorified.

'Truly, truly, I say to you, unless a grain of wheat falls into the earth and dies, it remains alone; but if it dies, it bears much fruit.

'He who loves his life loses it, and he who hates his life in this world will keep it for eternal life. If any one serves me, he must follow me; and where I am, there shall my servant be also; if any one serves me, the Father will honour him.

'Now is my soul troubled. And what shall I say? "Father, save me from this hour?" No, for this purpose I have come to this hour.'

This is the Gospel of the Lord.

5. WALKING ON WATER

A reading from the prophet Isaiah   35:3-6.10

Strengthen the weak hands, and make firm the feeble knees. Say to those who are of a fearful heart, 'Be strong, fear not! Behold, your God will come with vengeance, with the recompense of God. He will come and save you.'

Then the eyes of the blind will be opened, and the ears of the deaf unstopped; then will the lame man leap like a hart, and the tongue of the dumb sing for joy.

And the ransomed of the Lord will return, and come to Zion with singing; everlasting joy shall be upon their heads; they shall obtain joy and gladness, and sorrow and sighing shall flee away.

This is the word of the Lord.

Responsorial Psalm   Ps 123 (124)

Response:
Our help is in the name of the Lord,
who made heaven and earth.

If the Lord had not been on our side
when men rose against us,
then would they have swallowed us alive
when their anger was kindled.   **R.**

Then would the waters have engulfed us,
the torrent gone over us;
over our head would have swept
the raging waters.   **R.**

Blessed be the Lord who did not give us
a prey to their teeth.
Our life, like a bird, has escaped
from the snare of the fowler.   **R.**

Indeed the snare has been broken
and we have escaped.
Our help is in the name of the Lord,
who made heaven and earth.   **R.**

SECOND READING

A reading from the first letter of St Paul to the Corinthians 15:51-57

Lo! I tell you a mystery. We shall not all sleep, but we shall all be changed, in a moment, in the twinkling of an eye, at the last trumpet. For the trumpet will sound, and the dead will be raised imperishable, and we shall be changed.

For this perishable nature must put on the imperishable, and this mortal nature must put on immortality. When the perishable puts on the imperishable, and the mortal puts on immortality, then shall come to pass the saying that is written: 'Death is swallowed up in victory. O death, where is thy victory? O death, where is thy sting?'

The sting of death is sin, and the power of sin is the law. But thanks be to God, who gives us the victory through our Lord Jesus Christ.

This is the word of the Lord.

Gospel Acclamation   Matthew 24:35

Alleluia, alleluia! [*Lent*: Praise to you, Lord Jesus Christ]
Heaven and earth will pass away,
but my words will not pass away,
says the Lord.
Alleluia! [*Lent*: Praise to you, Lord Jesus Christ]

GOSPEL

A reading from the holy Gospel according to Matthew   14:22-23

Then Jesus made the disciples get into the boat and go before him to the other side, while he dismissed the crowds. And after he had dismissed the crowds he went up into the hills by himself to pray.

When evening came, he was there alone, but the boat by this time was many furlongs distant from the land, beaten by the waves; for the wind was against them. And in the fourth watch of the night he came to them, walking on the sea. But when the disciples saw him walking on the sea, they were terrified, saying, 'It is a ghost!' And they cried out for fear. But immediately he spoke to them, saying, 'Take heart, it is I; have no fear.'

And Peter answered him, 'Lord, if it is you, bid me come to you on the water.' He said, 'Come.' So Peter got out of the boat and walked on the water and came to Jesus; but when he saw the wind, he was afraid, and beginning to sink he cried out, 'Lord, save me.' Jesus immediately reached out his hand and caught him, saying to him, 'O man of little faith, why did you doubt?'

And when they got into the boat, the wind ceased. And those in the boat worshipped him, saying, 'Truly you are the Son of God.'

This is the Gospel of the Lord.

6. BUILDING ON HIS WORDS

A reading from the prophet Isaiah   35:3-6.10

Strengthen the weak hands, and make firm the feeble knees. Say to those who are of a fearful heart, 'Be strong, fear not! Behold, your God will come with vengeance, with the recompense of God. He will come and save you.'

Then the eyes of the blind will be opened, and the ears of the deaf unstopped; then will the lame man leap like a hart, and the tongue of the dumb sing for joy.

And the ransomed of the Lord will return, and come to Zion with singing; everlasting joy shall be upon their heads; they shall obtain joy and gladness, and sorrow and sighing shall flee away.

This is the word of the Lord.

Responsorial Psalm   Ps 61(63):2-3.8.11-13

Response:
In God alone is my soul at rest.

In God alone is my soul at rest;
my help comes from him.
He alone is my rock, my stronghold,
my fortress: I stand firm.   **R**.

Take refuge in God all you people;
trust him at all times.
Pour out your hearts before him
for God is our refuge.   **R**.

Do not put your trust in oppression
nor vain hopes of plunder.
Do not set your heart on riches
even when they increase.   **R**.

For God has said only one thing:
only two do I know:
that to God alone belongs power
and to you, Lord, love.   **R**.

A reading from the first letter of St Paul to the Corinthians 2:1-6.9

When I came to you, brethren, I did not come proclaiming to you the testimony of God in lofty words or wisdom. For I decided to know nothing among you except Jesus Christ and him crucified. And I was with you in weakness and in much fear and trembling; and my speech and my message were not in plausible words of wisdom, but in demonstration of the Spirit and power, that your faith might not rest in the wisdom of men but in the power of God.

Yet among the mature we do impart wisdom, although it is not a wisdom of this age or of the rulers of this age, who are doomed to pass away. It is written, 'What no eye has seen, nor ear heard, nor the heart of man conceived, what God has prepared for those who love him,' God has revealed to us through the Spirit.

This is the word of the Lord.

Gospel Acclamation   Matthew 24:35
   Alleluia, alleluia! [*Lent*: Praise to you, Lord Jesus Christ]
   Heaven and earth will pass away,
   but my words will not pass away,
   says the Lord.
   Alleluia! [*Lent*: Praise to you, Lord Jesus Christ]

GOSPEL

A reading from the holy Gospel according to Matthew   7:24-27
Jesus said to his disciples:
   'Every one then who hears these words of mine and does them will be like a wise man who built his house upon the rock; and the rain fell, and the floods came, and the winds blew and beat upon that house, but it did not fall, because it had been founded on the rock.
   'And every one who hears these words of mine and does not do them will be like a foolish man who built his house upon the sand; and the rain fell, and the floods came, and the winds blew and beat against that house, and it fell; and great was the fall of it.'
   This is the Gospel of the Lord.

7. HARVEST TIME OF THE SPIRIT

FIRST READING

A reading from the book of Ecclesiastes   3:1-8.11
For everything there is a season, and a time for every matter under heaven:
   a time to be born, and a time to die;

a time to plant, and a time to pluck up what is planted;
a time to kill, and a time to heal;
a time to break down, and a time to build up;
a time to weep, and a time to laugh;
a time to mourn, and a time to dance;
a time to cast away stones, and a time to gather stones together;
a time to embrace, and a time to refrain from embracing;
a time to seek, and a time to lose;
a time to keep, and a time to cast away;
a time to rend, and a time to sew;
a time to keep silence, and a time to speak;
a time to love, and a time to hate;
a time for war, and a time for peace.
God has made everything beautiful in its time.
This is the word of the Lord.

Responsorial Psalm   Ps 125 (126)

Response:
Those who are sowing in tears
will sing when they reap.

When the Lord delivered Sion from bondage,
it seemed like a dream.
Then was our mouth filled with laughter,
on our lips there were songs.   **R.**

The heathens themselves said:
'What marvels the Lord worked for them!
What marvels the Lord worked for us!
Indeed we were glad.   **R.**

Deliver us, O Lord, from our bondage
as streams in dry land.
Those who are sowing in tears
will sing when they reap.   **R.**

They go out, they go out, full of tears,
carrying seed for the sowing:
they come back, they come back, full of song,
carrying their sheaves.   **R.**

SECOND READING

A reading from the letter of St Paul to the Galatians   6:7-10
Do not be deceived; God is not mocked, for whatever a man sows,
that he will also reap. For he who sows to his own flesh will from the

flesh reap corruption; but he who sows to the Spirit will from the Spirit reap eternal life.

And let us not grow weary in well-doing, for in due season we shall reap, if we do not lose heart. So then, as we have opportunity, let us do good to all men, and especially to those who are of the household of faith.

This is the word of the Lord.

Gospel Acclamation   Matthew 24:35

Alleluia, alleluia! [*Lent*: Praise to you, Lord Jesus Christ]
Heaven and earth will pass away,
but my words will not pass away,
says the Lord.
Alleluia! [*Lent*: Praise to you, Lord Jesus Christ]

GOSPEL

A reading from the holy Gospel according to Matthew   13:4-9

Jesus spoke this parable to the people:

'A sower went out to sow. And as he sowed, some seeds fell along the path, and the birds came and devoured them.

'Other seeds fell on rocky ground, where they had not much soil, and immediately they sprang up, since they had no depth of soil, but when the sun rose they were scorched; and since they had no root they withered away.

'Other seeds fell upon thorns, and the thorns grew up and choked them.

'Other seeds fell on good soil and brought forth grain, some a hundredfold, some sixty, some thirty. He who has ears, let him hear.'

This is the Gospel of the Lord.

8. GOING HOME

FIRST READING

A reading from the prophet Isaiah   49:8.13-16

Thus says the Lord: 'In a time of favour I have answered you, in a day of salvation I have helped you.' Sing for joy, O heavens, and exult, O earth; break forth, O mountains, into singing! For the Lord has comforted his people, and will have compassion on his afflicted.

But Zion said, 'The Lord has forsaken me, my Lord has forgotten me.' 'Can a woman forget her sucking child, that she should have no compassion on the son of her womb? Even these may forget, yet I will not forget you. Behold, I have graven you on the palms of my hands.'
    This is the word of the Lord.

Responsorial Psalm   Ps 83(84):4-8.12.
    Response:
My soul is longing for the courts of the Lord.

The sparrow finds herself a home
and the swallow a nest for her brood;
she lays her young by your altars,
Lord of hosts, my king and my God.   **R**.

They are happy, who dwell in your house,
for ever singing your praise.
They are happy, whose strength is in you,
in whose hearts are the roads to Sion.   **R**.

As they go through the Bitter Valley
they make it a place of springs.
They walk with ever growing strength,
they will see the God of gods in Sion.   **R**.

For the Lord God is a rampart, a shield;
he will give us his favour and glory.
The Lord will not refuse any good
to those who walk without blame.   **R**.

SECOND READING

A reading from the second letter of St Paul to the Corinthians 5:1.6-10

For we know that if the earthly tent we live in is destroyed, we have a building from God, a house not made with hands, eternal in the heavens. So we are always of good courage; we know that while we are at home in the body we are away from the Lord, for we walk by faith, not by sight.
    We are of good courage, and we would rather be away from the body and at home with the Lord. So whether we are at home or away, we make it our aim to please him. For we must all appear before the judgement seat of Christ, so that each one may receive good or evil, according to what he has done in the body.
    This is the word of the Lord.

Gospel Acclamation   John 16:28
Alleluia, alleluia! [*Lent*: Praise to you, Lord Jesus Christ]
I came from the Father and have come into the world;
again, I am leaving the world and going to my Father,
says the Lord.
Alleluia! [*Lent*: Praise to you, Lord Jesus Christ]

GOSPEL

A reading from the holy Gospel according to John   14:1-6
Jesus said to his disciples:
  'Let not your hearts be troubled; believe in God, believe also in
me. In my Father's house are many rooms; if it were not so, would I
have told you that I go to prepare a place for you? And when I go
and prepare a place for you, I will come again and will take you to
myself, that where I am you may be also. And you know the way
where I am going.'
  Thomas said to him, 'Lord, we do not know where you are going;
how can we know the way?' Jesus said to him, 'I am the way, and the
truth, and the life; no one comes to the Father, but by me.'
  This is the Gospel of the Lord.

---

9. THE GREAT LOSS

FIRST READING

A reading from the prophet Ezekiel   34:11-12.15-16
Thus says the Lord God, 'Behold, I myself will search for my sheep,
and will seek them out. As a shepherd seeks out his flock when some
of his sheep have been scattered abroad, so will I seek out my sheep;
and I will rescue them from all places where they have been scattered on a day of clouds and thick darkness.
  'I myself will be the shepherd of my sheep, and I will make them
lie down. I will seek the lost, and I will bring back the strayed, and I
will bind up the crippled, and I will strengthen the weak, and the fat
and the strong I will watch over; I will feed them in justice.'
  This is the word of the Lord.

Responsorial Psalm   Ps 22(23)

Response:
The Lord is my shepherd;
there is nothing I shall want.

The Lord is my shepherd;
there is nothing I shall want.
Fresh and green are the pastures
where he gives me repose.
Near restful waters he leads me,
to revive my drooping spirit.   **R**.

He guides me along the right path;
he is true to his name.
If I should walk in the valley of darkness
no evil would I fear.
You are there with your crook and your staff;
with these you give me comfort.   **R**.

You have prepared a banquet for me
in the sight of my foes.
My head you have anointed with oil;
my cup is overflowing.   **R**.

Surely goodness and kindness shall follow me
all the days of my life.
In the Lord's own house shall I dwell
for ever and ever.   **R**.

SECOND READING

A reading from the first letter of St Paul to the Thessalonians   4:13-18

But we would not have you ignorant, brethren, concerning those who are asleep, that you may not grieve as others do who have no hope. For since we believe that Jesus died and rose again, even so, through Jesus, God will bring with him those who have fallen asleep. For this we declare to you by the word of the Lord, that we who are alive, who are left until the coming of the Lord, shall not precede those who have fallen asleep.

For the Lord himself will descend from heaven with a cry of command, with the archangel's call, and with the sound of the trumpet of God. And the dead in Christ will rise first; then we who are alive, who are left, shall be caught up together with them in the clouds to meet the Lord in the air; and so we shall always be with the Lord.

Therefore comfort one another with these words.

This is the word of the Lord.

Gospel Acclamation   John 10:27

Alleluia, alleluia! [*Lent*: Praise to you, Lord Jesus Christ]
My sheep hear my voice, and I know them,
and they follow me; and I give them eternal life,
says the Lord.
Allelluia! [*Lent*: Praise to you, Lord Jesus Christ]

GOSPEL

A reading from the holy Gospel according to John   10:14-15.27-30
Jesus said:

'I am the good shepherd; I know my own and my own know me,
as the Father knows me and I know the Father; and I lay down my
life for my sheep.

'My sheep hear my voice, and I know them, and they follow me;
and I give them eternal life, and they shall never perish, and no one
shall snatch them out of my hand. My Father, who has given them to
me, is greater than all, and no one is able to snatch them out of the
Father's hand. I and the Father are one.'

This is the Gospel of the Lord.

10. PARTING TIME

FIRST READING

A reading from the book of Wisdom   3:1-6.9

The souls of the righteous are in the hands of God, and no torment
will ever touch them. In the eyes of the foolish they seemed to have
died, and their departure was thought to be an affliction, and their
going from us to be their destruction; but they are at peace.

For though in the sight of men they were punished, their hope is
full of immortality. Having been disciplined a little, they will receive
great good, because God tested them and found them worthy of
himself; like gold in the furnace he tried them, and like a sacrificial
burnt offering he accepted them.

Those who trust in him will understand truth, and the faithful will
abide with him in love, because grace and mercy are upon his elect,
and he watches over his holy ones.

This is the word of the Lord.

Responsorial Psalm   Ps 15(16):5-11

Response:
Preserve me, God, I take refuge in you.

O Lord, it is you who are my portion and cup;
it is you yourself who are my prize.
The lot market out for me is my delight:
welcome indeed the heritage that falls to me.   **R**.

I will bless the Lord who gives me counsel,
who even at night directs my heart.
I keep the Lord ever in my sight:
since he is at my right hand,
I shall stand firm.   **R**.

And so my heart rejoices, my soul is glad;
even my body shall rest in safety.
For you will not leave my soul among the dead,
nor let your beloved know decay.   **R**.

You will show me the path of life,
the fulness of joy in your presence,
at your right hand happiness for ever.   **R**.

SECOND READING

A reading from the first letter of St Paul to the Thessalonians   4:13-18

But we would not have you ignorant, brethren, concerning those
who are asleep, that you may not grieve as others do who have no
hope. For since we believe that Jesus died and rose again, even so,
through Jesus, God will bring with him those who have fallen
asleep. For this we declare to you by the word of the Lord, that we
who are alive, who are left until the coming of the Lord, shall not
precede those who have fallen asleep.

For the Lord himself will descend from heaven with a cry of command, with the archangel's call, and with the sound of the trumpet of
God. And the dead in Christ will rise first; then we who are alive, who
are left, shall be caught up together with them in the clouds to meet the
Lord in the air; and so we shall always be with the Lord.

Therefore comfort one another with these words.

This is the word of the Lord.

Gospel Acclamation   John 16:28

Alleluia, alleluia! [*Lent*: Praise to you, Lord Jesus Christ]
I came from the Father and have come into the world;
again, I am leaving the world and going to my Father,

says the Lord.
Alleluia! [*Lent*: Praise to you, Lord Jesus Christ]

GOSPEL

A reading from the holy Gospel according to John   16:16-22
Jesus said to his disciples:

'A little while, and you will see me no more; again a little while, and you will see me.' Some of his disciples said to one another, 'What is this that he says to us, "A little while, and you will not see me, and again a little while, and you will see me"; and, "because I go to the Father"?' They said, 'What does he mean by "a little while"? We do not know what he means.'

Jesus knew that they wanted to ask him; so he said to them, 'Is this what you are asking yourselves, what I meant by sahing, "A little while, and you will not see me, and again a little while, and you will see me"?

'Truly, truly, I say to you, you will weep and lament, but the world will rejoice; you will be sorrowful, but your sorrow will turn into joy. When a woman is in travail she has sorrow, because her hour has come; but when she is delivered of her child, she no longer remembers the anguish, for joy that a child is born into the world. So you have sorrow now, but I will see you again and your hearts will rejoice, and no one will take your joy from you.'

This is the Gospel of the Lord.

11. ENCOUNTER WITH CHRIST

FIRST READING

A reading from the prophet Isaiah   25:6-9

On this mountain the Lord of hosts will make for all peoples a feast of fat things. And he will destroy on this mountain the covering that is cast over all peoples, the veil that is spread over all nations.

He will swallow up death for ever, and the Lord God will wipe away tears from all faces, and the reproach of his people he will take away from all the earth; for the Lord has spoken.

It will be said on that day, 'Lo, this is our God; we have waited for him, that he might save us. This is the Lord; we have waited for him; let us be glad and rejoice in his salvation.'

This is the word of the Lord.

Responsorial Psalm   Ps 41(42):2.3.9.12

Response:
My soul is thirsting for God,
the God of my life.

Like a deer that yearns
for running streams,
so my soul is yearning
for you, my God.   **R**.

My soul is thirsting for God,
the God of my life;
when can I enter and see
the face of God?   **R**.

By day the Lord will send
his loving kindness;
by night I will sing to him,
praise the God of my life.   **R**.

Why are you cast down, my soul,
why groan within me?
Hope in God;
I will praise him still,
my saviour and my God.   **R**.

SECOND READING

A reading from the first letter of St Paul to the Corinthians 13:8-12

Love never ends; as for prophecies, they will pass away; as for
tongues, they will cease; as for knowledge, it will pass away. For our
knowledge is imperfect and our prophecy is imperfect; but when the
perfect comes, the imperfect will pass away.

When I was a child, I spoke like a child, I thought like a child, I
reasoned like a child; when I became a man, I gave up childish ways.
For now we see in a mirror dimly, but then face to face. Now I know
in part; then I shall understand fully, even as I have been fully
understood.

This is the word of the Lord.

Gospel Acclamation   John 10:10
Alleluia, alleluia! [*Lent*: Praise to you, Lord Jesus Christ]
I came that you may have life,
and have it abundantly,
says the Lord.
Alleluia! [*Lent*: Praise to you, Lord Jesus Christ]

GOSPEL

A reading from the holy Gospel according to Luke   7:11-17

Soon afterward Jesus went to a city called Naim, and his disciples and a great crowd went with him. As he drew near to the gate of the city, behold, a man who had died was being carried out, the only son of his mother, and she was a widow; and a large crowd from the city was with her.

And when the Lord saw her, he had compassion on her and said to her, 'Do not weep.' And he came and touched the bier, and the bearers stood still. And he said, 'Young man, I say to you, arise.' And the dead man sat up, and began to speak. And he gave him to his mother.

Fear seized them all; and they glorified God, saying, 'A great prophet has arisen among us!' and 'God has visited his people!'

This is the Gospel of the Lord.

ALTERNATIVE GOSPEL

A reading from the holy Gospel according to Luke   23:33.39-43

And when they came to the place which is called The Skull, there they crucified him, and the criminals, one on the right and one on the left.

One of the criminals who were hanged railed at him, saying, 'Are you not the Christ? Save yourself and us!' But the other rebuked him, saying, 'Do you not fear God, since you are under the same sentence of condemnation? And we indeed justly; for we are receiving the due reward of our deeds; but this man has done nothing wrong.'

And he said, 'Jesus, remember me when you come in your kingly power.' And Jesus said to him, 'Truly, I say to you, today you will be with me in Paradise.'

This is the Gospel of the Lord.

Comment

Here was a man who had travelled a dark path, and who had done nothing to merit salvation. Yet, through an unplanned encounter with Christ, the light of God's mercy suddenly illuminated his path and he walked straight into Paradise. Hence, we must not make the outcome of the final encounter with Christ dependent on our good works.

12. THE LIGHT OF LIFE

A reading from the prophet Isaiah   9:2.6

The people who walked in darkness have seen a great light; those who dwelt in a land of deep darkness, on them has light shined. For to us a child is born, to us a Son is given; and the government will be upon his shoulder, and his name will be called 'Wonderful Counsellor, Mighty God, Everlasting Father, Prince of Peace.'
    This is the word of the Lord.

Responsorial Psalm   Ps 26(27):1.4.10.13.14

Response:
The Lord is my light and my help.

The Lord is my light and my help;
whom shall I fear?
The Lord is the stronghold of my life;
before whom shall I shrink?   **R**.

There is one thing I ask of the Lord,
for this I long,
to live in the house of the Lord
all the days of my life.   **R**.

Do not abandon or forsake me,
O God my help.
Though father and mother forsake me,
the Lord will receive me.   **R**.

I am sure I shall see the Lord's goodness
in the land of the living.
Hope in him, hold firm and take heart.
Hope in the Lord.   **R**.

A reading from the first letter of St Paul to the Corinthians 13:8-12

Love never ends; as for prophecies, they will pass away; as for tongues, they will cease; as for knowledge, it will pass away. For our knowledge is imperfect and our prophecy is imperfect; but when the perfect comes, the imperfect will pass away.
    When I was a child, I spoke like a child, I thought like a child, I

reasoned like a child. When I became a man, I gave up childish ways. For now we see in a mirror dimly, but then face to face. Now I know in part; then I shall understand fully, even as I have been fully understood.

This is the word of the Lord.

Gospel Acclamation   John 8:12

Alleluia, alleluia! [*Lent*: Praise to you, Lord Jesus Christ]
I am the light of the world;
he who follows me will not walk in darkness,
but will have the light of life,
says the Lord.
Alleluia! [*Lent*: Praise to you, Lord Jesus Christ]

GOSPEL

A reading from the holy Gospel according to Mark   10:46-51

And they came to Jericho; and as he was leaving Jericho with his disciples and a great multitude, Bartimaeus, a blind beggar, was sitting by the roadside. And when he heard that it was Jesus of Nazareth, he began to cry out and say, 'Jesus, Son of David, have mercy on me!' And many rebuked him, telling himm to be silent; but he cried out all the more, 'Son of David, have mercy on me!'

And Jesus stopped and said, 'Call him.' And they called the blind man, saying to him, 'Take heart; rise, he is calling you.' And throwing off his mantle he sprang up and came to Jesus. And Jesus said to him, 'What do you want me to do for you?' And the blind man said to him, 'Master, let me receive my sight.' And Jesus said to him, 'Go your way; your faith has made you well.' And immediately he received his sight and followed him on the way.

This is the Gospel of the Lord.

13. THE HUNGER FOR ETERNAL LIFE

FIRST READING

A reading from the first book of Kings   19:4-8

Elijah went a day's journey into the wilderness, and came and sat down under a broom tree; and he asked that he might die, saying, 'It is enough; now, O Lord, take away my life; for I am no better than my fathers.'

And he lay down and slept under a broom tree; and behold, an angel touched him, and said to him, 'Arise and eat.' And he looked, and behold, there was at his head a cake baked on hot stones and a jar of water. And he ate and drank, and lay down again.

And the angel of the Lord came again a second time, and touched him, and said, 'Arise and eat, else the journey will be too great for you.' And he arose, and ate and drank, and went in the strength of that food forty days and forty nights to Horeb the mount of God.

This is the word of the Lord.

Responsorial Psalm   Ps 41(42):2.3.9.12

Response:
My soul is thirsting for God,
the God of my life.

Like a deer that yearns
for running streams,
so my soul is yearning
for you, my God. **R**.

My soul is thristing for God,
the God of my life;
when can I enter and see
the face of God? **R**.

By day the Lord will send
his loving kindness;
by night I will sing to him,
praise the God of my life. **R**.

Why are you cast down, my soul,
why groan within me?
Hope in God; I will praise him still,
my saviour and my God. **R**.

SECOND READING

A reading from the first letter of St Paul to the Corinthians   2:1-6.9

When I came to you, brethren, I did not come proclaiming to you the testimony of God in lofty words or wisdom. For I decided to know nothing among you except Jesus Christ and him crucified. And I was with you in weakness and in much fear and trembling; and my speech and my message were not in plausible words of wisdom, but in demonstration of the Spirit and power, that your faith might not rest in the wisdom of men but in the power of God.

Yet among the mature we do impart wisdom, although it is not a wisdom of this age or of the rulers of this age, who are doomed to pass away. It is written, 'What no eye has seen, nor ear heard, nor the heart of man conceived, what God has prepared for those who love him,' God has revealed to us through the Spirit.

This is the word of the Lord.

Gospel Acclamation   John 6:35

Alleluia, Alleluia! [*Lent*: Praise to you, Lord Jesus Christ]
I am the bread of life, says the Lord.
He who comes to me shall not hunger.
Alleluia! [*Lent*: Praise to you, Lord Jesus Christ]

GOSPEL

A reading from the holy Gospel according to John   6:44-51
Jesus said:

'No one can come to me unless the Father who sent me draw him; and I will raise him up at the last day. It is written in the prophets, "And they shall all be taught by God." Every one who has heard and learned from the Father comes to me. Not that any one has seen the Father except him who is from God; he has seen the Father.

'Truly, truly, I say to you, he who believes has eternal life. I am the bread of life. Your fathers ate the manna in the wilderness, and they died. This is the bread which comes down from heaven, that a man may eat of it and not die. I am the living bread which came down from heaven; if any one eats of this bread, he will live for ever.'

This is the Gospel of the Lord.

14. THE RESURRECTION AND THE LIFE

FIRST READING

A reading from the book of Lamentations   3:17-26

My soul is bereft of peace, I have forgotten what happiness is; so I say, 'Gone is my glory, and my expectation from the Lord.' Remember my affliction and my bitterness, the wormwood and the gall! My soul continually thinks of it and is bowed down within me.

But this I call to mind, and therefore I have hope: The steadfast love of the Lord never ceases, his mercies never come to an end; they are new every morning; great is thy faithfulness. The Lord is my portion', says my soul, 'therefore I will hope in him.'

The Lord is good to those who wait for him, to the soul that seeks him.
It is good that one should wait quietly for the salvation of the Lord.
    This is the word of the Lord.

Responsorial Psalm   Ps 138(139):7-12.23-24
Response:
O Lord, you search me and you know me.

O where can I go from your spirit,
or where can I flee from your face?
If I climb the heavens, you are there.
If I lie in the grave, you are there.   **R**.

If I take the wings of the dawn
and dwell at the sea's furthest end,
even there your hand would lead me,
your right hand would hold me fast.   **R**.

If I say: 'Let the darkness hide me
and the light around me be night,'
even darkness is not dark for you
and the night is as clear as the day.   **R**.

O search me, God, and know my heart.
O test me and know my thoughts.
See that I follow not the wrong path
and lead me in the path of life eternal.

SECOND READING

A reading from the first letter of St Paul to the Corinthians 15:51-57
Lo! I tell you a mystery. We shall not all sleep, but we shall all be
changed, in a moment, in the twinkling of an eye, at the last
trumpet. For the trumpet will sound, and the dead will be raised
imperishable, and we shall be changed.
    For this perishable nature must put on the imperishable, and this
mortal nature must put on immortality. When the perishable puts on
the imperishable, and the mortal puts on immortality, then shall
come to pass the saying that is written: 'Death is swallowed up in
victory. O death, where is thy victory? O death, where is they sting?'
    The sting of death is sin, and the power of sin is the law. But thanks
be to God, who gives us the victory through our Lord Jesus Christ.
    This is the word of the Lord.

Gospel Acclamation   John 11:25
    Alleluia, alleluia! [*Lent*: Praise to you, Lord Jesus Christ]

I am the resurrection and the life, says the Lord.
He who believes in me, though he die, yet shall he live.
Alleluia! [*Lent*: Praise to you, Lord Jesus Christ]

GOSPEL

A reading from the holy Gospel according to John   11:17-27

Now when Jesus came, he found that Lazarus had already been in the tomb four days. Bethany was near Jerusalem, about two miles off, and many of the Jews had come to Martha and Mary to console them concerning their brother. When Martha heard that Jesus was coming, she went and met him, while Mary sat in the house.

Martha said to Jesus, 'Lord, if you had been here, my brother would not have died. And even now I know that whatever you ask from God, God will give you.' Jesus said to her, 'Your brother will rise again.' Martha said to him, 'I know that he will rise again in the resurrection at the last day.' Jesus said to her, 'I am the resurrection and the life; he who believes in me, though he die, yet shall he live, and whoever lives and believes in me shall never die. Do you believe this?' She said to him, 'Yes, Lord; I believe that you are the Christ, the Son of God, he who is coming into the world.'

This is the Gospel of the Lord.

---

15. THE PEARL OF GREAT PRICE

FIRST READING

A reading from the book of Wisdom   7:7-11

Therefore I prayed, and understanding was given me; I called upon God, and the spirit of wisdom came to me. I preferred her to sceptres and thrones, and I accounted wealth as nothing in comparison with her. Neither did I liken to her any priceless gem, because all gold is but a little sand in her sight, and silver will be accounted as clay before her.

I loved her more than health and beauty, and I chose to have her rather than light, because her radiance never ceases. All good things came to me along with her, and in her hands uncounted wealth.

This is the word of the Lord.

Responsorial Psalm   Ps 18(19):8-11

Response:
The law of the Lord is perfect.

The law of the Lord is perfect,
it revives the soul.
The rule of the Lord is to be trusted,
it gives wisdom to the simple. **R.**

The precepts of the Lord are right,
they gladden the heart.
The command of the Lord is clear,
it gives light to the eyes. **R.**

The fear of the Lord is holy,
abiding for ever.
The decrees of the Lord are truth
and all of them just. **R.**

They are more to be desired than gold,
than the purest of gold,
and sweeter are they than honey,
than honey from the comb. **R.**

SECOND READING

A reading from the first letter of St Paul to the Corinthians 2:1-6.9

When I came to you, brethren, I did not come proclaiming to you
the testimony of God in lofty words or wisdom. For I decided to
know nothing among you except Jesus Christ and him crucified.
And I was with you in weakness and in much fear and trembling;
and my speech and my message were not in plausible words of
wisdom, but in demonstration of the Spirit and power, that your
faith might not rest in the wisdom of men but in the power of God.

Yet among the mature we do impart wisdom, although it is not a
wisdom of this age or of the rulers of this age, who are doomed to
pass away. It is written, 'What no eye has seen, nor ear heard, nor
the heart of man conceived, what God has prepared for those who
love him,' God has revealed to us through the Spirit.

This is the word of the Lord.

Gospel Acclamation   Matthew 6:33

Alleluia, alleluia! [*Lent*: Praise to you, Lord Jesus Christ]
Seek first the kingdom of God and his righteousness,
and all these things shall be yours as well,

says the Lord.
Alleluia! [*Lent*: Praise to you, Lord Jesus Christ]

GOSPEL

A reading from the holy Gospel according to Matthew   13:44-46

Jesus spoke these parables to the people:

'The kingdom of heaven is like treasure hidden in a field, which a man found and covered up; then in his joy he goes and sells all that he has and buys that field.

'Again, the kingdom of heaven is like a merchant in search of fine pearls, who, on finding one pearl of great value, went and sold all that he had and bought it.'

This is the Gospel of the Lord.

---

16. BEARING ONE'S OWN PARTICULAR FRUIT

FIRST READING

A reading from the book of Sirach   2:1-9

If you come forward to serve the Lord, prepare yourself for temptation. Set your heart right and be steadfast, and do not be hasty in time of calamity. Cleave to him and do not depart, that you may be honoured at the end of your life.

Accept whatever is brought upon you, and in changes that humble you be patient. For gold is tested in the fire, and acceptable men in the furnace of humiliation. Trust in him, and he will help you; make your ways straight, and hope in him.

You who fear the Lord, wait for his mercy; and turn not aside, lest you fall. You who fear the Lord, trust in him, and your reward will not fail; you who fear the Lord, hope for good things, for everlasting joy and mercy.

This is the word of the Lord.

Responsorial Psalm   Ps 8(9):3-9

Response:
How great is your name, O Lord our God,
through all the earth.

Your majesty is praised above the heavens;
on the lips of children and of babes
you have found praise to foil your enemy,
to silence the foe and the rebel.   **R.**

When I see the heavens, the work of your hands,
the moon and the stars which you arranged,
what is man that you should keep him in mind,
mortal man that you care for him?   **R**.

Yet you have made him little less than a god;
with glory and honour you crowned him,
gave him power over the works of your hand,
put all things under his feet.   **R**.

All of them, sheep and cattle,
yes, even the savage beasts,
birds of the air, and fish
that make their way through the waters.   **R**.

SECOND READING

A reading from the first letter of St Paul to the Corinthians 12:31-13:1-7
Earnestly desire the higher gifts. And I will show you a still more
excellent way.

If I speak in the tongues of men and of angels, but have no love, I
am a noisy gong or a clanging cymbal. And If I have prophetic
powers, and understand all mysteries and all knowledge, and if I
have all faith, so as to remove mountains, but have not love, I am
nothing. If I give away all I have, and if I deliver my body to be
burned, but have not love, I gain nothing.

Love is patient and kind; love is not jealous or boastful; it is not
arrogant or rude. Love does not insist on its own way; it is not
irritable or resentful; it does not rejoice at wrong, but rejoices in the
right. Love bears all things, believes all things, hopes all things,
endures all things. Love never ends.

This is the word of the Lord.

Gospel Acclamation   Matthew 25:23
Alleluia, alleluia! [*Lent*: Praise to you, Lord Jesus Christ]
Well done, good and faithful servant;
enter into the joy of your master.
Alleluia! [*Lent*: Praise to you, Lord Jesus Christ]

GOSPEL

A reading from the holy Gospel according to Matthew 25:14-15.19-23
Jesus spoke the following parable to his disciples:
'The kingdom of heaven will be as when a man going on a journey
called his servants and entrusted to them his property; to one he

gave five talents, to another two, to another one, to each according
to his ability. Then he went away.

'Now after a long time the master of those servants came and
settled accounts with them. And he who had received the five
talents came forward, bringing five talents more, saying, "Master,
you delivered to me five talents; here I have made five talents
more." His master said to him, "Well done, good and faithful
servant; you have been faithful over a little, I will set you over
much; enter into the joy of your master."

'And he also who had the two talents came forward, saying,
"Master, you delivered to me two talents; here I have made two
talents more." His master said to him, "Well done, good and
faithful servant; you have been faithful over a little, I will set you
over much; enter into the joy of your master." '

This is the Gospel of the Lord.

---

17. THE FALL OF A SPARROW
Death of an infant

FIRST READING

A reading from the prophet Isaiah   49:8.14-16

Thus says the Lord: 'In a time of favour I have answered you, in a
day of salvation I have helped you.' But Zion said, 'The Lord has
forsaken me.'

'Can a woman forget her sucking child, that she should have no
compassion on the son of her womb? Even these may forget, yet I will
not forget you. Behold, I have graven you on the palms of my hands.'

This is the word of the Lord.

Responsorial Psalm   Ps 83(84):4-8.12

Response:
My soul is longing for the courts of the Lord.

The sparrow finds herself a home
and the swallow a nest for her brood;
she lays her young by your altars,
Lord of hosts, my king and my God.   **R.**

They are happy, who dwell in your house,
for ever singing your praise.
They are happy, whose strength is in you,
in whose hearts are the roads to Sion.   **R.**

As they go through the Bitter Valley
they make it a place of springs.
They walk with ever growing strength,
they will see the God of gods in Sion.   **R**.

For the Lord God is a rampart, a shield;
he will give us his favour and glory.
The Lord will not refuse any good
to those who walk without blame.   **R**.

SECOND READING

A reading from the first letter of St John   3:1-2

See what love the Father has given us, that we should be called
children of God, and so we are. The reason why the world does not
know us is that it did not know him. Beloved, we are God's children
now; it does not yet appear what we shall be, but we know that when
he appears we shall be like him, for we shall see him as he is.
     This is the word of the Lord.

Gospel Acclamation   Luke 18:16

     Alleluia, alleluia! [*Lent*: Praise to you, Lord Jesus Christ]
     Let the children come to me, and do not hinder them;
     for to such belongs the kingdom of God,
     says the Lord.
     Alleluia! [*Lent*: Praise to you, Lord Jesus Christ]

GOSPEL

A reading from the holy Gospel according to Matthew   10:28-31

Jesus said to his disciples:
     'Do not fear those who kill the body but cannot kill the soul;
rather fear him who can destroy both soul and body in hell.
     'Are not two sparrows sold for a penny? And not one of them will
fall to the ground without your Father's will. But even the hairs of
your head are all numbered.
     'Fear not, therefore; you are of more value than many sparrows.'
     This is the Gospel of the Lord.

18. LET THE LITTLE ONES COME TO ME   1
Death of a child or youth through illness

A reading from the book of Wisdom   4:7-15

But the righteous man, though he die early, will be at rest. For old age is not honoured for length of time, nor measured by number of years; but understanding is grey hair for men, and a blameless life is ripe old age.

There was one who pleased God and was loved by him, and while living among sinners he was taken up. He was caught up lest evil change his understanding or guile deceive his soul. For the fascination of wickedness obscures what is good, and roving desire perverts the innocent mind.

Being perfected in a short time, he fulfilled long years; for his soul was pleasing to the Lord, therefore he took him quickly from the midst of wickedness. Yet the peoples saw and they did not understand, nor take such a thing to heart, that God's grace and mercy are with his elect, and he watches over his holy ones.

This is the word of the Lord.

Responsorial Psalm   Ps 130

Response:
Hope in the Lord both now and for ever.

O Lord, my heart is not proud
nor haughty my eyes.
I have not gone after things too great
nor marvels beyond me.   **R.**

Truly I have set my soul
in silence and peace.
A weaned child on its mother's breast,
even so is my soul.   **R.**

O Israel, hope in the Lord
both now and for ever.   **R.**

A reading from the letter of St Paul to the Romans   8:14-18

All who are led by the Spirit of God are sons of God. For you did not receive the spirit of slavery to fall back into fear, but you have received the spirit of sonship. When we cry, 'Abba! Father!' it is the

Spirit himself bearing witness with our spirit that we are children of God, and if we are children, then heirs, heirs of God and fellow heirs with Christ, provided we suffer with him in order that we may also be glorified with him.

I consider that the sufferings of this present time are not worth comparing with the glory that is to be revealed to us.

This is the word of the Lord.

Gospel Acclamation   Luke 18:16

Alleluia, alleluia! [*Lent*: Praise to you, Lord Jesus Christ]
Let the children come to me, and do not hinder them;
for to such belongs the kingdom of God,
says the Lord.
Alleluia! [*Lent*: Praise to you, Lord Jesus Christ]

GOSPEL

A reading from the holy Gospel according to Matthew   11:25-30

At that time Jesus declared, 'I thank thee, Father, Lord of heaven and earth, that thou hast hidden these things from the wise and understanding and revealed them to babes; yea, Father, for such was thy gracious will.

'All things have been delivered to me by my Father; and no one knows the Son except the Father, and no one knows the Father except the Son and any one to whom the Son chooses to reveal him.

'Come to me, all who labour and are heavy laden, and I will give you rest. Take my yoke upon you, and learn from me; for I am gentle and lowly in heart, and you will find rest for your souls. For my yoke is easy, and my burden is light.'

This is the Gospel of the Lord.

ALTERNATIVE GOSPEL (Matthew 18:1-4;19:13-15)   p. 132

---

19. LET THE LITTLE ONES COME TO ME   2
Death of a child or youth through tragedy

FIRST READING

A reading from the prophet Isaiah   49:8.14-16

Thus says the Lord: 'In a time of favour I have answered you, in a day of salvation I have helped you.' But Zion said, 'The Lord has forsaken me.'

'Can a woman forget her sucking child, that she should have no compassion on the son of her womb? Even these may forget, yet I will not forget you. Behold, I have graven you on the palms of my hands.'
This is the word of the Lord.

Responsorial Psalm   Ps 22(23)

Response:
The Lord is my shepherd;
there is nothing I shall want.

The Lord is my shepherd;
there is nothing I shall want.
Fresh and green are the pastures
where he gives me repose.
Near restful waters he leads me,
to revive my drooping spirit.   **R.**

He guides me along the right path;
he is true to his name.
If I should walk in the valley of darkness
no evil would I fear.
You are there with your crook and your staff;
with these you give me confort.   **R.**

You have prepared a banquet for me
in the sight of my foes.
My head you have anointed with oil;
my cup is overflowing.   **R.**

Surely goodness and kindness shall follow me
all the days of my life.
In the Lord's own house shall I dwell
for ever and ever.   **R.**

SECOND READING

A reading from the letter of St Paul to the Romans   8:14-18

All who are led by the Spirit of God are sons of God. For you did not receive the spirit of slavery to fall back into fear, but you have received the spirit of sonship. When we cry, 'Abba! Father!' it is the Spirit himself bearing witness with our spirit that we are children of God, and if we are children, then heirs, heirs of God and fellow heirs with Christ, provided we suffer with him in order that we may also be glorified with him.

I consider that the sufferings of this present time are not worth comparing with the glory that is to be revealed to us.
This is the word of the Lord.

Gospel Acclamation   Matthew 18:3
Alleluia, alleluia! [*Lent*: Praise to you, Lord Jesus Christ]
Unless you become like little children,
you will never enter the kingdom of heaven,
says the Lord.
Alleluia! [*Lent*: Praise to you, Lord Jesus Christ]

GOSPEL

A reading from the holy Gospel according to Matthew   18:1-4;19:13-15
At that time the disciples came to Jesus, saying, 'Who is the greatest
in the kingdom of heaven?' And calling to him a child, he put him in
the midst of them, and said, 'Truly, I say to you, unless you turn and
become like children, you will never enter the kingdom of heaven.
Whoever humbles himself like this child, he is the greatest in the
kingdom of heaven.'
Then children were brought to him that he might lay his hands on
them and pray. The disciples rebuked the people; but Jesus said,
'Let the children come to me, and do not hinder them; for to such
belongs the kingdom of heaven.'
And he laid his hands on them and went away.
This is the Gospel of the Lord.

ALTERNATIVE GOSPEL (Matthew 11:25-30) ———————— p. 130

20. A TIME OF RIPENING
Death of an elderly person   1

FIRST READING

A reading from the book of Ecclesiastes   3:1-8.11
For everything there is a season, and a time for every matter under
heaven:
a time to be born, and a time to die;
a time to plant, and a time to pluck up what is planted;
a time to kill, and a time to heal;
a time to break down, and a time to build up;
a time to weep, and a time to laugh;
a time to mourn, and a time to dance;
a time to cast away stones, and a time to gather stones together;
a time to embrace, and a time to refrain from embracing;
a time to seek, and a time to lose;

a time to keep, and a time to cast away;
a time to rend, and a time to sew;
a time to keep silence, and a time to speak;
a time to love, and a time to hate;
a time for war, and a time for peace.
God has made everything beautiful in its time.
This is the word of the Lord.

Responsorial Psalm   Ps 91(92):2-6.13-16

Response:
It is good to give thanks to the Lord.

It is good to give thanks to the Lord
to make music to your name, O Most High,
to proclaim your love in the morning
and your truth in the watches of the night.   **R.**

Your deeds, O Lord, have made me glad;
for the work of your hands I shout with joy.
O Lord, how great are your works,
how deep are your designs.   **R.**

The just will flourish like the palm-tree
and grow like a Lebanon cedar.
Planted in the house of the Lord
they will flourish in the courts of our God.   **R.**

Still bearing fruit when they are old,
still full of sap, still green,
to proclaim that the Lord is just;
in him, my rock, there is no wrong.   **R.**

SECOND READING

A reading from the second letter of St Paul to the Corinthians 4:14-5:1

He who raised the Lord Jesus will raise us also with Jesus and bring us with you into his presence. For it is all for your sake, so that as grace extends to more and more people it may increase thanksgiving, to the glory of God.

So we do not lose heart. Though our outer nature is wasting away, our inner nature is being renewed every day. For this slight momentary affliction is preparing for us an eternal weight of glory beyond all comparison, because we look not to the things that are seen, but to the things that are unseen; for the things that are seen are transient, but the things that are unseen are eternal.

For we know that if the earthly tent we live in is destroyed, we have a building from God, a house not made with hands, eternal in the heavens.

This is the word of the Lord.

Gospel Acclamation   Matthew 6:33

Alleluia, alleluia! [*Lent*: Praise to you, Lord Jesus Christ]
Seek first the kingdom of God and his righteousness,
and all these things shall be yours as well.
Alleluia! [*Lent*: Praise to you, Lord Jesus Christ]

GOSPEL

A reading from the holy Gospel according to Luke   12:22-31

Jesus said to his disciples:

'Therefore I tell you, do not be anxious about your life, what you shall eat, nor about your body, what you shall put on. For life is more than food, and the body more than clothing.

'Consider the ravens: they neither sow nor reap, they have neither storehouse nor barn, and yet God feeds them. Of how much more value are you than the birds!

'And which of you by being anxious can add a cubit to his life span? If then you are not able to do as small a thing as that, why are you anxious about the rest?

'Consider the lilies, how they grow; they neither toil nor spin; yet I tell you, even Solomon in all his glory was not arrayed like one of these. But if God so clothes the grass which is alive in the field today and tomorrow is thrown into the oven, how much more will he clothe you, O men of little faith!

'And do not seek what you are to eat and what you are to drink, nor be of anxious mind. For all the nations of the world seek these things; and your Father knows that you need them. Instead, seek his kingdom, and these things shall be yours as well.'

This is the Gospel of the Lord.

21. MISSION ACCOMPLISHED
Death of an elderly person   2

FIRST READING

A reading from the book of Lamentations   3:17-26

My soul is bereft of peace, I have forgotten what happiness is; so I say, 'Gone is my glory and my expectation from the Lord.' Remember my affliction and my bitterness, the wormwood and the gall! My soul continually thinks of it and is bowed down within me.

But this I call to mind, and therefore I have hope: The steadfast love of the Lord never ceases, his mercies never come to an end; they are new every morning; great is thy faithfulness. 'The Lord is my portion,' says my soul, 'therefore I will hope in him.'

The Lord is good to those who wait for him, to the soul that seeks him. It is good that one should wait quietly for the salvation of the Lord.

This is the word of the Lord.

Responsorial Psalm   Ps 91(92):2-6,13-16

Response:
It is good to give thanks to the Lord.

It is good to give thanks to the Lord
to make music to your name, O Most High,
to proclaim your love in the morning
and your truth in the watches of the night. **R.**

Your deeds, O Lord, have made me glad;
for the work of your hands I shout with joy.
O Lord, how great are your works,
how deep are your designs. **R.**

The just will flourish like the palm-tree
and grow like a Lebanon cedar.
Planted in the house of the Lord
they will flourish in the courts of our God. **R.**

Still bearing fruit when they are old,
still full of sap, still green,
to proclaim that the Lord is just;
in him, my rock, there is no wrong. **R.**

SECOND READING

A reading from the second letter of St Paul to Timothy   4:6-8

I am already on the point of being sacrificed; the time of my departure has come. I have fought the good fight. I have finished the race. I have kept the faith. Henceforth there is laid up for me the crown of righteousness, which the Lord, the righteous judge, will award to me on that Day, and not only to me but also to all who have loved his appearing.

This is the word of the Lord.

Gospel Acclamation   John 10:10
Alleluia, alleluia! [*Lent*: Praise to you, Lord Jesus Christ]
I came that you may have life,
and have it abundantly,
says the Lord.
Alleluia! [*Lent*: Praise to you, Lord Jesus Christ]

GOSPEL

A reading from the holy Gospel according to John   17:1-5
When Jesus had spoken these words, he lifted up his eyes to heaven
and said, 'Father, the hour has come; glorify thy Son that the Son
may glorify thee, since thou hast given him power over all flesh, to
give eternal life to all whom thou hast given him. And this is eternal
life, that they know thee the only true God, and Jesus Christ whom
thou hast sent.

'I glorified thee on earth, having accomplished the work which thou
gavest me to do; and now, Father, glorify thou me in thy own presence
with the glory which I had with thee before the world was made.'

This is the Gospel of the Lord.

---

22. SHARING HIS SUFFERINGS

For one who bore a lot of suffering and/or illness

FIRST READING

A reading from the book of Wisdom   3:1-6.9
The souls of the righteous are in the hands of God, and no torment
will ever touch them. In the eyes of the foolish they seemed to have
died, and their departure was thought to be an affliction, and their
going from us to be their destruction; but they are at peace.

For though in the sight of men they were punished, their hope is
full of immortality. Having been disciplined a little, they will receive
great good, because God tested them and found them worthy of
himself; like gold in the furnace he tried them, and like a sacrificial
burnt offering he accepted them.

Those who trust in him will understand truth, and the faithful will
abide with him in love, because grace and mercy are upon his elect,
and he watches over his holy ones.

This is the word of the Lord.

Responsorial Psalm   Ps 114(115):1-8
  Response:
  I will walk in the presence of the Lord
  in the land of the living.

  I love the Lord for he has heard
  the cry of my appeal;
  for he turned his ear to me
  in the day when I called him.   **R**.

  They surrounded me, the snares of death,
  with the anguish of the tomb;
  they caught me, sorrow and distress.
  I called on the Lord's name.   **R**.

  How gracious is the Lord, and just;
  our God has compassion.
  The Lord protects the simple hearts;
  I was helpless so he saved me.   **R**.

  Turn back, my soul, to your rest
  for the Lord has been good;
  he has kept my soul from death,
  and my feet from stumbling.   **R**.

SECOND READING

A reading from the letter of St Paul to the Romans   8:14-18

All who are led by the Spirit of God are sons of God. For you did not
receive the spirit of slavery to fall back into fear, but you have
received the spirit of sonship. When we cry, 'Abba! Father!' it is the
Spirit himself bearing witness with our spirit that we are children of
God, and if we are children, then heirs, heirs of God and fellow
heirs with Christ, provided we suffer with him in order that we may
also be glorified with him.

  I consider that the sufferings of this present time are not worth
comparing with the glory that is to be revealed to us.
  This is the word of the Lord.

Gospel Acclamation   Matthew 7:13
  Alleluia, alleluia! [*Lent*: Praise to you, Lord Jesus Christ]
  Enter by the narrow gate,
  for the gate is narrow and the way is hard
  that leads to life,
  says the Lord.
  Alleluia! [*Lent*: Praise to you, Lord Jesus Christ]

GOSPEL

A reading from the holy Gospel according to John   12:23-27

Jesus said:

'The hour has come for the Son of man to be glorified.

'Truly, truly, I say to you, unless a grain of wheat falls into the earth and dies, it remains alone; but if it dies, it bears much fruit.

'He who loves his life loses it, and he who hates his life in this world will keep it for eternal life. If any one serves me, he must follow me; and where I am, there shall my servant be also; if any one serves me, the Father will honour him.

'Now my soul is troubled, and what shall I say? "Father, save me from this hour?" No, for this purpose I have come to this hour.'

This is the Gospel of the Lord.

---

23. WHEN THE LIGHTS GO OUT
Tragic death   1

FIRST READING

A reading from the prophet Isaiah   25:6-9

On this mountain the Lord of hosts will make for all peoples a feast of fat things. And he will destroy on this mountain the covering that is cast over all peoples, the veil that is spread over all nations.

He will swallow up death for ever, and the Lord God will wipe away tears from all faces, and the reproach of his people he will take away from all the earth; for the Lord has spoken.

It will be said on that day, 'Lo, this is our God; we have waited for him, that he might save us. This is our Lord; we have waited for him; let us be glad and rejoice in his salvation.'

This is the word of the Lord.

Responsorial Psalm   Ps 26(27):1.4.10.13.14

Response:
The Lord is my light and my help.

The Lord is my light and my help;
whom shall I fear?
The Lord is the stronghold of my life;
before whom shall I shrink?   **R**.

There is one thing I ask of the Lord,
for this I long,

to live in the house of the Lord
all the days of my life.   **R.**

Do not abandon or forsake me,
O God my help.
Though father and mother forsake me,
the Lord will receive me.   **R.**

I am sure I shall see the Lord's goodness
in the land of the living.
Hope in him, hold firm and take heart.
Hope in the Lord.   **R.**

SECOND READING

A reading from the letter of St Paul to the Romans   8:31-35.37-39

If God is for us, who is against us? He who did not spare his own Son
but gave him up for us all, will he not also give us all things with him?
Who shall bring any charge against God's elect? It is God who
justifies; who is to condemn? Is it Jesus Christ, who died, yes, who
was raised from the dead, who is at the right hand of God, who
indeed intercedes for us?

Who shall separate us from the love of Christ? Shall tribulation, or
distress, or persecution, or famine, or nakedness, or peril, or sword?
No, in all these things we are more than conquerors through him who
loved us. For I am sure that neither death, nor life, nor angels, nor
principalities, nor things present, nor things to come, nor powers, nor
height, nor depth, nor anything else in all creation, will be able to
separate us from the love of God in Christ Jesus our Lord.

This is the word of the Lord.

Gospel Acclamation   John 3:16

Alleluia, alleluia! [*Lent*: Praise to you, Lord Jesus Christ]
God so loved the world that he gave his only Son,
that whoever believes in him
should not perish but have eternal life.
Alleluia! [*Lent*: Praise to you, Lord Jesus Christ]

GOSPEL

A reading from the holy Gospel according to Luke   23:35-37.44-48

And the people stood by, watching; but the rulers scoffed at him,
saying, 'He saved others; let him save himself, if he is the Christ of
God, his Chosen One!'

The soldiers also mocked him, coming up and offering him vine-
gar, and saying, 'If you are the King of the Jews, save yourself!'

It was now about the sixth hour, and there was darkness over the whole land until the ninth hour, while the sun's light failed; and the curtain of the temple was torn in two. Then Jesus, crying with a loud voice, said, 'Father, into thy hands I commit my spirit!' And having said this he breathed his last.

Now when the centurion saw what had taken place, he praised God, and said, 'Certainly this man was innocent!' And all the multitudes who assembled to see the sight, when they saw what had taken place, returned home beating their breasts.

This is the Gospel of the Lord.

ALTERNATIVE GOSPEL

A reading from the holy Gospel according to Mark   4:35-41

On that day when evening had come, Jesus said to his apostles, 'Let us go across to the other side.' And leaving the crowd, they took him with them just as he was, in the boat. And other boats were with them.

And a great storm of wind arose, and the waves beat into the boat, so that the boat was already filling. But he was in the stern, asleep on the cushion; and they woke him and said to him, 'Teacher, do you not care if we perish?'

And he awoke and rebuked the wind, and said to the sea, 'Peace! Be still!' And the wind ceased, and there was a great calm. He said to them, 'Why are you afraid? Have you no faith?'

And they were filled with awe, and said to one another, 'Who then is this, that even wind and sea obey him?'

This is the Gospel of the Lord.

Comment on Alternative Gospel   Mk 4:35-41

A homily, even a whole liturgy, could be based on this Gospel.

The apostles were rowing across a placid lake in the cool of the evening. But as night came on, a freak storm arose and suddenly they are in mortal danger. In spite of the fact that they are experienced seamen, the ferocity of it paralyses them with fear. And where is Jesus? Sound asleep! They think he no longer cares about what happens to them. But he does. As soon as he awakes, he speaks to the wind, and there comes a great calm. Then he rebukes them for their lack of faith.

The freak storm could be used as a symbol of sudden and tragic death. It shatters the peace of our lives and leaves us paralysed with shock. We feel utterly helpless. We also feel that God no longer cares about us. If he did, he would not have allowed this 'storm' to assail us.

But God has not abandoned us. It is to him we must have recourse. We must awaken our faith in him. He will calm our fears, and give us courage and hope. He surrounds us with the love and support of the community. And we can be sure that he will snatch our loved one from the angry waters of death, and bring him (her) to the calm and peace of the eternal shore.

24. OUT OF THE DEPTHS WE CRY
Tragic death   2

FIRST READING

A reading from the prophet Isaiah   25:6-9

On this mountain the Lord of hosts will make for all peoples a feast of fat things. And he will destroy on this mountain the covering that is cast over all peoples, the veil that is spread over all nations.

He will swallow up death for ever, and the Lord God will wipe away tears from all faces, and the reproach of his people he will take away from all the earth; for the Lord has spoken.

It will be said on that day, 'Lo, this is our God; we have waited for him, that he might save us. This is our Lord; we have waited for him; let us be glad and rejoice in his salvation.'

This is the word of the Lord.

Responsorial Psalm   Ps 129(130)

Response:
Out of the depths I cry to you, O Lord.
Lord, hear my voice.

Out of the depths I cry to you, O Lord,
Lord, hear my voice.
O let your ears be attentive
to the voice of my pleading.   **R**.

If you, O Lord, should mark our guilt,
Lord, who would survive?
But with you is found forgiveness:
for this we revere you.   **R**.

My soul is waiting for the Lord,
I count on his word.
My soul is longing for the Lord
more than watchman for daybreak.   **R**.

Because with the Lord there is mercy
and fulness of redemption,
Israel indeed he will redeem
from all its iniquity.   **R**.

SECOND READING

A reading from the letter of St Paul to the Romans   8:31-35.37-39

If God is for us, who is against us? He who did not spare his own Son but gave him up for us all, will he not also give us all things with him? Who shall bring any charge against God's elect? It is God who justifies; who is to condemn? Is it Jesus Christ, who died, yes, who was raised from the dead, who is at the right hand of God, who indeed intercedes for us?

Who shall separate us from the love of Christ? Shall tribulation, or distress, or persecution, or famine, or nakedness, or peril, or sword? No, in all these things we are more than conquerors through him who loved us. For I am sure that neither death, nor life, nor angels, nor principalities, nor things present, nor things to come, nor powers, nor height, nor depth, nor anything else in all creation, will be able to separate us from the love of God in Christ Jesus our Lord.

This is the word of the Lord.

Gospel Acclamation   John 14:16
Alleluia, alleluia! [*Lent*: Praise to you, Lord Jesus Christ]
I am the way,m and the truth, and the life;
no one comes to the Father, but by me,
says the Lord.
Alleluia! [*Lent*: Praise to you, Lord Jesus Christ]

GOSPEL

A Reading from the holy Gospel according to Luke 24:13-17.19-31

That very day [Easter Day] two of Jesus' disciples were going to a village named Emmaus, about seven miles from Jerusalem, and talking about these things that had happened. While they were talking, Jesus himself drew near. But their eyes were kept from recognising him. And he said to them, 'What is this conversation which you are holding as you walk?' And they stood still, looking sad.

Then they said to him, 'Concerning Jesus of Nazareth, who was a prophet mighty in deed and word before God and all the people, and how our chief priests and rulers delivered him up and crucified him. But we had hoped that he was the one to redeem Israel. It is now the third day since this happened. Moreover, some women of our company amazed us. They were at the tomb early in the morning and did not find his body; and they came back saying that they had even seen a vision of angels, who said he was alive.'

And he said to them, 'O foolish men, and slow of heart to believe all the prophets have spoken! Was it not necessary that the Christ should suffer these things and enter into his glory?' And beginning with Moses and all the prophets, he interpreted to them in all the scriptures the things concerning himself.

So they drew near to the village to which they were going. He appeared to be going further, but they said, 'Stay with us, for the day is far spent.' So he went in to stay with them. When he was at table with them, he took the bread and blessed, and broke it, and gave it to them. And their eyes were opened and they recognised him; and he vanished out of their sight.

This is the Gospel of the Lord.

ALTERNATIVE GOSPEL (John 11:17-27)   p. 123

Comment on Alternative Gospel   John 11:17-27

This could also be used as the basis of a homily. Martha and Mary are plunged into gloom because of the death of their brother Lazarus. They blame Jesus for his death, or at least suggest that he could have prevented it, and should have. At the height of their grief, Jesus comes to them, shares their sorrow, and gives them hope by announcing eternal life present in himself.

Neither a good life nor a close friendship with Jesus will save a person from death, even tragic death. Fortunately we are not left alone. Like Martha and Mary we are surrounded by the love and support of the community. But what can we do? Nothing, except what Martha did – run to the Lord, pour out our story to him, and he will give us hope.

The minister can do no more than be with the bereaved, share their sorrow, and announce eternal life through faith in Jesus.

25. A WITNESS TO CHRIST

FIRST READING

A reading from the book of Job   19:23-27

Oh that my words were written! Oh that they were inscribed in a book! Oh that with an iron pen and lead they were graven in the rock for ever!

For I know that my Redeemer lives, and at last he will stand upon the earth; and after my skin has been thus destroyed, then from my flesh I shall see God, whom I shall see on my side.

This is the word of the Lord.

Responsorial Psalm   Ps 15(16):5-11

Response:
Preserve me, God, I take refuge in you.

O Lord, it is you who are my portion and cup;
it is you yourself who are my prize.
The lot marked out for me is my delight:
welcome indeed the heritage that falls to me.   **R**,

I will bless the Lord who gives me counsel,
who even at night directs my heart.
I keep the Lord ever in my sight:
since he is at my right hand, I shall stand firm.   **R**.

And so my heart rejoices, my soul is glad;
even my body shall rest in safety.
For you will not leave my soul among the dead,
nor let your beloved know decay.   **R**.

You will show me the path of life,
the fulness of joy in your presence,
at your right hand happiness for ever.   **R**.

SECOND READING

A reading from the first letter of St Peter   1:3-4.6-9

Blessed be the God and Father of our Lord Jesus Christ! By his great
mercy we have been born anew to a living hope through the resurrection of Jesus Christ from the dead, and to an inheritance which is
imperishable, undefiled, and unfading, kept in heaven for you.

In this you rejoice, though now for a little while you may have to
suffer various trials, so that the genuineness of your faith, more precious than gold which though perishable is tested by fire, may redound
to praise and glory and honour at the revelation of Jesus Christ.

Without having seen him you have loved him; though you do not
now see him you believe in him and rejoice with unutterable and
exalted joy. As the the outcome of your faith you obtain the
salvation of your souls.

This is the word of the Lord.

Gospel Acclamation   Matthew 10:39

Alleluia, alleluia! [*Lent*: Praise to you, Lord Jesus Christ]
He who finds his life will lose it,
and he who loses his life for my sake will find it,
says the Lord.
Alleluia! [*Lent*: Praise to you, Lord Jesus Christ]

GOSPEL

A reading from the holy Gospel according to Matthew   10:26-32

Jesus said to his disciples:

'So have no fear of them; for nothing is covered that will not be revealed, or hidden that will not be known. What I tell you in the dark, utter in the light; and what you hear whispered, proclaim upon the housetops.

'And do not fear those who kill the body but cannot kill the soul; rather fear him who can destroy both soul and body in hell. Are not two sparrows sold for a penny? And not one of them will fall to the ground without your Father's will. But even the hairs of your head are all numbered. Fear not, therefore; you are of more value than many sparrows.

'So every one who acknowledges me before men, I also will acknowledge before my Father who is in heaven.'

This is the Gospel of the Lord.

ALTERNATIVE GOSPEL

A reading from the holy Gospel according to Matthew   5:13-16

Jesus said to his disciples:

'You are the salt of the earth; but if salt has lost its taste, how shall its saltness be restored? It is no longer good for anything except to be thrown out and trodden under foot by men.

'You are the light of the world. A city set on a hill cannot be hid. Nor do men light a lamp and put it under a bushel, but on a stand, and it gives light to all in the house. Let your light so shine before men, that they may see your good works and give glory to your Father who is in heaven.'

This is the Gospel of the Lord.

26. A WITNESS TO LOVE

FIRST READING

A reading from the prophet Isaiah   58:6-9.11

'Is not this the fast that I choose: to loose the bonds of wickedness, to undo the thongs of the yoke, to let the oppressed go free, and to break every yoke? Is it not to share your bread with the hungry, and bring the homeless poor into your house; when you see the naked, to cover him, and not to hide yourself from your own flesh?

Then shall your light break forth like the dawn, and your healing shall spring up speedily; your righteousness shall go before you, the glory of the Lord shall be your rearguard. Then you shall call, and the Lord will answer; you shall cry, and he will say, Here I am.

And the Lord will guide you continually, and satisfy your desire with good things, and make your bones strong; and you shall be like a watered garden, like a spring of water, whose waters fail not.'

This is the word of the Lord.

Responsorial Psalm   Ps 102(103):8,10-14,17-18

Reponse:
Lord is compassion and love.

The Lord is compassion and love,
slow to anger and rich in mercy.
He does not treat us according to our sins
nor repay us according to our faults.   **R.**

For as the heavens are high above the earth
so strong is his love for those who fear him.
As far as the east is from the west
so far does he remove our sins.   **R.**

As a father has compassion on his children,
the Lord has pity on those who fear him;
for he knows of what we are made,
he remembers that we are dust.   **R.**

The love of the Lord is everlasting
upon those who fear him;
his justice reaches out to children's children
when they keep his covenant in truth.   **R.**

SECOND READING

A reading from the first letter of St John   4:7-12.17

Let us love one another; for love is of God, and he who loves is born of God and knows God. He who does not love does not know God; for God is love.

In this the love of God was made manifest among us, that God sent his only Son into the world, so that we might live through him. In this is love, not that we loved God but that he loved us and sent his Son to be the expiation for our sins.

If God so loved us, we also ought to love one another. No man has ever seen God; if we love one another, God abides in us and his love

is perfected in us. In this is love perfected with us, that we may have confidence for the day of judgement.
This is the word of the Lord.

ALTERNATIVE SECOND READING

A reading from the first letter of St Paul to the Corinthians   13:1-7
If I speak in the tongues of men and of angels, but have no love, I am a noisy gong or a clanging cymbal. And if I have prophetic powers, and understand all mysteries and all knowledge, and if I have all faith, so as to remove mountains, but have not love, I am nothing. If I give away all I have, and if I deliver my body to be burned, but have not love, I gain nothing.

Love is patient and kind; love is not jealous or boastful; it is not arrogant or rude. Love does not insist on its own way; it is not irritable or resentful; it does not rejoice at wrong, but rejoices in the right. Love bears all things, believes all things, hopes all things, endures all things. Love never ends.
This is the word of the Lord.

Gospel Acclamation   Matthew 25:34
Alleluia, alleluia! [*Lent*: Praise to you, Lord Jesus Christ]
Come, O blessed of my Father,
inherit the kingdom prepared for you
from the foundation of the world.
Alleluia! [*Lent*: Praise to you, Lord Jesus Christ]

GOSPEL

A reading from the holy Gospel according to Matthew   25:31-40
Jesus said to his disciples:
'When the Son of man comes in his glory, and all the angels with him, then he will sit on his glorious throne. Before him will be gathered all the nations, and he will separate them one from another as a shepherd separates the sheep from the goats, and he will place the sheep at his right hand, but the goats at the left.

'Then the King will say to those at his right hand, "Come, O blessed of my Father, inherit the kingdom prepared for you from the foundation of the world; for I was hungry and you gave me good, I was thirsty and you gave me drink, I was a stranger and you welcomed me, I was naked and you clothed me, I was sick and you visited me, I was in prison and you came to me."

'Then the righteous will answer him, "Lord, when did we see thee hungry and feed thee, or thirsty and give thee drink? And when did we see thee a stranger and welcome thee, or naked and clothe thee?

And when did we see thee sick or in prison and visit thee?"

'And the King will answer them, "Truly I say to you, as you did it to one of the least of these my brethren, you did it to me." '

This is the Gospel of the Lord.

ALTERNATIVE GOSPEL

A reading from the holy Gospel according to John　　　　13:33-35

Jesus said to his disciples:

'Little children, yet a little while I am with you. You will seeks me; and as I said to the Jews so now I say to you, "Where I am going you cannot come."

'A new commandment I give to you, that you love one another; even as I have loved you, that you also love one another. By this all men will know that you are my disciples, if you have love for one another.'

This is the Gospel of the Lord

OTHER ALTERNATIVE GOSPELS

Luke 10:29-37 (The Good Samaritan).

This would be very suitable for a caring doctor or nurse.

Mark 14:3-9 (The anointing at Bethany).

This would also be a very appropriate Gospel to use in regard to people who were known for their love. The 'fragrance' of their kindness filled not only their own house, but the whole neighbourhood. Wherever their name is mentioned, the story of their good deeds will be told. It would be particularly appropriate in the case of a mother.

---

27. A DEDICATED PERSON

FIRST READING

A reading from the book of Sirach　　　　　　　　　　2:1-9

If you come forward to serve the Lord, prepare yourself for temptation. Set your heart right and be steadfast, and do not be hasty in time of calamity. Cleave to him and do not depart, that you may be honoured at the end of your life.

Accept whatever is brought upon you, and in changes that humble you be patient. For gold is tested in the fire, and acceptable men in the furnace of humiliation. Trust in him, and he will help you; make your ways straight, and hope in him.

You who fear the Lord, wait for his mercy; and turn not aside, lest

you fall. You who fear the Lord, trust in him, and your reward will not fail; you who fear the Lord, hope for good things, for everlasting joy and mercy.
This is the word of the Lord.

Responsorial Psalm   Ps 125(126)
Response:
Those who are sowing in tears
will sing when they reap.

When the Lord delivered Sion from bondage,
it seemed like a dream.
Then was our mouth filled with laughter,
on our lips there were songs. **R**.

The heathens themselves said:
'What marvels the Lord worked for them!'
What marvels the Lord worked for us!
Indeed we were glad. **R**.

Deliver us, O Lord, from our bondage
as streams in dry land.
Those who are sowing in tears
will sing when they reap. **R**.

They go out, they go out, full of tears,
carrying seed for the sowing:
they come back, they come back, full of song,
carrying their sheaves. **R**.

SECOND READING
A reading from the first letter of St Paul to the Corinthians 9:24-27
Do you not know that in a race all the runners compete, but only one receives the prize? So run that you may obtain it. Every athlete exercises self-control in all things. They do it to receive a perishable wreath, but we an imperishable.
Well, I do not run aimlessly, I do not box as one beating the air; but I pommel my body and subdue it, lest after preaching to others I myself should be disqualified.
This is the word of the Lord.

Gospel Acclamation   Matthew 7:13
Alleluia, alleluia! [*Lent*: Praise to you, Lord Jesus Christ]
Enter by the narrow gate,
for the gate is narrow and the way is hard

that leads to life,
says the Lord.
Alleluia! [*Lent*: Praise to you, Lord Jesus Christ]

A reading from the holy Gospel according to John   10:11-15.17-18
Jesus said:

'I am the good shepherd. The good shepherd lays down his life for
the sheep. He who is a hireling and not a shepherd, whose own the
sheep are not, sees the wolf coming and leaves the sheep and flees;
and the wolf snatches them and scatters them. He flees because he is
a hireling and cares nothing for the sheep.

'I am the good sheherd; I know my own and my own know me, as
the Father knows me and I know the Father; and I lay down my life
for the sheep.

'For this reason the Father loves me, because I lay down my life,
that I may take it up again. No one takes it from me, but I lay it down
of my own accord. I have power to lay it down, and I have power to
take it up again; this charge I have received from my Father.'

This is the Gospel of the Lord.

---

28. A FAITHFUL SERVANT

A reading from the book of Sirach   2:1-9

If you come forward to serve the Lord, prepare yourself for temptation. Set your heart right and be steadfast, and do not be hasty in
time of calamity. Cleave to him and do not depart, that you may be
honoured at the end of your life.

Accept whatever is brought upon you, and in changes that humble you be patient. For gold is tested in the fire, and acceptable men
in the furnace of humiliation. Trust in him, and he will help you;
make your ways straight, and hope in him.

You who fear the Lord, wait for his mercy; and turn not aside, lest
you fall. You who fear the Lord, trust in him, and your reward will

not fail; you who fear the Lord, hope for good things, for everlasting joy and mercy.
This is the word of the Lord.

Responsorial Psalm   Ps 115(116):12-19
Response:
Precious in the eyes of the Lord
is the death of his faithful.

How can I repay the Lord
for his goodness to me?
The cup of salvation I will raise;
I will call on the Lord's name.   **R.**

My vows to the Lord I will fulfil
before all his people.
O precious in the eyes of the Lord
is the death of his faithful.   **R.**

Your servant, Lord, your servant am I;
you have loosened my bonds.
A thankgiving sacrifice I make:
I will call on the Lord's name.   **R.**

My vows to the Lord I will fulfil
before all his people,
in the courts of the house of the Lord,
in your midst, O Jerusalem.   **R.**

SECOND READING

A reading from the second letter of St Paul to Timothy   4:6-8
I am already on the point of being sacrificed; the time of my departure has come. I have fought the good fight. I have finished the race. I have kept the faith. Henceforth there is laid up for me the crown of righteousness, which the Lord, the righteous judge, will award to me on that Day, and not only to me but also to all who have loved his appearing.
This is the word of the Lord.

Gospel Acclamation   Matthew 7:13
Alleluia, alleluia! [*lent*: Praise to you, Lord Jesus Christ]
Enter by the narrow gate,
for the gate is narrow and the way is hard
that leads to life,
says the Lord.

Alleluia! [*Lent*: Praise to you, Lord Jesus Christ]

GOSPEL

A reading from the holy Gospel according to Luke   12:35-40.42-44
Jesus said to his disciples:

'Let your loins be girded and your lamps burning, and be like men
who are waiting for their master to come home from the marriage
feast, so that they may open to him at once when he comes and
knocks. Blessed are those servants whom the master finds awake
when he comes; truly, I say to you, he will gird himself and have
them sit at his table, and he will come and serve them. If he comes in
the second watch, or in the third, and finds them so, blessed are
those servants!

'But know this, that if the householder had known at what hour
the thief was coming, he would have been awake and would not
have let his house to be broken into. You also must be ready; for the
Son of man is coming at an hour you do not expect.

'Who then is the faithful and wise steward, whom his master will
set over his household, to give them their portion of food at the
proper time? Blessed is that servant whom his master when he
comes will find so doing. Truly, I tell you, he will set him over all his
possessions.'

This is the Gospel of the Lord.

ALTERNATIVE GOSPEL

Matthew 25:14-15.19-23 (The talents)   p. 126

---

29. COME TO ME, ALL YOU WHO LABOUR

FIRST READING

A reading from the book of Genesis   1:27-31

God created man in his own image, in the image of God he created
him; male and female he created them. And God blessed them and
said to them, 'Be fruitful and multiply, and fill the earth and subdue
it; and have dominion over the fish of the sea and over the birds of
the air and over every living thing that moves upon the earth.'

And God said, 'Behold, I have given you every plant yielding
seed which is upon the face of the earth, and every tree with seed in
its fruit; you shall have them for food. And to every beast of the
earth, and to every bird of the air, and to everything that creeps on

the earth, everything that has the breath of life, I have given every green plant for food.'

And God saw everything that he had made, and behold, it was very good. And there was evening and there was morning, a sixth day.

This is the word of the Lord.

Responsorial Psalm   Ps 89(90):1-2.12-17

Response:
O Lord, you have been our refuge
from one generation to the next.

O Lord you have been our refuge
from one generation to the next.
Before the mountains were born
you are God, without beginning or end. **R**.

Our life is over like a sigh;
our days pass swiftly and we are gone.
Make us know the shortness of our life,
that we may gain wisdom of heart. **R**.

In the morning, fill us with your love;
we shall exult and rejoice all our days.
Give us joy to balance our affliction
for the years when we knew misfortune. **R**.

Show forth your work to your servants;
let your glory shine on their children.
Let the favour of the Lord be upon us:
give success to the work of our hands. **R**.

SECOND READING

A reading from the letter of St Paul to the Colossians 3:14-15.17.23-24

Above all these put on love, which binds everything together in perfect harmony. And let the peace of Christ rule in your hearts, to which indeed you were called in the one body. And be thankful. Whatever you do, in word or deed, do everything in the name of the Lord Jesus, giving thanks to God the Father through him.

Whatever your task, work heartily, as serving the Lord and not men, knowing that from the Lord you will receive the inheritance as your reward.

This is the word of the Lord.

Gospel Acclamation   Revelation 14:13

Alleluia, alleluia! [*Lent*: Praise to you, Lord Jesus Christ]

Blessed are the dead who die in the Lord;
they can rest from their labours,for their deeds follow them.
Alleluia! [*Lent*: Praise to you, Lord Jesus Christ]

A reading from the holy Gospel according to Matthew   11:28-30
Jesus said:

'Come to me, all who labour and are heavy laden, and I will give you rest. Take my yoke upon you, and learn from me; for I am gentle and lowly in heart, and you will find rest for your souls. For my yoke is easy, and my burden is light.'

This is the Gospel of the Lord.

---

30. THE EXPRESS STOPS AT A SMALL STATION
For one of the 'little ones' of the earth

FIRST READING

A reading from the book of Sirach   35:6-11

The offering of a righteous man anoints the altar, and its pleasing odour rises before the Most High. The sacrifice of a righteous man is acceptable, and the memory of it will not be forgotten.

Glorify the Lord generously, and do not stint the first fruits of your hands. With every gift show a cheerful face, and dedicate your tithe with gladness. Give to the Most High as he has given, and as generously as your hand has found. For the Lord is the one who repays, and he will repay you sevenfold.

This is the word of the Lord.

Responsorial Psalm   Ps 137(138):1-3.6-7

Response:
Your love, O Lord, is eternal.

I thank you, Lord, with all my heart,
you have heard the words of my mouth.
Before the angels I will bless you.
I will adore before your holy temple.   **R.**

I thank you for your faithfulness and love
which excel all we ever knew of you.
On the day I called, you answered;
you increased the strength of my soul.   **R.**

The Lord is high yet he looks on the lowly
and the haughty he knows from afar.
Though I walk in the midst of affliction
you give me life and frustrate my foes. **R**.

You stretch out your hand and save me,
your hand will do all things for me.
Your love, O Lord, is eternal,
discard not the work of your hands. **R**.

SECOND READING

A reading from the first letter of St Paul to the Corinthians 2:1-6.9

When I came to you, brethren, I did not come proclaiming to you the testimony of God in lofty words or wisdom. For I decided to know nothing among you except Jesus Christ and him crucified. And I was with you in weakness and in much fear and trembling; and my speech and my message were not in plausible words of wisdom, but in demonstration of the Spirit and power, that your faith might not rest in the wisdom of men but in the power of God.

Yet among the mature we do impart wisdom, although it is not a wisdom of this age or of the rulers of this age, who are doomed to pass away. It is written, 'What no eye has seen, nor ear heard, nor the heart of man conceived, what God has prepared for those who love him,' God has revealed to us through the Spirit.

This is the word of the Lord.

Gospel Acclamation   Matthew 11:28

Alleluia, alleluia! [*Lent*: Praise to you, Lord Jesus Christ]
Come to me, all who labour and are heavy laden,
and I will give you rest,
says the Lord.
Alleluia. [*Lent*: Praise to you, Lord Jesus Christ]

GOSPEL

A reading from the holy Gospel according to Mark   12:41-44

Jesus sat down opposite the treasury, and watched the multitude putting money into the treasury. Many rich people put in large sums. And a poor widow came, and put in two copper coins, which make a penny. And he called his disciples to him, and said to them, 'Truly, I say to you, this poor widow has put in more than all those who are contributing to the treasury. For they all contributed out of their abundance; but she out of her poverty has put in everything she had, her whole living.'

This is the Gospel of the Lord.

31. THE DEAD ARE ALIVE

FIRST READING

A reading from the second book of the Maccabees   12:43-45

Judas, the leader of the Jews, took up a collection, man by man, to the amount of two thousand drachmas of silver, and sent it to Jerusalem to provide for the sin offering. In doing this he acted very well and honourably, taking account of the resurrection.

For if he were not expecting that those who had fallen would rise again, it would have been superfluous and foolish to pray for the dead. But if he was looking to the splendid reward that is laid up for those who fall asleep in godliness, it was a holy and pious thought. Therefore he made atonement for the dead, that they might be delivered from their sin.

This is the word of the Lord.

Responsorial Psalm   Ps 123(124)

Response:
Our help is in the name of the Lord,
who made heaven and earth.

If the Lord had not been on our side
when men rose against us,
then would they have swallowed us alive
when their anger was kindled.   **R**.

Then would the waters have engulfed us,
the torrent gone over us;
over our head would have swept
the raging waters.   **R**.

Blessed be the Lord who did not give us
a prey to their teeth.
Our life, like a bird, has escaped
from the snare of the fowler.   **R**.

Indeed the snare has been broken
and we have escaped.
Our help is in the name of the Lord,
who made heaven and earth.   **R**.

SECOND READING

A reading from the first letter of St Paul to the Corinthians 15:12-20

Now if Christ is preached as raised from the dead, how can some of you say that there is no resurrection of the dead? But if there is no resurrection of the dead, then Christ has not been raised; if Christ has not been raised, then our preaching is in vain and your faith is in vain. We are even found to be misrepresenting God, because we testified of God that he raised Christ, whom he did not raise if it is true that the dead are not raised.

For if the dead are not raised, then Christ has not been raised. If Christ has not been raised, your faith is futile and you are still in your sins. Then those also who have fallen asleep in Christ have perished. If for this life only we have hoped in Christ, we are of all men most to be pitied.

But in fact Christ has been raised from the dead, the first fruits of those who have fallen asleep.

This is the word of the Lord.

Gospel Acclamation   John 10:10

Alleluia, alleluia! [*Lent*: Praise to you, Lord Jesus Christ]
I came that you may have life,
and have it abundantly,
says the Lord.
Alleluia. [*Lent*: Praise to you, Lord Jesus Christ]

GOSPEL

A reading from the holy Gospel according to Luke   24:1-8

But on the first day of the week, at early dawn, they went to the tomb, taking the spices which they had prepared. And they found the stone rolled away from the tomb, but when they went in they did not find the body.

While they were perplexed about this, behold, two men stood by them in dazzling apparel; and as they were frightened and bowed their faces to the ground, the men said to them, 'Why do you seek the living among the dead? He is not here, but has risen. Remember how he told you, while he was still in Galilee, that the Son of Man must be delivered into the hands of sinful men, and be crucified, and on the third day rise.' And they remembered his words.

This is the Gospel of the Lord.

32. REMEMBERING

A reading from the prophet Isaiah   49:8.13-16
Thus says the Lord: 'In a time of favour I have answered you, in a
day of salvation I have helped you.' Sing for joy, O heavens, and
exult, O earth; break forth, O mountains, into singing! For the Lord
has comforted his people, and will have compassion on his afflicted.
   But Zion said, 'The Lord has forsaken me, my Lord has forgotten
me.' 'Can a woman forget her sucking child, that she should have no
compassion on the son of her womb? Even these may forget, yet I will
not forget you. Behold, I have graven you on the palms of my hands.'
   This is the word of the Lord.

Responsorial Psalm   Ps 29(30):3-8.12-23
   Response:
   I will praise you, Lord, you have rescued me.

   O Lord, I cried to you for help
   and you, my God, have healed me.
   O Lord, you have raised my soul from the dead,
   restored me to life from those who sink into the grave.   **R.**

   Sing psalms to the Lord, you who love him,
   give thanks to his holy name.
   His anger lasts but for a moment; his favour through life.
   At night there are tears, but joy comes with dawn.   **R.**

   I said to myself in my good fortune:
   'Nothing will ever disturb me.'
   Your favour had set me on a mountain fastness,
   then you hid your face and I was put to confusion.   **R.**

   For me you have changed my mourning into dancing,
   you removed my sackcloth and girdled me with joy.
   So my soul sings psalms to you unceasingly.
   O Lord my God, I will thank you for ever.   **R.**

A reading from the first letter of St Paul to the Corinthians 15:20-26
Christ has been raised from the dead, the first fruits of those who
have fallen asleep. For as by a man came death, by a man has come

also the resurrection of the dead. For as in Adam all die, so also in Christ shall all be made alive. But each in his own order: Christ the first fruits, then at his coming those who belong to Christ.

Then comes the end, when he delivers the kingdom to God the Father after destroying every rule and every authority and power. For he must reign until he has put all his enemies under his feet. The last enemy to be destroyed is death.

This is the word of the Lord.

Gospel Acclamatiom   Matthew 24:35

Alleluia, alleluiia! [*Lent*: Praise to you, Lord Jesus Christ]
Heaven and earth will pass away,
but my words will not pass away,
says the Lord.
Alleluia. [*Lent*: Praise to you, Lord Jesus Christ]

GOSPEL

A reading from the holy Gospel according to Luke   22:14-20

And when the hour came, Jesus sat at table, and the apostles with him. And he said to them, 'I have earnestly desired to eat this passover with you before I suffer; for I tell you I shall not eat it until it is fulfilled in the kingdom of God.'

And he took a cup, and when he had given thanks he said, 'Take this, and divide it among yourselves; for I tell you that from now on I shall not drink of the fruit of the vine until the kingdom of God comes.'

And he took the bread, and when he had given thanks he broke it and gave it to them, saying, 'This is my body which is given for you. Do this in remembrance of me.' And likewise the cup after supper, saying, 'This cup which is poured out for you is the new covenant in my blood.'

This is the Gospel of the Lord.

ALTERNATIVE GOSPEL

A reading from the holy Gospel according to John   20:11-18

But Mary stood weeping outside the tomb, and as she wept she stooped to look into the tomb; and she saw two angels in white, sitting where the body of Jesus had lain, one at the head and one at the feet.

They said to her, 'Woman, why are you weeping?' She said to them, 'Because they have taken away my Lord, and I do not know where they had laid him.' Saying this, she turned around and saw Jesus standing, but she did not know it was Jesus.

Jesus said to her, 'Woman, why are you weeping? Whom do you seek?' Supposing him to be the gardener, she said to him, 'Sir, if you have carried him away, tell me where you have laid him, and I will take him away.' Jesus said to her, 'Mary.' She turned and said to him in Hebrew, 'Rab-boni!' (which means Teacher). Jesus said to her, 'Do not hold me, for I have not yet ascended to the Father; but go to my brethren and say to them, I am ascending to my Father and to your Father, to my God and to your God.'

Mary Magdalen went and said to the disciples, 'I have seen the Lord' and she told them that he had said these things to her.

This is the Gospel of the Lord.

Comment on Alternative Gospel   John 20:11-18

Mary Magdaalen wanted to cling to Christ. We too want to cling to our departed loved ones. We do not want to let go of them. But we must let go of them. What helps us to do this is the knowledge that they are going to better things. They too are going to the Father.

---

33. RESTORING BROKEN RELATIONSHIPS

FIRST READING

A reading from the prophet Isaiah   35:3-6.10

Strengthen the weak hands, and make firm the feeble knees. Say to those who are of a fearful heart, 'Be strong, fear not! Behold, your God will come with vengeance, with the recompense of God. He will come and save you.'

Then the eyes of the blind will be opened, and the ears of the deaf unstopped; then will the lame man leap like a hart, and the tongue of the dumb sing for joy.

And the ransomed of the Lord will return, and come to Zion with singing; everlasting joy shall be upon their heads; they shall obtain joy and gladness, and sorrow and sighing shall flee away.

This is the word of the Lord.

Responsorial Psalm   Ps 89(90):1-2.12-17

Response:
O Lord, you have been our refuge
from one generation to the next.

O Lord, you have been our refuge
from one generation to the next.
Before the mountains were born
you are God, without beginning or end. **R.**

Our life is over like a sigh;
our days pass swiftly and we are gone.
Make us know the shortness of our life,
that we may gain wisdom of heart.   **R**.

In the morning, fill us with your love;
we shall exult and rejoice all our days.
Give us joy to balance our affliction
for the years when we knew misfortune.   **R**.

Show forth your work to your servants;
let your glory shine on their children.
Let the favour of the Lord be upon us:
give success to the work of our hands.   **R**.

SECOND READING

A reading from the second letter of St Paul to the Corinthians 5:1.6-10

For we know that if the earthly tent we live in is destroyed, we have
a building from God, a house not made with hands, eternal in the
heavens. So we are always of good courage; we know that while we
are at home in the body we are away from the Lord, for we walk by
faith, not by sight.

We are of good courage, and we would rather be away from the
body and at home with the Lord. So whether we are at home or
away, we make it our aim to please him. For we must all appear
before the judgement seat of Christ, so that each one may receive
good or evil, according to what he has done in the body.

This is the word of the Lord.

Gospel Acclamation   John 8:12
    Alleluia, alleluia! [*Lent*: Praise to you, Lord Jesus Christ]
    I am the light of the world;
    he who follows me will not walk in darkness,
    but will have the light of life,
    says the Lord.
    Alleluia! [*Lent*: Praise to you, Lord Jesus Christ]

GOSPEL

A reading from the holy Gospel according to John   20:19-20.24-29

On the evening of that day, the first day of the week, the doors being
shut where the disciples were, for fear of the Jews, Jesus came and
stood among them and said to them, 'Peace be with you.' When he
had said this, he showed them his hands and his side. Then the
disciples were glad when they saw the Lord.

Now Thomas, one of the twelve, called the Twin, was not with them when Jesus came. So the other disciples told him, 'We have seen the Lord.' But he said to them, 'Unless I see in his hands the print of the nails, and place my finger in the mark of the nails, and place my hand in his side, I will not believe.'

Eight days later, his disciples were again in the house, and Thomas was with them. The doors were shut, but Jesus came and stood among them, and said, 'Peace be with you.' Then he said to Thomas, 'Put your finger here, and see my hands; and put out your hand, and place it in my side; do not be faithless, but believing.'

Thomas answered him, 'My Lord and my God!' Jesus said to him, 'Have you believed because you have seen me? Blessed are those who have not seen and yet believe.'

This is the Gospel of the Lord.

34. HEALING THE WOUNDS OF GRIEF

FIRST READING

A reading from the prophet Isaiah   61:1-3

The Spirit of the Lord God is upon me, because the Lord has anointed me to bring good tidings to the afflicted; he has sent me to bind up the brokenhearted, to proclaim liberty to the captives, and the opening of the prison to those who are bound; to proclaim the year of the Lord's favour, and the day of vengeance of our Lord; to comfort all who mourn; to give them a garland instead of ashes, the oil of gladness instead of mourning.

This is the word of the Lord.

Responsorial Psalm   Ps 33(34):1-3.8-9.18-21

Response:
I will bless the Lord at all times.

I will bless the Lord at all times,
his praise always on my lips;
in the Lord my soul shall make its boast.
The humble shall hear and be glad. **R.**

The angel of the Lord is encamped
around those who revere him,
to rescue them.

Taste and see that the Lord is good.
He is happy who seeks refuge in him.   **R.**

They call and the Lord hears
and rescues them in all their distress.
The Lord is close to the broken-hearted;
those whose spirit is crushed he will save.   **R.**

Many are the trials of the just
but from them all the Lord will rescue them.
He will keep guard over all their bones,
not one of their bones shall be broken.   **R.**

SECOND READING

A reading from the apocalypse of St John   21:1-4

Then I saw a new heaven and a new earth; for the first heaven and
the first earth had passed away, and the sea was no more. And I saw
the holy city, new Jerusalem, coming down out of heaven from
God, prepared as a bride adorned for her husband; and I heard a
great voice from the throne saying, 'Behold, the dwelling of God is
with men. He will dwell with them, and they shall be his people, and
God himself will be with them; and he will wipe away every tear
from their eyes, and death shall be no more, neither shall there be
mourning nor crying nor pain any more, for the former things have
passed away.'
    This is the word of the Lord.

Gospel Acclamation   Matthew 11:28

Alleluia, alleluia! [*Lent*: Praise to you, Lord Jesus Christ]
Come to me, all who labour and are heavy laden,
and I will give you rest,
says the Lord.
Alleluia! [*Lent*: Praise to you, Lord Jesus Christ]

GOSPEL

A reading from the holy Gospel according to Luke   24:36-48

As they were saying this, Jesus himself stood among them, and said
to them, 'Peace to you!' But they were startled and frightened, and
supposed that they saw a spirit. And he said to them, 'Why are you
troubled, and why do questions rise in your hearts? See my hands
and my feet, that it is I myself; handle me, and see; for a spirit has
not flesh and bones as you see that I have.'
    And when he had said this, he showed them his hands and his
feet. And while they still disbelieved for joy, and wondered, he said

to them, 'Have you anything here to eat?' They gave him a piece of broiled fish, and he took it and ate before them.

Then he said to them, 'These are my words which I spoke to you, while I was still with you, that everything written about me in the law of Moses and the prophets and the psalms must be fulfilled.' Then he opened their minds to understand the scriptures, and said to them, 'Thus it is written, that the Christ should suffer and on the third day rise from the dead, and that repentance and forgiveness of sins should be preached in his name to all nations, beginning from Jerusalem. You are witnesses of these things.'

This is the Gospel of the Lord.

---

35. RE-BUILDING OUR LIVES

FIRST READING

A reading from the prophet Isaiah   52:7-10

How beautiful upon the mountains are the feet of him who brings good tidings, who publishes peace, who brings good tidings of good, who publishes salvation, who says to Zion, 'Your God reigns.'

Hark, your watchmen lift up their voice, together they sing for joy; for eye to eye they see the return of the Lord to Zion.

Break forth together into singing, you waste places of Jerusalem; for the Lord has comforted his people, he has redeemed Jerusalem.

The Lord has bared his holy arm before the eyes of all the nations; and all the ends of the earth shall see the salvation of our God.

This is the word of the Lord.

Responsorial Psalm   Ps 29(30):3-8.12-13

Response:
I will praise you, Lord, you have rescued me.

Lord, I cried to you for help
and you, my God, have healed me.
O Lord, you have raised my soul from the dead,
restored me to life from those who sink into the grave. **R.**

Sing psalms to the Lord, you who love him,
give thanks to his holy name.
His anger lasts but for a moment; his favour through life.
At night there are tears, but joy comes with dawn. **R.**

I said to myself in my good fortune:
'Nothing will ever disturb me.'
Your favour had set me on a mountain fastness,
then you hid your face and I was put to confusion. **R.**

For me you have changed my mourning into dancing,
you removed my sackcloth and girdled me with joy.
So my soul sings psalms to you unceasingly.
O Lord my God, I will thank you ever. **R.**

SECOND READING

A reading from the first letter of St Paul to the Corinthians 15:51-57

Lo! I tell you a mystery. We shall not all sleep, but we shall all be changed, in a moment, in the twinkling of an eye, at the last trumpet. For the trumpet will sound, and the dead will be raised imperishable, and we shall be changed.

For this perishable nature must put on the imperishable, and this mortal nature must put on immortality. When the perishable puts on the imperishable, and the mortal puts on immortality, then shall come to pass the saying that is written: 'Death is swallowed up in victory. O death, where is thy victory? O death, where is thy sting?'

The sting of death is sin, and the power of sin is the law.

But thanks be to God, who gives us the victory through our Lord Jesus Christ.

This is the word of the Lord.

Gospel Acclamation   John 3:16

Alleluia, alleluia! [*Lent*: Praise to you, Lord Jesus Christ]
God so loved the world that he gave his only Son,
that whoever believes in him should not perish
but have eternal life,
says the Lord.
Alleluia! [*Lent*: Praise to you, Lord Jesus Christ]

GOSPEL

A reading from the holy Gospel according to Luke 24:13-17.19-31

That very day [Easter Day] two of Jesus' disciples were going to a village named Emmaus, aboout seven miles from Jerusalem, and talking about these things that had happened. While they were talking, Jesus himself drew near. But their eyes were kept from recognising him. And he said to them, 'What is this conversation which you are holding as you walk?' And they stood still, looking sad.

Then they said to him, 'Concerning Jesus of Nazareth, who was a prophet mighty in deed and word before God and all the people, and how our chief priests and rulers delivered him up and crucified him. But we had hoped that he was the one to redeem Israel. It is now the third day since this happened. Moreover, some women of our company amazed us. They were at the tomb early in the morning and did not find his body; and they came back saying that they had even seen a vision of angels, who said he was alive.'

And he said to them, 'O foolish men, and slow of heart to believe all that the prophets have spoken! Was it not necessary that the Christ should suffer these things and enter into his glory?' And beginning with Moses and all the prophets, he interpreted to them in all the scriptures the things concerning himself.

So they drew near to the village to which they were going. He appeared to be going further, but they said, 'Stay with us, for the day is far spent.' So he went in to stay with them. When he was at table with them, he took the bread and blessed, and broke it, and gave it to them. And their eyes were opened and they recognised him; and he vanished out of their sight.

And they rose that same hour and returned to Jerusalem. Then they told the others what had happened on the road and how he was known to them in the breaking of bread.

This is the Gospel of the Lord.

36. THE COMING OF THE SPIRIT

FIRST READING

A reading from the book of Lamentations   3:17-26

My soul is bereft of peace, I have forgotten what happiness is; so I say, 'Gone is my glory, and my expectation from the Lord.' Remember my affliction and my bitterness, the wormwood and the gall! My soul continually thinks of it and is bowed down within me.

But this I call to mind, and therefore I have hope: The steadfast love of the Lord never ceases, his mercies never come to an end; they are new every morning; great is thy faithfulness. 'The Lord is my portion,' says my soul 'therefore I will hope in him.'

The Lord is good to those who wait for him, to the soul that seeks him. It is good that one should wait quietly for the salvation of the Lord.

This is the word of the Lord.

Responsorial Psalm   Ps 26(27):1.4.10.13.14

Response:
The Lord is my light and my help.

The Lord is my light and my help;
whom shall I fear?
The Lord is the stronghold of my life;
before whom shall I shrink?   **R.**

There is one thing I ask of the Lord
for this I long,
to live in the house of the Lord
all the days of my life.   **R.**

Do not abandon or forsake me,
O God my help.
Though father and mother forsake me,
the Lord will receive me.   **R.**

I am sure I shall see the Lord's goodness
in the land of the living.
Hope in him, hold firm and take heart.
Hope in the Lord.   **R.**

SECOND READING

A reading from the first letter of St Paul to the Thessalonians   4:13-18

But we would not have you ignorant, brethren, concerning those
who are asleep, that you may not grieve as others do who have no
hope. For since we believe that Jesus died and rose again, even so,
through Jesus, God will bring with him those who have fallen
asleep. For this we declare to you by the word of the Lord, that we
who are alive, who are left until the coming of the Lord, shall not
precede those who have fallen asleep.

For the Lord himself will descend from heaven with a cry of command, with the archangel's call, and with the sound of the trumpet of
God. And the dead in Christ will rise first; then we who are alive, who
are left, shall be caught up together with them in the clouds to meet the
Lord in the air; and so we shall always be with the Lord.

Therefore comfort one another with these words.

This is the word of the Lord.

Gospel Acclamation   John 16:7

Alleluia, alleluia! [*Lent*: Praise to you, Lord Jesus Christ]
It is to your advantage that I go away,
for if I do not go away, the Holy Spirit will not come to you;

but if I go, I will send him to you,
says the Lord.
Alleluia! [*Lent*: Praise to you, Lord Jesus Christ]

GOSPEL

A reading from the holy Gospel according to John   16:1-7
Jesus said to his disciples:

'I have said all this to you to keep you from falling away. They will put you out of the synagogues; indeed, the hour is coming when whoever kills you will think he is offering service to God. And they will do this because they have not known the Father, nor me. But I have said these things to you, that when their hour comes you may remember that I told you of them.

'I did not say these things to you from the beginning, because I was with you. But now I am going to him who sent me; yet none of you asks me, "Where are you going?" But because I have said these things to you, sorrow has filled your hearts. Nevertheless I tell you the truth: it is to your advantage that I go away, for if I do not go away, the Counsellor will not come to you; but if I go, I will send him to you.'

This is the Gospel of the Lord.

Reflections

1. Trust in God

Lord,
I have no idea where I'm going.
I do not see the road ahead of me.
I cannot know for certain where it will end.

Nor do I really know myself.
And the fact that I think I am doing your will,
does not mean that I am actually doing it.
But I believe that the desire to please you,
does in fact please you,
and I hope that I have this desire.

I know that if I do this,
you will lead me by the right road,
though I may know nothing about it.
Therefore I trustyou always.

Though I may seem to be lost
and in the shadow of death,
I will not fear, for you are with me,
and you will never leave me face my perils alone.

Thomas Merton

From *Thoughts in Solitude*

2. Trust in Christ

Our span of life is brief
and our hold on it precarious.
The years scurry along
like dead leaves blown in the wind.

I sometimes wonder where I'm going
and what is the meaning of my life.
I wonder especially what the future holds.
But then I remember that Christ came on earth;
that he made himself my companion on the road of life,
and that this road leads to the Father's kingdom.

So I say to my soul: 'Go out into the darkness
and put your hand in the hand of Christ, your Brother.

That will be to you better than a light,
and safer than a known way.'

3. Footprints in the Sand

One night a man had a dream.
He dreamt that he was walking
along a beach with the Lord.
Across the sky flashed the scenes of his life.
For each scene he noticed
not one but two sets of footprints in the sand.
He understood immediately that one belonged to him,
and the other to the Lord.

But then he noticed a curious thing.
At the lowest and saddest times in his life
there was only one set of footprints.
This bothered him, so he asked the Lord:
'How come that during the most difficult times in my life,
the very times when I most needed you,
you left me on my own?'

Then the Lord replied:
'My friend, during your trials and sufferings,
when you see only one set of footprints,
those footprints are mine.
It was then that I carried you.'

4. Stranger at Our Side

All through life's day
our risen Lord walks with us.
Often, however, he is a stranger to us,
for he never forces himself upon us.

Before the day's end we will ask many questions,
experience many failures,
disappointments and heartaches.
And then, suddenly,
whether we are young, middle-aged, or old,
we will find that the shadows are lengthening and night is fast
    approaching.

In that moment we pray
that, like the disciples on the road to Emmaus,
our eyes will be opened,

and that we will recognise *him* –
the stranger who walked at our side -
as our risen Lord.

And he will not vanish from our sight.
Instead he will guide us
through the dark valley of death
to the safety of the Father's house.

5. Journey of Life

For each of us life is like a journey.
Birth is the beginning of this journey,
and death is not the end but the destination.

It is a journey that takes us
from youth to age,
from innocence to awareness,
from ignorance to knowledge,
from foolishness to wisdom,
from weakness to strength and often back again,
from offence to forgiveness,
from loneliness to friendship,
from pain to compassion,
from fear to faith,
from defeat to victory and from victory to defeat,
until, looking backward or ahead,
we see that victory does not lie
at some high point along the way,
but in having made the journey,
stage by stage.

Adapted from an old Hebrew prayer.

6. Your Stay Was so Short

My little one, down what centuries
of light did you travel
to reach us here,
your stay so short-lived;
in the twinkling of an eye
you were moving on,
bearing our name and a splinter
of the human cross we suffer;
flashed upon us like a beacon
we wait in darkness for that light

to come round, knowing at heart
you shine forever for us.

Hugh O'Donnell, S.D.B.

7. Finding One's Work

Blessed are those who have found their work.
I often feel that I am as rich as Croesus,
not in money,
but rich because I have found my work,
something to which I can devote myself heart and soul,
and which gives meaning and inspiration to my life.

I think it is a very great blessing
when people find their work,
and even though I have lots of difficulties,
and there are many gloomy days in my life,
I count myself among the fortunate.

If at times I feel rising within me
the desire for a life of ease,
I go back fondly to a life of hardship,
convinced that I learn more from it.
This is not the road on which one perishes.

Vincent Van Gogh.

8. One's Daily Work

When God's Son became man
he didn't become a king or a great political leader.
He became a workingman.

The Gospels show us Christ
as a healer, teacher and wonder-worker.
But these activities lasted only three years.
For the rest of his life on earth
he worked as a village carpenter.

There was nothing spectacular about his work.
He didn't make benches and tables by means of miracles,
but by the hammer and the saw.
And, as far as we know,
nothing he made ever became a collector's item.

Our daily tasks may be dull and insignificant,
but we must not underestimate their importance.

In the long run,
the only thing that ripens and bears fruit
is the meagre work of every day.

9. The Things I Fail to Do

It isn't the things you do,
it's the things you leave undone
which give you a little heartache
at the setting of the sun.

The gentle word forgotten,
the letter you didn't write;
the flowers you might have sent
are your haunting ghosts tonight.

The stone you might have lifted
out of your brother's way;
the little heart-felt counsel
you were hurried too much to say.

The tender touch of the hand,
the gentle and kindly tone,
which we have no time or thought for,
with troubles enough of our own.

Anonymous.

10. Before I Sleep

Whose woods these are I think I know.
His house is in the village though;
He will not see me stopping here
To watch his woods fill up with snow.

My little horse must think it queer
To stop without a farmhouse near
Between the woods and frozen lake
The darkest evening of the year.

He gives his harness bells a shake
To ask if there is some mistake.
The only other sound is the sweep
Of easy wind and downy flake.

The woods are lovely, dark and deep;
But I have promises to keep,

And miles to go before I sleep,
And miles to go before I sleep.

Robert Frost.

11. The Two Roads

Christ spoke about two roads.

The first is broad and easy to travel.
All you have to do is follow the crowd.
It is the way of comfort and ease,
popularity and fame,
and is lit by glittering neon lights.
Many are fooled and travel down this road,
but in the end it leads nowhere;
they die in the desert.

The second road is narrow and difficult.
You will often have to go it alone.
It is the way of sacrifice and struggle.
At times you will have no light to guide you
save that of the stars.
Few take this road.
But they are the lucky ones,
for this road leads to the Promised Land.

12. Dying to Self

Each of us is like a grain of wheat
planted by the heavenly Father.
Just as a grain of wheat must die
if it is to produce a harvest,
so the false self in us must die
in order that the true self, made in God's image,
may be born.

This dying to self is a gradual process
and happens in very ordinary ways.
Every act of love involves a dying to selfishness.
Every act of humility involves a dying to pride.
Every act of courage involves a dying to cowardice.

It is the true self alone
that will inherit eternal life.
There is no place for what is false

in the presence of God.
It would melt like snow before the sun.

13. Go Peacefully

Go peacefully amid the noise and the haste,
and remember what peace there may be in silence.
As far as possible,
without surrendering what you believe in,
be on good terms all persons.

Keep interested in your own career,
however humble;
it is a real possession in the changing fortunes of time.
And be careful not to be taken in,
for the world is full of trickery;
but let this not blind you to what good there is:
many persons strive for high ideals,
and everywhere life is full of heroism.

Above all, be at peace with God.
And whatever your labours and aspirations
in the noisy confusion of life,
keep peace with your soul.
For in spite of all its sham, drudgery and broken dreams,
it is still a beautiful world.

Desiderata.

14. A Simple Life but Close to God

It is a simple life we lived here,
but nobody could say that it was comfortable.
Often during life I have known God's holy help,
because I was often in the grip of a sorrow
from which I could not escape.
When the need was greatest,
God would lay his merciful eye on me,
and the clouds of sorrow would be gone without a trace.
In their place would be a spiritual joy
whose sweetness I cannot describe here.

There are people who think this island is a lonely place,
but the peace of the Lord is here.
We helped each other,
and lived in the shelter of each other.

But now my life is spent, like a candle,
and my hope is rising every day
that I'll be called into the eternal kingdom.
May God guide me on this long road
I have not travelled before.
I think everything is folly except for loving God.

Peig Sayers.

From *An Old Woman Remembers*, translated by Séamus Ennis, Oxford University Press.

15. What Is Essential Is Invisible

'People,' said the Little Prince,
'set out on their way in express trains,
but they do not know what they are looking for.
They rush about, and get excited, and turn round and round.

'They raise five thousand roses in the same garden,
and they do not find in it what they are looking for.
Yet what they are looking for
could be found in a single rose,
or in a little water.

'It is only with the heart that one can see rightly;
what is essential is invisible to the eye.'

Antoine de Saint Exupery.

16. A Light That Shines in the Dark

We are told that the Magi were led to Christ
by the light of a bright star.
But they only saw the star
because they were not afraid to travel in the dark.

The fact is,
we cannot see the stars in the bright light of day,
but only in the darkness of night;
and the darker the night,
the brighter they shine.

Those who have to travel by night
need no longer fear the darkness,
because since the coming of Christ
a light has come into the world,

a light that shines in the dark,
a light that darkness cannot overpower.

17. Do Not Be Afraid of Misfortune

Live with a steady superiority over life.
Don't be afraid of misfortune,
and don't yearn after happiness;
for the bitter doesn't last for ever,
and the sweet never fills the cup to overflowing.

It is enough that you don't freeze in the cold,
and if thirst and hunger don't claw at your insides.
If your back isn't broken,
if your feet can walk,
if both arms can bend,
if both eyes can see,
and if both ears can hear,
then whom should you envy?

So rub your eyes and purify your heart,
and prize above all else in the world
those who love you and who wish you well.
Do not hurt them or scold them,
and never part from any of them in anger:
after all, you simply do not know,
but it might be your last act,
and that will be how you are imprinted in their memory.

Alexander Solzhenitsyn.

18. A Powerful Stream

Vincent Van Gogh experienced many difficulties
in the course of his short life as a painter.
From a worldly point of view
that life seemed to be a total failure.
But he didn't see it like this.

He said:

'It is true that sometimes I have earned my bread,
and sometimes a friend has given it to me in charity.
It is true that my financial affairs are in a sad state.
It is true that my future looks gloomy.
It is true that I might have done better.

It is true that my studies have been neglected,
and that my needs are greater than my possessions.

'But is this what you call going downhill?
Is this what you call doing nothing?
On the contrary, this is a powerful stream
that will bear me safely to port.'

19. The Facts of Life

The American writer, Thoreau,
lived for two years in a shack in the woods.
'I went into the woods,' he says,
'to confront the essential facts of life,
lest when I come to die,
I should discover that I had not lived.

'I love a broad margin to my life.
Sometimes on a summer morning
I sat amidst the pines,
in undisturbed solitude and stillness,
while the birds sang around me.

'I grew in those seasons like corn in the night.
They were not time subtracted from my life,
but so much over and above my usual allowance.
It's not enough to be industrious,
so are the ants.
What are you industrious about?'

20. Living in the Present

Sadly, I am often tempted to postpone life.
I refuse sympathy and intimacy with people,
as if expecting a better intimacy to come.

I am thirty-four years old.
Already my friends and fellow workers
are dying from me.
I rarely see new people approaching me.
I am too old to bother about fashion;
too old to expect the patronage of the powerful.

Let me, therefore, suck the sweetness
of those relationships that grow near me,
which divine Providence offers me.

The days come and go like muffled figures
sent from a distant friendly land.
If we do not use the gifts they bring,
they carry them as silently away.

Emerson.

21. Dying in Order To Live More Fully

I believe in death.
I believe that it is part of life.

I believe that we are born to die,
to die that we may live more fully;
born to die a little each day
to selfishness,
to pretence, and to sin.

I believe that every time we pass
from one stage of life to another,
something in us dies
and something new is born.

I believe we taste death
in moments of loneliness and rejection,
in moments of sorrow and disappointment,
when we are afraid, lose courage and give up,
when we see our dreams broken,
and every time we say goodbye.

I believe, too, that we are dying before our time
when we live in bitterness,
in hatred,
and in isolation.

I believe that each day
we are creating our own death
by the way we live.

To those who believe in Christ,
death is a gateway,
a gateway to eternal life.

22. Builders of Eternity

Isn't it strange that princes and kings
and clowns that caper in sawdust rings,

and ordinary folks like you and me
are builders of eternity.

To each is given a bag of tools,
an hour-glass and a book of rules;
and each must build, ere time is flown,
a stumbling block or a stepping stone.

Anonymous.

23. Gone only from Our Sight

I am standing on the seashore.
Suddenly a ship at my side
spreads her white sails to the morning breeze,
and starts out for the blue ocean.
She is an object of beauty and strength,
and I stand and watch her
until at length she is only a ribbon of white cloud
just above where sea and sky mingle with each other.
Then someone at my side says:
'There! She's gone!'

Gone where?
Gone from my sight – that is all.
She is just as large in mast and hull and spar
as she was when she left my side,
and just as able to bear her load of living freight
to the place of destination.
Her diminished size is in me, not in her,
and just at the moment when someone at my side says:
'There! She's gone!'
there are other voices ready to take the glad shout,
'There! She comes!'

And that is dying.

Words found in the wallet of Colonel Marcus, of the Israeli Army, when he was killed
in action on June 11th, 1948.

24. Death Is Only an Horizon

We give them back to you, O Lord,
who first gave them to us;
and as you did not lose them in the giving,
so we do not lose them in the return.

Not as the world gives do you give,
O Lover of souls.
For what is yours is ours also,
if we belong to you.

Life is unending because love is undying,
and the boundaries of this life are but an horizon,
and an horizon is but the limit of our vision.

Lift us up, strong Son of God,
that we may see further.
Strengthen our faith that we may see beyond the horizon.

And while you prepare a place for us,
as you have promised,
prepare us also for that happy place;
that where you are we may be also,
with those we have loved, forever.

Bede Jarrett, O.P.

25. Remembering

Everybody loves to be remembered.
But if we want to be remembered
we have a duty also to remember.

Memory is a powerful thing.
Wrongly used it can bring death rather than life.
Rightly used it is a form of immortality.
It keeps the past alive.
Those we remember never die.
They continue to walk and talk with us.
Their influence is still felt among us.
Their is nothing stronger or more helpful
than a good remembrance.

N. our brother (sister), we want you to know
that we haven't forgotten you.
We remember you.
And your memory most definitely
brings life to us today.
May it also assure us of life for you,
that eternal life Christ came on earth to give us.

26. Faith in Immortality

Thoreau tells the following story
in one of his books.

There was an old table made of apple-tree wood.
It had stood for sixty years in a farmer's kitchen,
first in Connecticut, and afterwards in Massachusetts.
One day, to the surprise of everybody,
a strange and beautiful bug came out of the table leaf.
Seemingly what had happened was this.

An egg had been deposited
in the living tree many years earlier,
as appeared by counting the layers beyond it.
The bug was hatched out by the heat of the fire.
Slowly it knawed its way out of its tomb,
spread its wings, and flew off.

Who would not have his faith in a resurrection
and immortality strengthened by hearing this?

27. Love Is like Fire

What a bleak place the world would be without fire.
However, the heat a fire gives off
depends not on the amount
but on the quality of the firewood.

You may pile on a mountain of wet, green firewood,
but all you'll get will be smoke and sparks.
Whereas if you put on a little seasoned firewood,
there will hardly be any smoke at all –
just a steady blaze which will roast you,
because its heart is on fire.

There are some people who give off a lot of smoke and sparks,
but who leave you cold,
because they have no love in their hearts.
But there are other people who glow quietly,
radiating friendship and hospitality,
so that people are warmed simply by being near them.

28. Children

Our children are not really our children.
They are sons and daughters of God our Father.

Though they come into this world through us,
they do not come from us.
And no matter how long they are with us,
they never belong to us.
And while we can provide a home for their bodies,
we cannot provide a home for their souls.

Parents are the launching pad from which
their children, like living space ships, are dispatched.
The fact that death takes them out of our sight,
doesn't mean they have ceased to exist.
It simply means they have broken free
from the constraints of the body,
and have become free spirits,
travelling onward and outward
towards God's eternal kingdom.

Every time we remember them
they remind us of our own eternal destiny.

29. Walking in Beauty and Wisdom

O Great Spirit,
whose voice I hear in the winds
and whose breath gives life to the world,
hear me.

I come to you as one of your many children.
I am small and weak.
I need your strength and your wisdom.

May I walk in beauty.
Make my eyes ever behold the red and purple sunset.
Make my hands respect the things you have made,
and my ears sharp to hear your voice.

Make me wise so that I may know
the things you have taught your children,
the lessons you have hidden in every leaf and rock.

Make me strong,
so that I may not be superior to other people,
but able to fight my greatest enemy,
which is myself.

Make me ever ready to come to you with straight eyes,

so that when life fades as the fading sunset,
my spirit may come to you without shame.

Prayer of an American Indian.

30. When Death Will Knock at Your Door

On the day when death will knock at your door
what will you offer to him?

Oh, I will set before my guest
the full vessel of my life.
I will never let him go with empty hands.

All the sweet vintage
of all my autumn days and summer nights,
all the earnings and gleanings of my busy life
will I place before him
at the close of my days
when death will knock at my door.

Tagore.

From *Gitanjali*, reproduced by permission of Macmillan, London and Basingstoke.

31. With Expectant Heart

At this time of my parting,
wish me good luck, my friends.
The sky is flushed with the dawn
and my path lies beautiful.

Ask not what I have with me to take there.
I start on my journey with empty hands
and expectant heart.

I shall put on my wedding garland.
Mine is not the red-brown dress of the traveller,
and though there are dangers on the way
I have no fear in my mind.

The evening star will come out when my voyage is done
and the plaintive notes of the twilight melodies
be struck up from the King's gateway.

Tagore.

From *Gitanjali*, reproduced by permission of Macmillan, London and Basingstoke.

32. Ready for the Journey

I have got my leave.
Bid me farewell, my brothers.
I bow to you all and take my departure.

Here I give back the keys of my door,
and I give up all claims to my house.
I only ask for last kind words from you.

We were neighbours for long,
but I have received more than I could give.
Now the day has dawned
and the lamp that lit my dark corner is out.
A summons has come
and I am ready for my journey.

Tagore.

From *Gitanjali*, reproduced by permission of Macmillan, London and Basingstoke.

Prayer Services

These prayer services, or wake services, are intended for use at the funeral home, or at the reception of the remains at the church. Nowadays, due to pressure of work, the funeral Mass is frequently attended only by the family, relatives and close friends of the deceased. For the majority of people the prayer service is the only opportunity to participate in the funeral rites of the deceased. Hence its importance.

Once again, the Word of God is given the central place. In view of what was said in the Introduction, a brief homily would be appropriate. If there is a homily, it would, of course, come after the Scripture readings. A reflection could also be used at some point in the service. Where customary, a decade of the Rosary could accompany the Our Father. I have offered ten services. But any of the liturgies in this book could be adapted for use as a prayer service.

---

1   ETERNAL LIFE: GOD'S GIFT TO HIS CHILDREN

INTRODUCTION

In the name of the Father and of the Son and of the Holy Spirit.

The grace of our Lord Jesus Christ, the love of God, and the fellowship of the Holy Spirit be with you all.

We all give and receive gifts. The best gift of all is the one which takes us by surprise and makes us ask, 'What did I do to deserve this?'

God is the greatest giver of all. He offers us the thing we all long for, namely, eternal life. Eternal life is not something we can earn through our own efforts. It is a gift from God, a gift he freely offers to all his children.

God loves us and wants us to live, yes, to live eternally. He did not make us for extinction, but for life. Let us pause for a moment to reflect on the great gift God is offering us in and through his Son.

(Moment of silent reflection).

Since God did not spare his own Son, but gave him up to death for us, he will not refuse us anything we ask. So let us turn to him now with unlimited trust.

Let us pray.

Father, eternal life is a gift, a gift which you offer to us not because we have earned it or deserved it, but simply because we are your children and you love us. Look with compassion on our brother (sister) N. As you gave him (her) the gift of life on earth, give him (her) now the gift of eternal life in your kingdom. We ask this through Christ our Lord.

A reading from the letter of St Paul to the Ephesians   2:4-10

God, who is rich in mercy, out of the great love with which he loved us, even when we were dead through our trespasses, made us alive together with Christ, and raised us up with him, and made us sit with him in the heavenly places in Christ Jesus, that in the coming ages he might show the immeasurable riches of his grace in kindness toward us in Christ Jesus.

For by grace you have been saved through faith; and this is not your own doing, it is the gift of God – not because of works, lest any man should boast. For we are his workmanship, created in Christ Jesus for good works, which God prepared beforehand, that we should walk in them.

This is the word of the Lord.

Responsorial Psalm   Ps 102(103):8.10-14.17-18

Response:
The Lord is compassion and love.

The Lord is compassion and love,
slow to anger and rich in mercy.
He does not treat us according to our sins
nor repay us according to our faults.   **R**.

For as the heavens are high above the earth
so strong is his love for those who fear him.
As far as the east is from the west
so far does he remove our sins.   **R**.

As a father has compassion on his children,
the Lord has pity on those who fear him;
for he knows of what we are made,
he remembers that we are dust.   **R**.

The love of the Lord is everlasting
upon those who fear him;

his justice reaches out to children's children
when they keep his covenant in truth.   **R.**

GOSPEL

A reading from the holy Gospel according to John   3:16-18

God so loved the world that he gave his only Son, that whoever believes in him should not perish but have eternal life. For God sent the Son into the world, not to condemn the world, but that the world might be saved through him. He who believes in him is not condemned.

This is the Gospel of the Lord.

PRAYER OF THE FAITHFUL

President: God so loved the world that he gave his only Son, that whoever believes in him should not perish but have eternal life. Let us therefore pray to him with unlimited confidence. *Response*: Father, hear us in your love.

Reader(s): N. was linked to Christ at Baptism; may he (she) now live with him in the glory of the Father's kingdom. We pray in faith.

That God in his great mercy may blot out the sins he (she) committed through human frailty. We pray in faith.

That God, the consoler of all who are afflicted, may comfort those who mourn for N., especially his (her) family and relatives. We pray in faith.

For all present here: that, having experienced the love of God in our own lives, we may grow in love for our brothers and sisters. We pray in faith.

For our brothers and sisters who have gone to their rest believing in Christ: that God may bring them into the light of his presence. We pray in faith.

(Pause for silent prayer).

President: Father, may you support us all day long, till the shadows lengthen and evening falls, and the busy world is hushed, and the fever of life is over, and our work is done; then in your mercy grant us a safe lodging, a holy rest, and peace at last. We ask this through Christ our Lord.

INTRODUCTION TO THE LORD'S PRAYER

God the Father is rich in mercy. In Christ we have seen and experienced his kindness and love. Let us pray to him with the words our Saviour gave us.

BLESSING

It is not any good works that we might do that will gain us eternal life, but faith in God. May the Lord confirm your faith.

And may almighty God bless you, the Father, the Son, and the Holy Spirit.

---

2 SHARING CHRIST'S VICTORY

INTRODUCTION

In the name of the Father and of the Son and of the Holy Spirit.

The Lord be with you.

Death, from which none of us can escape, is an overwhelming reality. It defeats all our efforts, ends all our dreams, and leaves us speechless and helpless. We can do nothing to save ourselves. Only God can save us. Fortunately, in his love for us, he has not left us without help. He has sent his Son to our rescue.

Christ has gained a victory over death. He overcame it, not by avoiding it, but by undergoing it and triumphing over it. He wants us to share in his victory. This is a cause of joy and hope for us. Let us reflect on what our faith teaches, namely, that in and through Christ we can overcome death.

(Moment of silent reflection).

With the confidence that Christ gives us, let us now have recourse in prayer to our heavenly Father.

OPENING PRAYER

Let us pray:

Father, by undergoing death your Son broke the power of death for us your adopted children, and by rising from the dead he opened for us the way to eternal life. Our brother (sister) N. has passed through the gates of death. Let your gentle mercy shine on him (her), and grant him (her) a share in your Son's victory over death. We ask this through Christ our Lord.

FIRST READING

A reading from the first letter of St Paul to the Corinthians 15:53-57

This perishable nature must put on the imperishable, and this mortal nature must put on immortality. When the perishable puts on the imperishable, and the mortal puts on immortality, then shall come to pass the saying that is written: 'Death is swallowed up in victory. O death, where is thy victory? O death, where is thy sting?'

The sting of death is sin, and the power of sin is the law. But thanks be to God, who gives us the victory through our Lord Jesus Christ.

This is the word of the Lord.

Responsorial Psalm   Ps 114(115):1-8

Response:
I will walk in the presence of the Lord
in the land of the living.

I love the Lord for he has heard
the cry of my appeal;
for he turned his ear to me
in the day when I called him.   **R**.

They surrounded me, the snares of death,
with the anguish of the tomb;
they caught me, sorrow and distress.
I called on the Lord's name.   **R**.

How gracious is the Lord, and just;
our God has compassion.
The Lord protects the simple hearts;
I was helpless so he saved me.   **R**.

Turn back, my soul, to your rest
for the Lord has been good;
he has kept my soul from death,
and my feet from stumbling.   **R**.

GOSPEL

A reading from the holy Gospel according to John   12:23-26

Jesus said to the people, 'The hour has come for the Son of man to be glorified. Truly, truly, I say to you, unless a grain of wheat falls into the earth and dies, it remains alone; but if it dies, it bears much fruit. He who loves his life loses it, and he who hates his life in this world will keep it for eternal life. If any one serves me, he must follow me; and where I am, there shall my servant be also; if any one serves me, the Father will honour him.'

This is the Gospel of the Lord.

PRAYER OF THE FAITHFUL

President: God the Father has removed the sting from our death through the Easter victory of his Son. So, even though we are saddened by death, we know that we can overcome it through the power of Christ's resurrection. Let us then pray with confidence to our heavenly Father in our hour of need. *Response*: Hear us, O Lord.

Reader(s): N. died with Christ at Baptism; may he (she) now enjoy the fulness of that eternal life Christ won for us by his own death. Let us pray.

That all the trials and hardships he (she) suffered during life may be crowned with the full pardon of his (her) sins. Let us pray.

Christ himself experienced the anguish of death; may he console those who mourn for N. especially his (her) family. Let us pray.

For all here present: that with the grace of Christ we may die to sin and live to holiness and goodness. Let us pray.

For all those who have no hope of a life beyond the grave: that they too may hear and believe the Good News of Christ's Easter victory over death. Let us pray.

For all who have died in the peace of Christ. Let us pray.
(Pause for silent prayer).

President: Father, your Son died so that we might have life. Help us so to follow him in this life that we may come to share the fruits of his victory in the next, where he lives and reigns with you and the Holy Spirit, one God for ever and ever.

INTRODUCTION TO THE LORD'S PRAYER

God our Father loves us and wants us to share in the victory of his Son. Let us pray to him with confidence as Christ, our Brother, taught us.

BLESSING

God the Father has given us victory over death through the resurrection of his Son. May he now strengthen your hope and keep you faithful in love.

And may almighty God bless you, the Father, the Son, and the Holy Spirit.

---

3   HOPING FOR A LIFE WITHOUT END

INTRODUCTION

In the name of the Father and of the Son and of the Holy Spirit.

The grace of our Lord Jesus Christ, the love of God, and the fellowship of the Holy Spirit be with you all.

Nobody can live without hope. We spend our entire lives longing, waiting, hoping for one thing or another. To give up hope is to go on a hunger strike of the spirit.

But our hopes go beyond this world. We also hope for a life without end. Only our faith gives us a basis for such a hope. This is why faith is the most important thing in the world. It means that, though we die in the dark, we die in hope. To die in hope is to die in expectation of the dawn. Let us reflect briefly on the great hope our faith holds out to us – the hope of a life without end.

(Moment of silent reflection)

Only God can fulfil our hope. Let us have recourse to him with great faith on behalf of our brother (sister) N.

OPENING PRAYER

Let us pray:

Father, your Son has given us the hope of eternal life, and has come on earth to help us attain it. Grant that our brother (sister) N. who has finished with earthly things may now come to that land where there are no more shattered hopes and broken dreams. Give him (her) a merciful judgement and grant him (her) a speedy entrance into your kingdom. We ask this through Christ our Lord.

FIRST READING

A reading from the first letter of St Peter   1:3-7

Blessed be the God and Father of our Lord Jesus Christ! By his great mercy we have been born anew to a living hope through the resurrection of Jesus Christ from the dead, and to an inheritance which is imperishable, undefiled, and unfading, kept in heaven for you, who by God's power are guarded through faith for a salvation ready to be revealed in the last time.

In this you rejoice, though now for a little while you may have to suffer various trials, so that the genuineness of your faith, which is more precious than gold, may redound to praise and glory and honour at the revelation of Jesus Christ.

This is the word of the Lord.

Responsorial Psalm   Ps 123 (124)

Response:
Our help is in the name of the Lord,
who made heaven and earth.

If the Lord had not been on our side
when men rose against us,
then would they have swallowed us alive
when their anger was kindled.   **R.**

Then would the waters have engulfed us,
the torrent gone over us;
over our head would have swept
the raging waters.   **R**.

Blessed be the Lord who did not give us
a prey to their teeth.
Our life, like a bird, has escaped
from the snare of the fowler.   **R**.

Indeed the snare has been broken
and we have escaped.
Our help is in the name of the Lord,
who made heaven and earth.   **R**.

GOSPEL

A reading from the holy Gospel according to John   11:21-27

Martha said to Jesus, 'Lord, if you had been here, my brother would not have died. And even now I know that whatever you ask from God, God will give you.' Jesus said to her, 'Your brother will rise again.' Martha said to him, 'I know that he will rise again in the resurrection at the last day.' Jesus said to her, 'I am the resurrection and the life; he who believes in me, though he die, yet shall he live, and whoever lives and believes in me shall never die. Do you believe this?' She said to him, 'Yes, Lord; I believe that you are the Christ, the Son of God, he who is coming into the world.'
  This is the Gospel of the Lord.

PRAYER OF THE FAITHFUL

President: God the Father raised Jesus from the dead so that we might have a sure hope of an inheritance that will never fade. This is a source of immense consolation to us who are now walking in the land and in the shadow of death. Let us pray as members of a hopeful people. *Response*: Lord, hear our prayer.

Reader(s): N. was given the promise of eternal life at Baptism; may he (she) now see that promise fulfilled in the kingdom of heaven.Let us pray to the Lord.

  That Christ who showed such mercy towards sinners, may now forgive N. his (her) sins and open for him (her) the gates of paradise. Let us pray to the Lord.

  For those who mourn N's death: that they may find strength and consolation in the hope we have through the resurrection of Jesus from the dead. Let us pray to the Lord.

  For all here present: that we may strive to grow in faith which is more precious than gold. Let us pray to the Lord.

For all our brothers and sisters who have gone to their rest in the hope of rising again: that the Lord may bring them into the light of his presence. Let us pray to the Lord.

(Pause for silent prayer).

President: Father, through the resurrection of your Son, you have kindled in our hearts the bright hope of eternal life. Guard this hope with your grace, and bring it to fulfilment in the kingdom of heaven. We ask this through Christ our Lord.

INTRODUCTION TO THE LORD'S PRAYER

Through faith in Christ his Son, our heavenly Father has given us the hope of an inheritance which is imperishable, undefiled, and unfading. Let us pray to him in the words our Saviour gave us.

BLESSING

Faith is our consolation, and hope is our anchor. May the Lord enliven your faith and strengthen your hope.

And may almighty God bless you, the Father, the Son, and the Holy Spirit.

---

4 SHEEP OF HIS FLOCK

INTRODUCTION

In the name of the Father and of the Son and of the Holy Spirit.

The grace and peace of God our Father and the Lord Jesus Christ be with you all.

In order to live a happy life we need to know that we matter to at least one person. Our faith tells us that each of us is important and special to God. Though everyone else might abandon us, God will never abandon us. We are members of Christ's flock. He is our shepherd. He knows each of us, and has proved his love for us by giving his life for us.

One of Christ's flock has died – our brother (sister) N. As we gather to pray for N. let us reflect for a moment on the fact that each of us is known and loved by Christ.

(Moment of silent reflection).

OPENING PRAYER

Let us pray:

Father, you showed your great love for us when you sent your only Son to us. He willingly laid down his life so that we might die to sin. He rose again so that we might rise to a new life, a life that will one day blossom into eternal life. Our brother (sister) N. shared the risen life of Christ at baptism. May he (she) now enjoy the fulness of that life in heaven. We ask this through Christ our Lord.

FIRST READING

A reading from the first letter of St Peter   2:21-24

Christ suffered for you, leaving you an example, that you should follow in his steps. He committed no sin; no guile was found on his lips. When he was reviled, he did not revile in return; when he suffered, he did not threaten; but he trusted to him who judges justly.

He himself bore our sins in his body on the tree, that we might die to sin and live to righteousness. By his wounds you have been healed. For you were straying like sheep, but you have now returned to the Shepherd and Guardian of your souls.

This is the word of the Lord.

Responsorial Psalm   Ps 22(23)

Response:
The Lord is my shepherd;
there is nothing I shall want.

The Lord is my shepherd;
there is nothing I shall want.
Fresh and green are the pastures
where he gives me repose.
Near restful waters he leads me,
to revive my drooping spirit.   **R**.

He guides me along the right path;
he is true to his name.
If I should walk in the valley of darkness
no evil would I fear.
You are there with your crook and your staff;
with these you give me comfort.   **R**.

You have prepared a banquet for me
in the sight of my foes.
My head you have anointed with oil;
my cup is overflowing.   **R**.

Surely goodness and kindness shall follow me
all the days of my life.

In the Lord's own house shall I dwell
for ever and ever.   **R.**

A reading from the holy Gospel according to John   10:10-14

Jesus said to his disciples, 'I came that you may have life, and have it
abundantly. I am the good shepherd. The good shepherd lays down
his life for the sheep. He who is a hireling and not a shepherd, whose
own the sheep are not, sees the wolf coming and leaves the sheep
and flees; and the wolf snatches them and scatters them. He flees
because he is a hireling and cares nothing for the sheep. I am the
good shepherd; I know my own and my own know me.'

This is the Gospel of the Lord.

PRAYER OF THE FAITHFUL

President: Christ is the shepherd and guardian of our souls. Let us
pray to him whose love for us is unfailing for N., for ourselves, and
for others. *Response*: Lord, hear our prayer.

Reader(s): Christ died that we might have eternal life; may he
lead our brother (sister) N. to the ever green pastures of his eternal
kingdom. Let us pray to the Lord.

Christ suffered for our sins on the cross; may the merits of his
passion and death gain for N. the full remission of all his (her) sins.
Let us pray to the Lord.

For those who mourn, especially N's family and friends: that
Christ the good shepherd may console them and heal the wounds of
their grief. Let us pray to the Lord.

For each of us: that we may listen to the voice of Christ so that he
may lead us along the path of eternal life. Let us pray to the Lord.

For this community: that we may realise that we are Christ's
flock, and strive to love one another as Christ has loved us. Let us
pray to the Lord.

For those who have no love in their lives, and who are not
important or precious to anyone: that they too may experience the
love of Christ, the good shepherd. Let us pray to the Lord.

(Pause for silent prayer).

President: Father, Christ your Son came that we might have life
and have it to the full. Help us to know him and to follow him in this
life so that when we die we may dwell in your house for ever and
ever. We ask this through Christ our Lord.

INTRODUCTION TO THE LORD'S PRAYER

Let us now pray to our heavenly Father using the words, and in the spirit, Christ has taught us.

BLESSING

May God, whose people we are and in whose eternal house we hope one day to dwell, increase your faith in his love, strengthen your hope in his promise, and deepen your love for one another.

And may almighty God bless you, the Father, the Son, and the Holy Spirit.

---

5   A LIGHT STRONGER THAN DEATH

INTRODUCTION

In the name of the Father and of the Son and of the Holy Spirit.

The grace and peace of God our Father and the Lord Jesus Christ be with you all.

With the death of N. a light has gone out in our midst. Our lives will be darker without him (her). Death causes a terrible darkness to descend upon us. One light, and one light only, is capable of dispelling the darkness of death. That light is the light of Christ.

It is to Christ that we now turn. As we commend our brother (sister) to God, let us also renew our belief in the light of Christ, a light which is stronger than death. Let us reflect briefly on the greatness of what happened to us at baptism when the lamp of faith was first lit in our hearts.

(Moment of silent reflection).

This is the hour to lift up the lamp of faith. We are confident that Christ will see our brother (sister) safely through the dark valley of death to the land of unending day.

OPENING PRAYER

Let us pray:

Father, from whom all light comes, look upon us your children as we stand in darkness and in the shadow of death. The night of death has come for our brother (sister) N. Grant him (her) a merciful judgement. May the light of Christ, who himself experienced the anguish of death, guide him (her) to your everlasting kingdom where the darkness of death will be banished for ever. We ask this through the same Christ our Lord.

A reading from the letter of St Paul to the Ephesians   5:8-14

Once you were darkness, but now you are light in the Lord; walk as children of light. The fruit of light is found in all that is good and right and true. Try to learn what is pleasing to the Lord.

Take no part in the unfruitful works of darkness, but instead expose them. For it is a shame even to speak of the things that they do in secret; but when anything is exposed by the light it becomes visible, for anything that becomes visible is light. Therefore it is said, 'Awake, O sleeper, and arise from the dead, and Christ shall give you light.'

This is the word of the Lord.

Responsorial Psalm   Ps 26(27):1.4.10.13.14

Response:
The Lord is my light and my help.

The Lord is my light and my help;
whom shall I fear?
The Lord is the stronghold of my life;
before whom shall I shrink?   **R**.

There is one thing I ask of the Lord,
for this I long,
to live in the house of the Lord
all the days of my life.   **R**.

Do not abandon or forsake me,
O God my help.
Though father and mother forsake me,
the Lord will receive me.   **R**.

I am sure I shall see the Lord's goodness
in the land of the living.
Hope in him, hold firm and take heart.
Hope in the Lord.   **R**.

GOSPEL

A reading from the holy Gospel according to John   8:12;12:34-36

Jesus said to the people, 'I am the light of the world; he who follows me will not walk in darkness, but will have the light of life. The light is with you for a little longer. Walk while you have the light, lest the darkness overtake you; he who walks in the darkness does not know where he goes. While you have the light, believe in the light, that you may become sons of the light.'

This is the Gospel of the Lord.

PRAYER OF THE FAITHFUL

President: Once we were in darkness, but the light of Christ has shone upon us. So, with Christ's light shining on us, we pray in hope. *Response*: Lord, graciously hear us.

Reader(s): N. was enlightened by Christ in baptism; may he (she) now come into possession of the kingdom of everlasting light. Lord, hear us.

That the darkness of his (her) sins may be banished by the light of God's mercy. Lord hear us.

For all those we are in darkness because of N's death: that the light of God's consolation may shine on them. Lord, hear us.

That God's eternal light may shine on all our departed relatives and friends. Lord, hear us.

That we who still enjoy the light of this life may strive to walk in goodness and holiness of life. Lord, hear us.

For those who walk in the darkness of doubt and unbelief: that they too may see the light of Christ, and so find their way into the kingdom of God. Lord, hear us.

(Pause for silent prayer).

President: Father, may the radiance of your glory light up our hearts and bring us safely through the shadows of this world until we reach our homeland of everlasting light. We ask this through Christ our Lord.

INTRODUCTION TO THE LORD'S PRAYER

Let us pray to our heavenly Father, who lets his light shine on all his children, deserving and undeserving.

BLESSING

May God in his great mercy dispel the darkness of your grief, and give you light and peace.

And may almighty God bless you, the Father, the Son, and the Holy Spirit.

---

6 TIME OF DEPARTURE

INTRODUCTION

In the name of the Father and of the Son and of the Holy Spirit.

The Lord be with you.

Life is full of partings. We have all seen friends off at airports and other places of departure. We go with them as far as we are allowed, and we linger with them as long as possible. But eventually we have to let them go. Before we do so, however, we bid them goodbye and wish them a safe journey.

Death is *the* moment of departure. We are gathered here to bid farewell to our brother (sister) N. We go with him (her) to the very threshold of the other world. Through our prayers we bid him (her) farewell and wish him (her) a safe journey to the kingdom of heaven. This is why we are gathered here. But first of all let us pause to reflect briefly on the great mystery of death.

(Moment of silent reflection).

It makes the moment of departure a little easier when we know that our friend is going to a better place. Our brother (sister) has gone to God.

OPENING PRAYER

Let us pray:

Heavenly Father, we bid farewell to N. with the hope our faith gives us that he (she) has gone to better things, and that we will see him (her) again when we will all meet in the everlasting kingdom your Son won for us through his death and resurrection. Save our brother (sister) from the corruption of sin and death, and bring him (her) safely to your kingdom of everlasting joy and peace. We ask this through Christ our Lord.

FIRST READING

A reading from the second letter of St Paul to Timothy   4:6-8

I am already on the point of being sacrificed; the time of my departure has come. I have fought the good fight. I have finished the race. I have kept the faith. Henceforth there is laid up for me the crown of righteousness, which the Lord, the righteous judge, will award to me on that Day, and not only to me but also to all who have loved his appearing.

This is the word of the Lord.

Responsorial Psalm   Ps 138(139):7-12.23-24

Response:

O Lord, you search me and you know me.

O where can I go from your spirit,
or where can I flee from your face?
If I climb the heavens, you are there.
If I lie in the grave, you are there.   **R.**

If I take the wings of the dawn

and dwell at the sea's furthest
end, even there your hand would lead me,
your right hand would hold me fast.   **R**.

If I say: 'Let the darkness hide
me and the light around me be night,'
even darkness is not dark for you
and the night is as clear as the day.   **R**.

O search me, God, and know my heart.
O test me and know my thoughts.
See that I follow not the wrong path
and lead me in the path of life eternal.   **R**.

GOSPEL

A reading from the holy Gospel according to John   16:16.20-22
Jesus said to his disciples, 'A little while, and you will see me no
more; again a little while, and you will see me, beacuse I go to the
Father. Truly, truly, I say to you, you will weep and lament, but the
world will rejoice; you will be sorrowful, but your sorrow will turn
into joy. When a woman is in travail she has sorrow, because her
hour has come; but when she is delivered of the child, she no longer
remembers the anguish, for the joy that a child is born into the
world. So you have sorrow now, but I will see you again and your
hearts will rejoice, and no one will take your joy from you.'
This is the Gospel of the Lord.

PRAYER OF THE FAITHFUL

President: It is from God that we come when we enter this life,
and it is to him we go when we leave it. Comforted by this faith, let
us pray with confidence for N., for ourselves, and for others.
Response: Father, hear us in your love.
Reader(s): That N. who has departed from us may reach the
safety of God's everlasting kingdom. We pray in faith.
That God, in his great mercy, may blot out the sins he (she)
committed through human weakness. We pray in faith.
For those who mourn for him (her): that God may deepen their
faith and strengthen their hope. We pray in faith.
That God may grant eternal life to all those whom we loved in this
life but whom death has taken away from us. We pray in faith.
For all here present: that we may so live here on earth that when
death comes we may pass with ease to that other shore. We pray in
faith.
(Pause for silent prayer).
President: Heavenly Father, into your hands we commend the

soul of N. May no torment touch him (her). May he (she) reach a place of refreshment, light and peace. We ask this through Christ our Lord.

INTRODUCTION TO THE LORD'S PRAYER

From the depths of our grief let us pray to our heavenly Father as Christ has taught us.

BLESSING

May God console you with the hope that we shall see our brother (sister) again in the kingdom of heaven.

And may God bless you now and for ever, the Father, the Son, and the Holy Spirit.

---

7 HARVEST OF THE SPIRIT

INTRODUCTION

In the name of the Father and of the Son and of the Holy Spirit.

The Lord be with you.

Death is like harvest time. In fact, it is the harvest time of the spirit. At an ordinary harvest one thing alone matters, namely, the grain. And at the harvest of the spirit one thing alone matters, namely, goodness of life. At death we reap the fruits of the good we have done during life.

The harvest time has come for our brother (sister) N. As we gather to pray for him (her), let us first pause for a moment to look into the field of our lives to see what is ripening there.

(Moment of silent reflection).

It is only with the help of God's grace that our lives become fruitful with the kind of fruit that endures to eternal life.

OPENING PRAYER

Let us turn to the Lord of the harvest and pray for our brother (sister):

Father, your Son said to his disciples, 'I am the vine, you are the branches; separated from me you can do nothing, but united with me you will bear much fruit.' Our brother (sister) N. was united with Christ in baptism, and remained faithful to him during life. May he (she) now reap the harvest of eternal life in your kingdom. We ask this through Christ our Lord.

FIRST READING

A reading from the letter of St Paul to the Galatians   6:7-10

Do not be deceived; God is not mocked, for whatever a man sows, that he will also reap. For he who sows to his own flesh will from the flesh reap corruption; but he who sows to the Spirit will from the Spirit reap eternal life.

And let us not grow weary in well-doing, for in due season we shall reap, if we do not lose heart. So then, as we have opportunity, let us do good to all men, and especially to those who are of the household of faith.

This is the word of the Lord.

Responsorial Psalm   Ps 125 (126)

Response:
Those who are sowing in tears
will sing when they reap.

When the Lord delivered Sion from bondage,
it seemed like a dream.
Then was our mouth filled with laughter,
on our lips there were songs.   **R**.

The heathens themselves said: 'What marvels
the Lord worked for them!'
What marvels the Lord worked for us!
Indeed we were glad.   **R**.

Deliver us, O Lord, from our bondage
as streams in dry land.
Those who are sowing in tears
will sing when they reap.   **R**.

They go out, they go out, full of tears,
carrying seed for the sowing:
they come back, they come back, full of song,
carrying their sheaves.   **R**.

GOSPEL

A reading from the holy Gospel according to John   4:31-32.34-36

Meanwhile the disciples besought Jesus, saying, 'Rabbi, eat.' But he said to them, 'I have food to eat of which you do not know. My food is to do the will of him who sent me, and to accomplish his work. Do you not say, "There are yet four months, then comes the harvest"? I tell you, lift up your eyes, and see how the fields are already white for harvest. He who reaps receives wages, and gathers

fruit for eternal life, so that sower and reaper may rejoice together.'
This is the Gospel of the Lord.

PRAYER OF THE FAITHFUL

President: Let us not grow weary in well-doing, for in due time we
will reap a harvest, provided we do not lose heart. Let us pray to the
Lord of the harvest with great trust and confidence. *Response*: Hear
us, O Lord.

Reader(s): That our brother (sister) N. may reap a rich harvest
from all the good he (she) did during life. Let us pray.

That God may consign to the flames of his mercy the weeds and
thorns of his (her) sins. Let us pray.

For those who mourn N's death: that they may find strength in the
knowledge that for many years to come they will continue to reap
the harvest of goodness he (she) sowed. Let us pray.

For this community: that we may realise that we are like seeds
planted by God in the same field, and so help one another grow. Let
us pray.

For all the faithful departed: that God may bring them to a place
of refreshment, light and peace. Let us pray.

(Pause for silent prayer).

President: Father with the help of your grace our lives can be
joyful and fruitful. Grant that, in spite of the many obstacles and
temptations we encounter, we may persevere in goodness, and so
one day come to reap an abundant harvest in your eternal kingdom.
We ask this through Christ our Lord.

INTRODUCTION TO THE LORD'S PRAYER

Let us pray the prayer Jesus taught his friends to say.

BLESSING

May God, who makes our lives fruitful through the grace of the
Holy Spirit, console you in your sorrow and help you to persevere in
goodness.

And may almighty God bless you, the Father, the Son, and the
Holy Spirit.

---

8 AN ETERNAL HOME

INTRODUCTION

In the name of the Father and of the Son and of the Holy Spirit.

The grace and peace of God our Father and the Lord Jesus Christ be with you all.

All creatures need a home to go to at the end of the day. Home means refreshment, company, and rest. We too need a home, not just here on earth, but an eternal home to which we can go when death brings down the curtain on the day of our life. Fortunately our faith assures us that we do have a home to go to. God, whose children we are, has not left us homeless. He has an eternal home prepared for us.

Our brother (sister) N. has left his (her) earthly home and set out for his (her) heavenly home. As we pray for him (her), let us reflect on our own lives and the splendid prospect of an eternal home which our faith holds out to us.

(Moment of silent reflection).

OPENING PRAYER

Let us pray:

Father, your Son has assured us that in your heavenly home there are many rooms. He himself has gone there to prepare a place for us. Be merciful to our brother (sister) N. May Christ come out to meet him (her) and lead him (her) to a place of refreshment, light and peace. We ask this through Christ our Lord.

FIRST READING

A reading from the second letter of Paul to the Corinthians 4:16-18;5:1

We do not lose heart. Though our outer nature is wasting away, our inner nature is being renewed every day. For this slight momentary affliction is preparing for us an eternal weight of glory beyond all comparison, because we look not to the things that are seen but to the things that are unseen; for the things that are seen are transient, but the things that are unseen are eternal.

For we know that if the earthly tent we live in is destroyed, we have a building from God, a house not made with hands, eternal in the heavens.

This is the word of the Lord.

Responsorial Psalm   Ps 138(139):7-12.23-24

Response:
O Lord, you search me and you know me.

O where can I go from your spirit,
or where can I flee from your face?
If I climb the heavens, you are there.
If I lie in the grave, you are there.   **R.**

If I take the wings of the dawn
and dwell at the sea's furthest end,
even there your hand would lead me,
your right hand would hold me fast.   **R.**

If I say: 'Let the darkness hide me
and the light around me be night,'
even darkness is not dark for you
and the night is as clear as the day.   **R.**

O search me, God, and know my heart.
O test me and know my thoughts.
See that I follow not the wrong path
and lead me in the path of life eternal.   **R.**

GOSPEL

A reading from the holy Gospel according to John   14:1-3

Jesus said to his disciples, 'Let not your hearts be troubled; believe in God, believe also in me. In my Father's house are many rooms; if it were not so, would I have told you that I go to prepare a place for you? And when I go and prepare a place for you, I will come again and will take you to myself, that where I am you may be also.'
This is the Gospel of the Lord.

PRAYER OF THE FAITHFUL

President: When the earthly tent we live in at present is destroyed by death, God has an eternal house built for us in heaven. Let us pray with confidence to the Father whose children we are. *Response*: Hear us, O Lord.

Reader(s): N. has departed his (her) earthly home; may he (she) safely reach the joy and peace of the Father's house. Let us pray.

That God may have mercy on him (her), forgive his (her) sins, and bring him (her) to everlasting life. Let us pray.

For those who mourn his (her) passing: that they may be comforted by the faith that tells them he (she) has gone to a better place. Let us pray.

For all here: that nothing in this life may cause us to forget the eternal home which is the final destination of our lives. Let us pray.

For all our deceased relatives and friends: that God may bring them into the light of his presence. Let us pray.

For those without faith and who are deprived of the hope of an eternal homeland. Let us pray.

(Pause for silent prayer).

President: Father, you made us for yourself, and our hearts will never rest until they rest in you. Grant that amidst the uncertainties of this changing world our hearts may be set on our eternal home where true joys are to be found. We ask this through Christ our Lord.

INTRODUCTION TO THE LORD'S PRAYER

Let us pray to our heavenly Father who sent his Son to us to guide us in the path of eternal life.

BLESSING

Let not your hearts be troubled. Believe in God, and believe also in Christ.

And may almighty God bless you, the Father, the Son, and the Holy Spirit.

---

9   DYING IN THE SPRINGTIME
For a child or young person

INTRODUCTION

In the name of the Father and of the Son and of the Holy Spirit.

The Lord be with you.

We are gathered in prayer before the mortal remains of N. who was only ... years old. We don't expect our children to die before us. We don't like to see them die in the springtime of life. Still, they die full of hope, full of promise and fragrant with innocence. And that is not a bad way in which to die.

Besides, we know that these little ones go straight to the kingdom of heaven. We have Christ's word for that. So we have the consolation of knowing that N. has gone to a better place. Before we pray, let us reflect for a moment on the fact that we were all young once, full of life, promise and hope, and also on the fact that before God we are still children.

(Moment of silent reflection).

OPENING PRAYER

Let us pray:

God our Father, your Son assured us that you notice and are concerned about a single sparrow that falls from the sky. We know that you have seen the fall of our little brother (sister) N. We are confident that he (she) has fallen into your hands and that you will take good care of him (her). Support us who grieve for him (her), and comfort us with your loving protection. We ask this through Christ our Lord.

A reading from the letter of St Paul to the Romans   8:14-18

All who are led by the Spirit of God are sons of God. For you did not receive the spirit of slavery to fall back into fear, but you have received the spirit of sonship. When we cry, 'Abba! Father!' it is the Spirit himself bearing witness with our spirit that we are children of God, and if children, then heirs, heirs of God and fellow heirs with Christ, provided we suffer with him in order that we may also be glorified with him.

    This is the word of the Lord.

Responsorial Psalm   Ps 83(84):4-8.12

Response:
My soul is longing for the courts of the Lord.

The sparrow finds herself a home
and the swallow a nest for her brood;
she lays her young by your altars,
Lord of hosts, my king and my God.   **R.**

They are happy, who dwell in your house,
for ever singing your praise.
They are happy, whose strength is in you,
in whose hearts are the roads to Sion.   **R.**

As they go through the Bitter Valley
they make it a place of springs.
They walk with ever growing strength,
they will see the God of gods in Sion.   **R.**

For the Lord God is a rampart, a shield;
he will give us his favour and glory.
The Lord will not refuse any good
to those who walk without blame.   **R.**

A reading from the holy Gospel according to Matthew   18:1-4

At that time the disciples came to Jesus, saying, 'Who is the greatest in the kingdom of heaven?' And calling to him a child, he put him in the midst of them, and said, 'Truly, I say to you, unless you turn and become like children, you will never enter the kingdom of heaven.

Whoever humbles himself like this child, he is the greatest in the kingdom of heaven.'
This is the Gospel of the Lord.

ALTERNATIVE GOSPEL

A reading from the holy Gospel according to Matthew   19:13-15
Children were brought to Jesus that he might lay his hands on them and pray. The disciples rebuked the people; but Jesus said, 'Let the children come to me, and do not hinder them; for to such belongs the kingdom of heaven.'
This is the Gospel of the Lord.

PRAYER OF THE FAITHFUL

President: Christ showed in word and deed that the little ones are precious to him and to the heavenly Father. We are confident then that he will hear our prayers on their behalf. *Response*: Lord, hear our prayer.
  Reader(s): That Christ may take N. by the hand and lead him (her) into that kingdom which he said belongs to all those who are little. Let us pray to the Lord.
  That from his (her) place in the kingdom of heaven he (she) may intercede for all of us. Let us pray to the Lord.
  For his (her) parents, family, and friends: that God may comfort them with the assurance that they will see him (her) again when we will all meet in Christ's everlasting kingdom. Let us pray to the Lord.
  For all the children and young people of the world: that we may never be a stumbling block to them, but rather that we may open the doors of life to them. Let us pray to the Lord.
  For all here present: that we may always be conscious of our great dignity as children of God, and strive to live lives that are worthy of that dignity. Let us pray to the Lord.
  (Pause for silent prayer).
  President: Father, in Christ you have shown us how much you love the little ones. Write N's name on the palm of your hand and give him (her) the freedom of your kingdom. We ask this through Christ our Lord.

INTRODUCTION TO THE LORD'S PRAYER

Let us pray to God our Father the prayer that Jesus, our Brother, has taught us to say.

BLESSING

May God, whose children we are, console you in your grief and strengthen your faith in his love.

And may almighty God bless you, the Father, the Son, and the Holy Spirit.

---

10 GOD IS ON OUR SIDE
Tragic death

INTRODUCTION

In the name of the Father and of the Son of the Holy Spirit.

The grace and peace of God our Father and the Lord Jesus Christ be with you all.

The N. family has suffered a great blow, a great loss. They have the consolation of knowing that the whole community feels their loss and supports them in it.

It is certainly not the will of God that such things should happen. No earthly father would will such a death on one of his children. Neither would God. In fact, God is the only one we can turn to in circumstances like these. He is on our side. So let us turn to him now. But first let us reflect briefly on how precarious is our hold on this precious thing we call 'life'.

(Moment of silent reflection).

PRAYER

Let us pray:

Father, your Son lived in our world, a world full of unrest and uncertainty. He did not hesitate to undergo the agony of the cross so that he might share with us the pain and anguish of death. But you raised him to life again and crowned him with glory. God of love, stand by us in our hour of need. Look with kindness on our brother (sister) N. whose earthly life has ended. Do not let him (her) be parted from you, but through your glorious power being him (her) to your kingdom of joy and peace. We ask this through Christ our Lord.

FIRST READING

A reading from the Letter of St Paul to the Romans   8:35.37-39

Who shall separate us from the love of Christ? Shall tribulation, or distress, or persecution, or famine, or nakedness, or peril, or sword? No, in all these things we are more than conquerors through him who loved us. For I am sure that neither death, nor life, nor angels, nor principalities, nor things present, nor things yet to come, nor powers, nor height, nor depth, nor anything else in all creation, will be able to separate us from the love of God in Christ Jesus our Lord.

This is word of the Lord.

Responsorial Psalm   Ps 22 (23)

Response:
The Lord is my shepherd;
there is nothing I shall want.

The Lord is my shepherd;
there is nothing I shall want.
Fresh and green are the pastures
where he gives me repose.
Near restful waters he leads me,
to revive my drooping spirit. **R.**

He guides me along the right path;
he is true to his name.
If I should walk in the valley of darkness
no evil would I fear.
You are there with your crook and your staff;
with these you give me comfort. **R.**

You have prepared a banquet for me
in the sight of my foes.
My head you have anointed with oil;
my cup is overflowing. **R.**

Surely goodness and kindness shall follow me
all the days of my life.
In the Lord's own house shall I dwell
for ever and ever. **R.**

Alternative Psalm   Ps 129 (130)

Response:
Out of the depths I cry to you, O Lord,
Lord, hear my voice.

Out of the depths I cry to you, O Lord,
Lord, hear my voice.
O let your ears be attentive
to the voice of my pleading. **R.**

If you, O Lord, should mark our guilt,
Lord, who would survive?
But with you is found forgiveness:
for this we revere you.   **R**.

My soul is waiting for the Lord,
I count on his word.
My soul is longing for the Lord
more than watchman for daybreak.   **R**.

Because with the Lord there is mercy
and fulness of redemption,
Israel indeed he will redeem
from all its iniquity.   **R**.

GOSPEL

A reading from the holy Gospel according to John   14:1-6

Jesus said to his disciples, 'Let not your hearts be troubled; believe in God, believe also in me. In my Father's house are many rooms; if it were not so, would I have told you that I go to prepare a place for you? And when I go and prepare a place for you, I will come again and will take you to myself, that where I am you may be also.'

Thomas said to him, 'Lord, we do not know where you are going; how can we know the way?' Jesus said to him, 'I am the way, the truth, and the life; no one comes to the Father, but by me.'

This is the Gospel of the Lord.

ALTERNATIVE GOSPEL

A reading from the holy Gospel according to John   11:21-27

Martha said to Jesus, 'Lord, if you had been here, my brother would not have died. And even now I know that whatever you ask from God, God will give you.' Jesus said to her, 'Your brother will rise again.' Martha said to him, 'I know that he will rise again in the resurrection at the last day.' Jesus said to her, 'I am the resurrection and the life; he who believes in me, though he die, yet shall he live, and whoever lives and believes in me shall never die. Do you believe this?' She said to him, 'Yes, Lord; I believe that you are the Christ, the Son of God, he who is coming into the world.'

This is the Gospel of the Lord.

PRAYER OF THE FAITHFUL

President: The night before his own death Christ said to his apostles, 'Let not your hearts be troubled; believe in God, believe also in me.' Though our hearts are deeply troubled we do believe in

God's love for us, and know that from this tragedy he can and will bring good. Let us therefore pray to him in our hour of darkness. *Response*: Father, hear us in your love.

Reader(s): That N., whose life was so cruelly cut short by tragedy, may now enter into the fulness of that life Christ won for us with his own death. We pray in faith.

For the family, relatives, and friends of N.: that they may find comfort in their faith in God, and strength through the support of the community. We pray in faith.

For all here present: that we may grow in faith so that we may be able to stand firm when misfortune or tragedy visits us. We pray in faith.

For all those who have left this world in God's friendship, especially those who were near and dear to us. We pray in faith.

(Pause for silent prayer).

President: Heavenly Father, give us the certainty that beyond death there is a life – where broken things are mended and lost things are found; where there is rest for the weary and joy for the sad; where all that we have loved and willed of good exists, and where we will meet again our loved ones. We ask this through Christ our Lord.

INTRODUCTION TO THE LORD'S PRAYER

The Father cares about what happens to his children. Let us pray to him with confidence in the words our Saviour gave us.

BLESSING

May the God of all consolation comfort you in your hour of need with hope, light and peace.

And may almighty God bless you, the Father, the Son, and the Holy Spirit.